SIGNS, WHISPERS, AND MIRACLES

FINDING GOD IN THE FABRIC OF LIFE

VIOLET BATEJAN

A TRUE STORY

Signs, Whispers, and Miracles: A True Story
Finding God in the Fabric of Life
by Violet Batejan
Published by Deer Point Press Copyright © 2021
All rights reserved.

This book is a memoir. It reflects the author's present recollections of experiences that occurred in the past. Some names and identifying characteristics have been changed, some events have been compressed, and some dialogue has been recreated.

Scripture taken from the New King James Version. Copyright 1982 by Thomas Nelson, Inc.
Used by permission. All rights reserved.

ISBN e-book: 978-1-7372167-0-4
ISBN paperback: 978-1-7372167-1-1

Edited by Jocelyn Carbonara
Cover design by Flip Design Studio
Author picture by Joanne Donato
Formatted by Nola Li Barr

CONTENTS

Foreword   v

Prologue   1
1. The Beginning   5
2. Elementary   9
3. Germany—Magstadt   16
4. Germany—Backnang and Europe   26
5. Trial by Fire   35
6. The Robe   40
7. Second Chance   47
8. The Accident   55
9. Prelude   63
10. Evil and Good   70
11. God Is Not Dead   78
12. Don't Go!   85
13. The Precipice   93
14. The Townhouse   101
15. Busted   105
16. Moving On   113
17. Transitions   121
18. New Beginnings   129
19. Family   135
20. Seers and Forbidden Things   146
21. Life and Death   153
22. Love's Spectrum   158
23. Wedding Plans and Reminiscence   168
24. The Wedding   174
25. Out of the City   183
26. God's Timing   191
27. Eden Hill   197
28. With Child   204
29. New Life Coming   211
30. Upside Down   219

31. Valley of the Shadow 227

32. Going Home 236

33. Oh Baby! 242

34. Broken 248

35. Learning Curve 252

36. Fighting the Dragon 257

37. Deception 263

38. Beauty for Ashes 268

39. Out of the Nest 278

40. Fanfare 283

41. Out to Dinner 290

42. Yoga 297

43. Dreams and Visions 302

44. Death of a Dream 309

45. The Butterfly 321

46. He Wants None To Perish 329

47. Final Decision 334

48. No Words 338

49. This Too Shall Pass 344

50. Celebration 348

51. Retirement 354

52. After All 364

Epilogue 372

Life Questions 373

Signs, Whispers, and Miracles: Scriptures 377

About the Author 383

Acknowledgments 389

Write a Review 391

FOREWORD

Where did all the miracles go?

This question rattles in my mind at times, typically when I can't see the forest through the trees. *Signs, Whispers, and Miracles* reminds me that God's hand never rests—threading me delicately and deliberately into the fabric of His purpose.

When Violet came to me with her book idea, she sent me a short sample. As an editor, ghostwriter, and publishing consultant for the past twenty years, I receive up to ten samples per week, from which I select those I may want to work with. Violet's struck me for three reasons.

First, her prose transported me—from her childhood forest perch overlooking the flowered river valley, to the dimly-lit bedside of a dying friend. Her skill at weaving words and imagery delighted me. I felt a rare "love at first read."

Second, her enthusiasm cemented that I must work with her. Ever dedicated to her craft of writing, and more committed to ensuring her reader would experience joy, I knew the process would delight me. More importantly, I knew the outcome would impact—and possibly even transform—others. Since my guiding principle is to engage in work that *improves lives*, I knew I wanted to help guide Violet's book development.

Third, her faith compelled me. I desired more—like a subtle thirst for a mountain spring just around the bend. She shared a glimpse into God that felt familiar, but still not clear to me. I knew that she trusted Him, but I would not yet know how—or what impact her words would have on my own faith journey.

In editing her first draft, she riveted me to her story—traveling by boat to Europe (who does that?), loving a drug dealer, maturing into a loving wife and mother, and helping others find healing through her physical therapy (and ultimately, prayer). Violet doesn't shy from honesty—whether about her life's trials or God's expansive hope. And her truth showers blessing on any reader willing to join.

I told her after her first edit that I wanted to see more detail of how her faith developed. It wasn't yet clear to me how a child who had endured some of her trials and doubts could become an adult who shared a seemingly innocent love for—and trust in—God. Knowing that she wanted any reader to feel at home in her book, regardless of their faith, I wasn't sure how she would accomplish this "telling" of her own personal walk with God.

Like a masterful writer, Violet revised—and she didn't just tell, she showed. Through shining light on the miracles that wove through her life—focusing her vision of God as her loving, active designer—she beckoned me into my own self. I found myself asking, "What miracles have I witnessed, even today?" and "What miracles can I expect tomorrow?" I began venturing *outside*—literally, into my flower garden, something we both share an affinity for—while letting His purpose reflect within me.

Like Violet—and most people I know—I've felt defeated at times by tragedy and trauma, like a wounded deer lying on the forest floor. Like Violet—I've seen "coincidences" that don't add up, pointing to God's hand at work.

His miracles are everywhere, if we listen to His whispers and notice his signs. Sometimes everything changes when we shift our view.

By reading Violet's story, my hope is that you, too, will find something already in front of you: God's ever-present hand—designing miracles, while weaving you into His everlasting garment.

— Jocelyn Carbonara

Editor, Ghostwriter, Publishing Consultant, and President of Spiritus Communications, Inc. (www.LeadtoEngage.com)

My Prayer

PRAYER

Oh, Lord, my God,

Hear my prayer with mercy.

May my faithfulness give You joy, O Lord.

Forgive my sins. Help me forgive others their sins.

Grant me a vibrant palette of words to exude Your pictures.

Color the words You give me with reality. Shine through them gloriously.

You are the color and description of all creation, far beyond our loveliest dreams.

**May this grateful prayer be pleasing to You and bring the colors of me and my

readers, Your creations,

to Your infinite mind,

in loving hues.   I

In Jesus'   I

name,   I

Amen   I

Amen   O

Amen

...the Word was God. John 1:1

Your word is a lamp to my feet and a light to my path.
Psalm 119:105

Then God made two great lights: the greater one to rule the day, and the
lesser light to rule the night.

He made the stars also.

Genesis 1:16

Then Jesus spoke to them saying," I am the light of the world. He who
follows Me shall not walk in darkness, but have
the light of life.

John 8:12

PROLOGUE

HOW DOES ONE FIND GOD? Finding God in hardship and joy involves an ongoing process throughout life—within each season. Life's seasons manifest in several ways. I'm beginning the *winter* of my life—at age seventy-one-in this season of retirement. Each of you is in a season of some sort—whether it's dictated by age or the "weather" you may be enduring at this time.

Finding God means *not ignoring Him as He makes himself evident*—and even before He has. Developing a deep trust in Him before walking through "the valley of the shadow of death" allows you to "fear no evil." Experiencing disability, disease, and tragedy remains painful, raw, intense, and even heart-shattering; but if His precious promises live in your heart, His joy and presence walk through those times with you.

Perhaps you need to "find" those promises and His love in the throes of an awful time. With God, all things are possible.

My husband, Michael, expressed surprise to me after reading several chapters in this book. "I've never had any experiences like these," he said.

To those of you who feel as he does, like my experiences don't parallel yours, you and he simply have *different expressions* of God in your lives. Each of us has one individual plan, one design—yet no two are alike. I believe despite our differences, all of us have God's presence in our lives, despite how we observe or experience it.

I write my story and insights so you also may choose to see the ongoing story of God's amazing grace woven throughout your life. Since He loves each of us equally, you also have this gift.

— Violet Batejan

Summer 2020

Live your life in joy and faith
Protected 'neath His wings;
Come and savor my Lord's grace
And listen to the angels sing...
— Violet Batejan

Use what talents you possess; the woods would be very silent if no
birds sang there except those that sang best.
— Henry van Dyke (1852-1933)

1

THE BEGINNING

"Then God saw everything that he had made, and indeed it was very good."
— *Genesis 1:31*

PERCHING HIGH in the red delicious apple tree, I look up and see the forest like a band of soldiers surrounding the house my mother's father built. The home rises, as if woven into the forest's edge; proud, it stands at the base of the towering trees. A stony, dirt driveway juts out from 5th Avenue, which dead-ends at the river.

The driveway access parallels our well-kept home: gray stone, cream stucco, wide-eyed picture windows, a flagstone patio. The driveway runs the length of the house and yard to a wood-frame, single-car garage. On the cusp of evening, the house glows sunset orange, burgundy, yellow, and hints of blue as the light blazes before giving in to darkness. Below the forest and home lie open, emerald meadows, rich with fruit trees. My six-year-old eyes see God's giving nature everywhere.

Although I can't see down the river road from my tree, I know silver, flashing water paints itself on the mountain base. A train whistles as it charges across, mid-mountain, above the river shore on the other side of the valley. I can't see the distant engineer from my apple tree. But he always blasts the whistle when I pull my raised fist down while standing on the nearby river's smooth stones, ankle deep in water. I can see it in my mind, high in my tree.

"Down the river," as we call it, is a magical place full of animal tracks, small life under rocks, birds that cry along the trail through silt basins, down to flowing water. Whenever I step in the river, I watch out for water moccasins. Even though snakes are part of God's creation, I don't have to get bit.

Still high in the tree, I turn my face into the evening wind. It rises, gusts, and flags my hair behind me, still with a hint of summer warmth. The breeze wafts down the unbuttoned V of my blouse— September's sigh at summer's passing.

I hear the crunch of tires on the gravel driveway. My father's black station wagon turns toward the garage. *It must be six o'clock, dinner in fifteen minutes.* I picture my mother in her favorite, second-hand apron. All our clothes are secondhand, except Dad's. He says he *needs new clothes because he works.*

I'm hungry now. I know there is a chicken in the roasting pan. I can see, even with my eye closed, as Mom pulls it out of the oven— crispy, brown, juicy. It smells rich and mouthwatering.

Dinner is always meat, fish, an occasional pizza or hoagie, two vegetables, salad, and dessert—sometimes homemade cake or pie. Mom says it's a "'balanced meal.'"

When Dad sits down, dinner is ready, and Mom serves. This rhythm is never broken without just cause; even when there is a good reason, the outcome may not be peaceful.

With that in mind, I know Mom is opening the back door to holler me home. I slither down the tree, swinging onto the lowest branch, still too high to touch the ground. Pumping my body, I whip back and forth—glory in the freedom of my swinging arc. My hands anchor me on the *banner,* my sister's and my word for a low branch that leads to earth. My fingers open. I fly toward the ground—practiced, arms aloft, back arched, feet in the right direction for return to the real world—a perfect landing. Only then, with impact, do I think about the unfinished homework in my bookbag.

Homework is done on yellowish-green paper with turquoise lines —two thick, and a skinny one in between, to show how tall the lowercase letters are as I print. On this day, I've already decided *that* paper is *lost*. Outside would become a mere daydream, if I were to say my homework is not done. I don't feel or understand the need to waste daylight on homework. While that's not how all the grownups in my life would see it, on this day, I'm not listening to them.

All through first grade and into second, I try to print letters and words, but they're a mystery to me without meaning. So even when stuck indoors with homework, I stare at the wall above my desk, travel out in the woods in my mind, walk on the river road, gallop in the meadow, until suddenly, it's dinner time.

The rule is homework is finished before dinner; but Mom doesn't ask to see it. And now it's *lost*, because outside is more important to me than homework after being cooped up in the classroom all day. Because I'm *slow*, I have many names, mostly from my Dad: *daydreamer, last rose of summer, slow poke, lazy bones, head in the clouds*, and just plain *lazy*.

I'm always last.

Dad teaches us to swim and do gymnastics. He keeps us safe while we learn. When he throws me up in the air, I know he'll catch me. Mom reads to us, buys us books, and talks to us like regular people when we're alone. These are good times, always in the shadow of the house my grandfather built. It feels safe there; though I never know what will happen next, between school and my parents. It feels safe even when voices are raised. It's a loved house on two acres of ground where I escape into the woods, down the river, or up a tree. The forest, house, fruit trees, and meadows wrap themselves around me; they are there for me, a gift from God.

I'm seven in December, two months from now. I am different from other kids: I can't read, spell, or do math or word flashcards. I can look into a teacher's eyes with tears of my own, because my homework is *lost*.

I know my family is different too. Even though I know Mom and Dad love me, they have secrets I can't tell anyone else. No one must know Mom works at night. No one must know we wear secondhand clothes.

Then there are the *commandments*, serious challenges. My sister and I must excel in school, then go to college. We must speak English correctly. Good manners are always observed, like the ones Mom teaches us. In public, children *must be seen and not heard*. We must have high Intelligence Quotients and land good paying jobs—like Dad in the IRS and US Army Reserves.

But how do I excel in school, if I can't read, spell, or memorize flashcards? Where is the bridge from the alphabet to reading? Why do other kids remember spelling words or answers to math flashcards?

Second grade is the year my parents learn the teacher's name for me, and they tell me I'm an "underachiever." That translates from my parents to me as *lazy*. By third grade, I know it must be true.

The House Mom's Father Built, Pen and ink drawing in 1947 by Dad's best friend, Robert Schmeer.

8

2

ELEMENTARY

"Take My yoke upon you and learn from Me, for I am gentle and lowly in heart, and you will find rest for your souls."
— *Matthew* 11:29

THE OAKTAG REPORT card slid out of its envelope. My sinking stomach lurched when the bold, red *U* beside "reading" jumped out at me.

"Oh, look!" The report card, wrenched from my hand, waved in the air. "Here's a first grader who's going to get her hide tanned tonight! She got a *U* in reading!" Howls, cackles, hoots, and whoops filled the bus as a mob of eyes cornered me. My spine collapsed as my body melted into the corner between window and seat. My heart pounded in my ears. I could feel my face, ripe-tomato red.

I looked at the laughing girl waving my report card. Boiling rage exploded inside my chest. My hand shot out and grabbed the card. Her look of surprise turned serious, with my angry eyes fixed on hers. She raised her eyebrows, shrugged her shoulders, and looked away.

The bus stopped. I stood up, straightening my back, eyes focused

9

on the door. My legs carried me surely down the aisle. Down the steps into the cool air outside, my shame dove underground.

The whipping waited until my father got home—the beaded belt blunted by my clothes. *He's not mean. I just have to figure out this reading thing.*

After second grade, the *underachiever* label stuck. My third-grade teacher, Miss Bellman, didn't question why I couldn't read or spell. She just believed the *lazy* label.

In her class, you could choose a sticker for a perfect spelling paper. The pony sticker—a gray pony with a dark mane and tail— looked like the pony I rode in my daydreams.

I studied, I didn't study, I stared at the spelling words. All the tests came back with a C, D, or red F on them. Letters didn't make sense strung together into words. Words did not mean anything but were a jumble of symbols. So, I tried something else.

"Miss Bellman, Violet's spelling book is open in her desk!" I froze as every head turned my direction.

"Stand here," Miss Bellman said, pinning me with her eyes while pointing next to her desk. "I'm going to call your mother and see what she has to say about her daughter cheating."

The sticker book lay open on the desk. P-O-N-Y printed under the handsome gray pony got my attention. *P-O-N-Y.* Miss Bellman spoke into the phone to Mom. My mind flashed with the connection: *P-O-N-Y spelled the letters on the sticker! P-O-N-Y—the name of the animal I liked to pet in the field. That's what reading means; the words are things!* No one ever explained words to me. For an instant, I felt stupid being the only one in the class that didn't understand this fact. But now, a switch had turned on the light. My heart beat faster; my skin tingled. I forced the corners of my mouth to turn down; *I have to look ashamed right now, even though I am going to read!* Miss Bellman announced to the class, "Violet's mother says she will be in for a surprise tonight." The teacher almost smiled; but her eyes were narrow and hard, like marbles.

Too happy to care about the whipping coming, I kept my face

serious. *Words mean things I can see and touch! I know how to spell pony! I can read!*

Each separate word pictured something, until strings of words became movies in my head. I sailed through the third-grade reader. There were ponies to ride—and magic carpets. A snowy, winged horse took me far into the clouds. I flew away from school and arguments and average report cards, away from anything upsetting. I escaped alongside the characters in each book.

Even though school got easier, my fifth-grade teacher saw something none of the other teachers did. Mom came for a parent-teacher conference. I sat outside the classroom, but I heard every word.

"Oh, Violet Finkle!" my teacher said. "Oh, I'm sorry; that was your name before you were married. Now it's Mrs. *Valor.*"

"Yes, Miss Flick. It's hard to believe you taught me in fifth grade, and now you have my daughter. How is she doing?"

"That's what I wanted to discuss with you. Violet is a bright child, but she doesn't learn like the other children."

"She didn't learn to read until third grade," Mom responded, "but no one said there was anything wrong."

"She needs instruction in different words, from a different angle to understand what the others get with traditional teaching." My teacher tried to paint the problem for my mom. "She needs pictures, sometimes, instead of verbal explanations. I'm afraid our public school system doesn't take needs like hers into consideration. A private school would, though."

"Isn't that expensive, Miss Flick? You know I trust your assessment; I think you're right. My husband... Well, I'll see what he says."

Dinner that night turned into a tense affair. Afterward, the *discussion* in the den became heated. I listened, sitting on the steps in the kitchen hallway, careful not to get caught.

"I never went to private school," my dad argued. "I studied correspondence courses in accounting and got where I am today!"

"But we're not talking about you, Rudy! She doesn't learn like the other children. Miss Flick..."

"Let Miss Flick pay for private school. Violet's grades are good enough to stay right where she is. She's just *lazy*. If she'd get her head out of the clouds and apply herself, she'd learn."

Mom tried. Money-talk always ended in an argument between Mom and Dad. Dad only saw dollar signs.

Yet he always filled the church envelope on Sunday.

Sunday loomed like a day without sun. Crinoline pricked my skin. Patent leather shoes with dressy coats, just for show. No one guessed it, but everything except my socks, shoes, and panties came from a secondhand shop.

By fifth grade, I understood my issues with church went lightyears beyond clothes. Sunday morning, buzzing voices carried beyond the outer doors, where the women hovered in small groups—like a social club Mom enjoyed. But they made me think of the cliques at school, full of catty girls.

Mom played piano for the service, while Lynne and I sang the first hymn before Sunday School started. I knew how I felt about God when I was looking over the house and grounds from the top of the apple tree: like God had painted a living scene and let me live in it. God made the wind rustle trees in the woods. He gave birds their songs and deer a place in the basins by the river.

But Jesus didn't seem alive from Sunday school lessons. I learned some things about Him—but *a living God that made all things* never seemed to enter the handsome brick building where we attended church.

One Sunday, Mom lost the gold charm bracelet her bosses gave her for Christmas. It must have come unlatched and fallen while she volunteered in the nursery. A printed "Lost" message in the bulletin met with silence and no bracelet. Mom seemed to lose her enthusiasm for church after that; I guess she thought the ladies weren't listening to Jesus.

Each morning, my sister and I straightened our rumpled twin beds; smoothed and tucked sheets and blankets; fluffed pillows; and pulled up light, identical bedspreads. Mom wanted to re-do our room, and we asked for bunk beds. A week later, she saw the "perfect girl's room" at a friend's house. After Dad's construction project, our whole room screamed pink. Walls; built-in, glass-topped desks; and glass-topped vanities with ruffled valences—all pink.

Neither of us liked pink.

And Mom sewed our twin mattresses together into one near king-sized bed. *No bunk beds.*

The first night in the stitched-together bed, Lynne and I crawled under one sheet with one blanket for the two of us. Waking in the dark, my teeth chattering, I sat up. Lynne had the blanket and sheet twisted around her. She batted at me with one arm when I tried to untangle the covers. I made do with an afghan, thin but warmer than nothing.

A sharp kick in the ribs awakened me. *Still dark out.* The night-light showed Lynne, spread-eagled, blanket and sheet wrapped around her trunk like a mummy with its arms and legs free. My sleeping sister occupied every inch of the bed. At dawn, I found a quilt, made a bed on the floor, and slept until morning.

"Sissy, why are you on the floor?" Lynne asked. I laughed at her tousled blonde hair and puzzled blue eyes peeking over the bed's edge. Two years younger than me, she was my best friend.

"It's okay, Lynney. You didn't know you kicked me out of bed in your sleep."

Her eyes widened above a little *oh* mouth. She reached to hug me. I got up and held her. "You didn't hurt me any. Come on. We have to make this stupid bed."

"It *is* a stupid bed," she said as we wrestled with the heavy bedspread Mom crafted on her sewing machine. Like the Limoges, porcelain vanity trays, silver brush and comb sets, and antique nail tools, the heavy spread with its pink dust ruffle could be called *elegant*. Mom's friends had complimented her on our "beautiful room." Elegant didn't interest Lynney and me. Gay, seven years younger than me, had a room of her own. But I liked sharing a room with Lynne.

The next night, I came prepared. A thick, blue blanket cushioned the floor while a soft, woolen, plaid blanket kept me warm. The big bed turned into a combat zone, unless I slept on the floor or the living room couch.

"Hye," Granny said in her German accent. "Violet Luise, what you doing on that floor?" Lynne still slept. I put a finger to my lips, hopped up, and motioned my grandmother to the living room. It didn't take long to explain.

"You come upstairs to sleep with me," Granny said. She typically slept on the pull-out couch in her living room, leaving her bed unoccupied in her apartment upstairs. I ran up the steps and sat on her queen-sized bed while Granny talked to Mom. That night, in her wide bed, I slept without waking until morning.

Upstairs, it felt like I had my own apartment under the eaves. A thick, gold, tapestry curtain hung between the living room and bedroom for privacy. Tall pine trees that spoke softly in the wind looked into an alcove through three, double-hung windows. The roof drummed with rain—rhythmic, soothing. Crickets and cicadas chirped and whirred, their voices carrying in on fresh, summer breezes. Winter's silence as snow fell on the pines became a "Silent Night" picture. I read late into the night, until my eyes fell closed with sleep. Granny's bedroom turned into my haven.

By sixth grade, I started reading the King James Bible I got at church. Granny poked her head in and laughed as I read one chapter each morning in her bathroom. She liked me reading the Bible; her opinion mirrored my own when it came to my parent's church. Invited by a neighbor, she had left Mom's and Dad's church for an independent chapel near home. Granny called her new church "fundamental."

It took me a year from the time Mom's bracelet went missing to speak up. I read that Jesus had called some of the priests *hypocrites*. Now I knew what it meant.

"Mom, how come you never got your bracelet back when one of the Commandments says, 'Thou shalt not steal'?"

"I'm not sure, but these things happen," she said.

I thought for a few seconds; the explanation wasn't enough. "Mom, I want to go to church with Granny. I'm not going back to that *church of hypocrites*."

Her eyes searched mine. Then, shoulders drooping, she nodded and left the room without saying a thing. I thought she'd argue....

As Granny and I attended what Dad called "the fire and brimstone" chapel, her gruff, German voice and ways grew softer edges. She seemed to appreciate me attending church with her. I felt a bond form that hadn't been there before the church change and my move upstairs.

"Hye, Violet Luise," Granny said in her German accent to get my attention. "Don't streak your hair back! You need height!" she pushed the plastic hair band forward towards my face, raising my hair in front.

It does look better, I thought, looking in the mirror. Granny patted my shoulder.

"We are good together at church, ja?"

Jesus remained less alive than I wanted; but I still said, "Ja" in return, arms around her hips, forehead buried in her belly. Her laughter traveled down, caressing my face. She gave me no hint how her upcoming plans would change my life, forever.

3

GERMANY—MAGSTADT

"How shall we sing the Lord's song in a foreign land?"
— *Psalm* 137:4

GRANNY CAME to dinner in February 1961 on a mission. Her thick, silver-streaked hair, caught in a bun, lay at the nape of her neck. Hardship and age creased her face, yet she still looked and moved like a younger woman with purpose.

As we sat down to eat, Granny said in her German-accented, broken English, "Hye, I hear from Emile in Magstadt. He wants me to visit. I take Violet Luise; she is oldest. Lynney comes too, if you pay," Granny gestured toward my father. Lynney hadn't come to the table yet.

Dad shifted in his chair—money at stake. His mouth, never generous, clamped shut in a thin line.

Mom recovered quickly from her stunned state. "Oh, Mother, that would be wonderful. I'd hate to separate Violet and Lynne. Gay is definitely too young. Mom turned to Dad, her expression of excited hope dying as she focused on his compressed lips and lined brow.

16

Balancing his children's interests against a substantial sum of his money placed Dad in an awkward position.

"When would you go, and how long would you stay?" he asked, buying some time.

"We see Emile and Marta, Hannelore and Lena. Then we travel and see some of Europe. We go in May and come back in September."

"How much are the airline tickets?" With each question, I could see Dad's internal calculator totaling.

My life's changing between bites of dinner, I thought.

"No air. Boat," she said, "to Bremerhaven, Deutschland."

"I'll look into prices and tickets," Dad said as he finished eating and left the table.

Lynne had no idea what had just happened. A trip to Germany for me alone would mean separation from her for more than a whole summer. I knew Dad would decide that Lynne couldn't go; it would be *too expensive,* because anything extra was too expensive. In two months, I could be on a ship crossing the Atlantic Ocean to foreign places I had never seen. Excited and anxious at the same time, I wondered what being away from home for a whole summer would be like.

"Violet," Mom caught my arm. "Come with me." I had to run to keep up with her. She sat on the couch and patted the spot beside her. "You understand you have to graduate sixth grade ahead of your classmates so you can leave in May." I nodded, even though it had not occurred to me. "I'll talk to Mr. Benz tomorrow. Please don't say anything to Lynne. Wait until your father makes his decision. I don't want her hurt." I nodded again as sadness rose. I already knew what his decision would be about including Lynne. So did Mom.

Lynney and I are going to be apart four and a half months. I swallowed hard as the reality sank in, and I realized: *This is an adventure outside of a book. Scary. You don't get hurt reading books.*

Dad had no clue the importance of this trip to Lynne and me. I sensed his impending refusal to pay for Lynne's passage would mark the rest of our lives. *I am going to Europe alone with Granny. Lynne must never know she could've come too,* I thought with an ache in my chest. *Sad.*

I thought about Dad's background, what pressures and layers had created his hardness. Born in Montana, he claimed first surviving son status, where cattle froze standing in the fields. Dirt poor, foreigners, his father had eked out a living in the coal mines. They moved to Hazelton, Pennsylvania, where Dad described running for his life, down back alleys, from local bullies. He told us how he helped his mother do the wash, ironing, and anything she asked, with pride. His story seemed strange, since he did none of these things at home. He always called it "women's work," if Mom asked for help. The condescending look on his face left no doubt about his feelings. Whenever Dad talked about his mother, Mom stared at her dinner plate or found something else to do. He never talked about his father.

Mom's history created different layers in her personality. She came from parents at opposite ends of the social stratum: Granny, a poor German immigrant, and Granddaddy, of English and Welsh origin whose family-owned antique stores and oil-painted portraits of their ancestors.

My grandfather died long before my birth. He rated "sun, moon, and stars" acclaim in all of Mom's childhood stories.

WWI forever scarred Granny, along with a generation of others. Mom painted a brave picture of Granny's escape from starvation by immigrating to America. Stern, gruff, no- nonsense—her smile shone as a God-given light in an otherwise severe, buttoned-down, stubborn woman. All those attributes placed the odds in favor of her survival.

With care and respect, Mom told me her own childhood story of pain and degradation at Granny's hands. Mom's beleaguered childhood lay rooted in events her mother had experienced with war, starvation, and trauma beyond Granny's ability to cope—or our ability to understand. By the time I turned twelve, I knew the story. By then, Granny and Mom shared a civil, occasionally barbed relationship—living under the same roof, two women in the same kitchen.

I think of my grandmother's history with a sense of nostalgia and respect. Although my grandmother could be difficult and crusty, she named Mom "Violet," a name that conveyed art and flowers, a name Mom loved. Being the firstborn, Mom named me Violet as well.

Long before my birth, Paris, France, claimed leadership in the fashion world—a world familiar to Mom as a runway model in the 1940s. Her air of elegance belied the frugal, savvy homemaker she became, one who kept her hands beautiful by wearing gardening gloves. With Dad's help for the larger bushes, she dug and transplanted perennials with care: wild rhododendron, azaleas, and mountain laurel. The gardens—splashed with low-growing daffodils, violas, mountain pink, and tulips—complemented taller lilacs, snowball bushes, and viburnum. The combination created an artistic, well-landscaped yard, where fruit trees already grew. Gardens framed the house her father built, a home she cherished in his memory and for its own beauty.

A practical woman who stretched the household budget with used clothing, Mom claimed the "secondhanding" legend title, known only in our home. She found fine, like-new, expensive clothing at a fraction of the original cost. Her eagle-eye for secondhand jewelry spotted diamond rings, sterling silver pins, cameos, and all sorts of fourteen-karat gold items, usually mixed in with jumbled costume jewelry. The way she crafted a secondhand ensemble made it look like she stepped out of a fashion magazine. No one ever guessed she shopped anywhere but the finest stores; and Mom *never* volunteered that information. *Each of us are made of our own, individual puzzle pieces. We fit into the world's puzzle, intersect with some people, never know others,* I thought. Granny labored most of her life as a live-in domestic before moving in with Mom and Dad. Since her pay had included room and board, she banked all her money. *Years and years of saving, and now she wants to take me to Europe!* Her last live-in job required cooking and housekeeping for Admiral Stump, famous in our house for "Stumpy scrambled eggs." His preferred recipe still made my mouth water: no milk, break the

19

eggs in a pan of sizzling butter, and stir until firm. Season to taste. *Delicious!*

School at Amber Elementary turned into a challenge. A thick, red folder begged to be opened when my sixth-grade teacher, Principal Benz, placed it on my desk. "Violet, you will have to complete all the work by May third that your classmates will finish by mid-June." He pointed to the packet as he lowered his tall frame into a chair beside me. "This is an exciting time for you. I know you will finish in time." I hadn't noticed his thoughtful, gray eyes before. His lightly creased face expressed a stern but caring spirit. "Each day, you'll complete part of the packet. I'll teach you the concepts you need for the work. If you want help, just raise your hand, and I'll make time."

I nodded, watching him rise. *I can trust him. I can do this.* Fear still hovered at the edges of my mind; yet I *would* leave all I knew, all I loved, and go to Germany.

At recess, a big tree on the edge of the playground welcomed me to lean against it. With school sorted out, I could think more clearly about Granny. I trusted her to keep me safe. Calm spread throughout —a sign of God, telling me *all would be well.*

Principal Benz patiently walked me through each part of the schoolwork. If I didn't understand something, he explained it a different way. With his help, I progressed through the sixth-grade requirements, completing the packet a week before our departure date.

"Violet," Dad strode toward me, his camera equipment in hand. "I want to teach you to use my camera, so you can take pictures of all the places you're going to see in Europe." My mouth opened in surprise. My three-year-old Kodak Brownie Star Flash still saw constant use. My photography, with Dad's camera, would rise to a whole different level.

Dad stood in back, wrapped around me, hands guiding my grip on the manual camera. "That's right," he said as I pressed the shutter. With an even voice, he repeated any instructions I needed when a blank stare gave me away. The shutter clicked through an entire role of twenty-four pictures, as he patiently taught the essentials. Directions on using the complicated light meter and manual aperture settings settled into my knowledge base with repetition.

In the house, Dad grabbed his car keys. "Let's take the film to be developed. I think there's an overnight service." My mind spun. *Overnight developing—expensive.* My ability to take pictures seemed really important to him.

The next day, we picked up the developed film. Dad sat close to me. "What do you think of this picture?" he asked. The picture of Lynne holding a branch of dogwood flowers next to her face went awry with her bare legs drawing the eye first.

"It's too far away," I said.

"Look what happens if we frame the picture like this." Dad drew a rectangle around Lynne's torso and head, cutting off her scratched up legs and dirty sneakers.

"That's much better," I said. We critiqued all the pictures together, intent on the final result. Dad made the lessons a priority, a pleasure, a treasure. I would guard his camera and light meter with my life. And I would bring home fantastic slides, so he could see Europe too.

Lynne—my joined-at-the-hip, ten-year-old sister—already started bonding more closely with Gay, five years her junior. Unperturbed that we would be separated, Lynne seemed to accept the fact that *the oldest daughter got to go with Granny.* Resigned to our parting, I began looking forward to the trip.

"Come help me! Look what I found!" Mom pulled me out the back door toward the station wagon. Two secondhand steamer trunks stood ready for transport into the house. Packing began. Clothes, toiletries, my journal and stuffed pony, Ginger, in suitcases. *The Little Lame Prince, The Littlest Princess,* pens and writing paper—all traveled in the trunk. Large, blue, trimmed S.S. America labels with Granny's name and address on them stood out, plastered to the center of the trunk. We were ready to go.

Crying never occurred to me at departure. Squirrelly with excitement, my mind ran in circles; but Mom's strict training in manners and deportment held the squirrel in check. S.S. America's majestic, black hull soared upward. The ship sported a thick red stripe where her hull met the water, rising into the sky with two massive smokestacks painted red, white, and blue. Hugs and last-minute goodbyes passed in a haze of unreality. *We're really leaving home, going far away.* With a tug to my hand, I blindly followed Granny.

Suddenly, we looked out over America's rail and threw confetti and streamers toward the dock. Lynney waved madly, jumping up and down. Mom held Gay, both waving and grinning. Dad's usually serious face smiled. Our eyes met. He saluted, as if in his Army Reserve dress uniform and cap. My mission: *take Kodachrome slides of everything, so the family could see Europe projected onto a bright screen in our dark basement.* His snappy salute also said, "God Speed."

The Statue of Liberty lofted her torch high—strong, graceful, swelling my chest, moistening my eyes. Saluting our flag with the Pledge of Allegiance and singing "America the Beautiful" choked me up, even in the classroom. Lady Liberty in real life magnified that feeling until I nearly burst with the magnificence of it all. We stood at the rail until the grand statute grew small and New York Harbor faded.

Below decks, our cabin's best attribute—the porthole—let in natural light. Bunk beds (me on top), a bathroom, and built-in dresser made the space tight but adequate—and relatively inexpensive.

I learned, the hard way, that seasickness is not resolved by staying in bed. The ship's nurse advised fresh air for the overwhelming nausea. Cocooned in a thick, red, plaid blanket, I rested on a deck chair facing the blue-gray ocean. Salt air and sea breeze whipped by, leaving my face tingling and rosy. Warmed in the blanket, the brisk air calmed my heaving gut until it finally felt peaceful.

I pointed Dad's camera and light meter at seascapes, sunrises, sunsets, an ice sculpture at dinner, the captain at his table, Granny at our table. Everything of interest had its likeness stored in the camera. The ship's library gave me *My Friend Flicka* and *The Diary of Anne Frank* to read on the deck as we knifed through the sea. Movies, shows, a saltwater pool, and souvenirs distracted me.

The port of Bremerhaven, Germany, came into view one sunset, only a surprise in its speed of arrival.

Onkel (Uncle) Emile, Granny's brother, greeted us with smiles and hugs. Not an American, all-out, grab-you kind of a hug that would pull you close; but more formal, even-keeled, with a joyful face and kind eyes. Our trunks shipped to Onkel's house. Darkness fell in a land that already felt distinctly different: in language, dress, and a more formal attitude as people greeted one another. Even the scents of this place registered as foreign: knockwurst and other sausages permeated the air surrounding a vendor's cart. People and suitcases loaded into a van. I curled up and slept, my head on Granny's lap, until we reached Magstadt beim Stuttgart, a town so tiny, locals said "by Stuttgart" to help locate it.

My second, less sleepy impression of Onkel Emile, and my first impression of *Tante (Aunt)* Marta, revolved around their differences. Onkel Emile's eyes were soft and encouraging with a pleasant, upturned, expressive face. Tante Marta's eyes were assessing, a bit critical, especially the set jawline and slight downturn of her mouth. Their voices followed suit: Onkel's a melodic tenor with a slower speech pattern; Tante's shorter, clipped speech pattern rang out with authority rather than melody.

Granny, Onkel Emile, and Tante Marta chattered in German that swirled over my head. Granny's and my room was an addition to the single-story house, built just for our visit, with hot and cold running water in the sink. I would realize that we spoiled Americans took hot, running water for granted.

After a cup of tea, we fell into bed, the night chill kept at bay with a massive, feather pillow that lay over the blanket and sheet. Warmed by tea, goose down, and a comfortable, firm bed, I slept.

Onkel Emile drove off to work by the time I awakened. Tante Marta had returned home from her daily bicycle trip to the market for the day's meals. Neighbor children—Uta, eight years old with wispy blonde hair like Lynney, and Hans, ten years old and a head taller than me—came over and played horses. Even though they were a few years younger than me, it didn't seem to matter. Teaching me German words seemed to delight them.

Since Granny's and my room boasted the only hot running water in our small sink, Granny heated water on the stove and washed my hair over the kitchen sink. Onkel Emile stopped me from taking a sip of tap water. Taking the glass from me, he said, "*Nein, Liebchen,*" (no, dear one), as he dumped the water down the drain. He gestured to a clear bottle in the refrigerator and said, "*Sprüdel.*" The naturally carbonated mineral water fizzed with a mountain-spring taste that was so refreshing, tap water held no temptation.

In the next few weeks, life in Magstadt became predictable. Little by little, German words flowed from my mouth, as the language became more familiar with the neighbor children's help. I began understanding simple German.

It took three weeks before Granny tried to take over Tante Marta's kitchen. My day-dreamy, inner world didn't fully register mounting tensions between Granny and Tante Marta, until the explosion finally detonated over a pie. A "best cook" title seemed to ignite competition between the two. Nearly drooling with anticipation, I shadowed Granny as she made my favorite: lemon meringue pie. I understood Tante Marta when she asked in German, "How can any pie be so wonderful that you stay at her side like this?" I smiled, but my suspicion—that Tante Marta had tried to veto the home addition, hot running water, and possibly our visit—hung like a storm cloud over me.

After two large pieces of pie—thick with lemon filling, topped by fluffy meringue—satisfied my sweet tooth, I followed Granny into the kitchen. Tante Marta, already stung by her family with the pie's success, spat a few words for Granny's ears alone and left the room. I watched Granny's facial expression change as she heard the remark. I, too, had seen Tante's narrowed eyes, lips curled in a near snarl, as the words leapt from her mouth. Rubor crept up Granny's neck, flushing her face. Without hesitation, she went after Tante Marta, railing at her in German.

Tante turned, face contorted in rage, and screamed in German, "Get out! Get out of my house!" By then, Onkel Emile held Marta's arm as I ushered Granny, still spitting mad, to our room.

Onkel Emile and Granny had a brother-to-sister, heart-to-heart talk later that evening. Although he wanted us to stay, Tante Marta's status as wife won out.

Even after the emotional fiasco, I slept deeply, warm—and awaited whatever came next. We couldn't stay in Magstadt; but *God must have something in mind.*

4

GERMANY—BACKNANG AND EUROPE

"He makes me lie down in green pastures;
He leads me beside still waters.
He restores my soul;
He leads me in the paths of righteousness for His Name's
sake."
— Psalm 23:2-3

OUR DESTINATION? Backnang, where we would be welcomed by Granny's younger kin, Hannelore, along with a woman Granny's age, Tante Lena (in my family, Aunt and Uncle were titles of affectionate respect, even if not used for true blood relations). This household—in town, beside a small stream—embraced us. We played board and dice games in the evening, interspersed with laughter and hugs. Each sentence turned into a German lesson, with kindness turning any mistakes into more lighthearted laughter.

Handsome Klaus Becker, the rosy-cheeked boy across the driveway, played cards and "Spiel," a board game. Exploring our cobblestoned neighborhood and the stream near home, he became a good companion.

Early Sunday mornings, Granny tapped me on the shoulder. "Time for *Kirch* (church)," she said. Snuggling deeper under my down quilt, I feigned sleep, clung to dreams: green, wooded stillness; leaping rapids down the river; a keening red-tailed hawk; my bare footprints next to deer tracks; toes feeling hot; silty dust of the river road with Lynney at my side. Granny never pressured me to go to church, although I could almost fully translate her disparaging comments to my aunts when I didn't. I never set foot in Backnang's white-steepled, Lutheran church. At age twelve, the idea of a large group of German speaking strangers surrounding me quenched any motivation to see inside its walls.

In mid-June, Hannelore, Tante Lena, and Granny began gabbing in excited German, with *Tyrol* the one consistent word I heard. Soon after, suitcases were flung open and packed for a trip: two weeks in the pastured foothills of Tyrol's Alps.

The tiny town, Haller am See, struck me as hand-carved with great skill, preserving the surrounding, natural beauty. Looking like a picture-book town whittled into the coast of a cold, blue lake, our chalet lay a mile up the mountainside, rising from its roots in a pasture. Wildflowers colored the grassy slope in scattered flecks. We could see the tranquil village, in miniature, from our deck. Coffee brown window boxes held a splash of red and white flowers. The chalet's great windows gazed over sloping hillside pastures that dropped sharply to the village below. The landscape ended with an expanse of serene, sky-blue water.

Trekking down the hill to town, Granny and I discovered a wood-carver's shop. We chose hand carved keepsakes: Two bucks, heads low, horns locked in deadly battle. A finely fashioned horse, rearing, mouth open—eight inches of wildness. The bust of a craggy man, eyes squinted, pipe held in his teeth, shaggy head topped with a Tyrolean hat—very like the wood-carver himself. Each figure, chiseled in wood and colored, was near-to-life.

But my favorite was an eight-inch, square, carved, inlayed chess/checker set with cunning drawers to store the pieces. The essence of Haller am See lived in each handmade work of art—reminders of the beloved town, mountainside, and lake—reminders of God's perfect creations.

Our shopping complete, I waded in the lake's chilly water. "Violet Luise, you think they like what we bought for home?" Granny asked.

"They'll love all the sculptures! Can't you see them on the den mantle?"

"Ja! A good idea. The carvings bring back this place, a little, to America."

Talking about home brought American life back into my senses—the landscape, scents, and people—so different from Germany or Austria. It felt odd to love the countryside, town, and people of Tyrol, yet feel homesick at the same time. Not in need of human comfort, I dove into a book when we returned to the chalet.

Some days, I climbed up the steep pasture until the chalet shrank to a dot below me. I toted a dense blanket with me to sit on—a soft cover over the prickly, wild grass. My book made a solid surface for thin, blue, airmail paper, so I could write my weekly letter home. I read in comfort beneath the glowing sun.

At milking time, the cows and goats ambled down the steep, grassy grade toward their milking shed. Many-pitched bells, one on each goat's collar, sounded—with every step forming harmony as a flock. The lead cow and several others wore deeper-toned bells, bass-like, that rang out with their swaying walk as they ambled home.

Tyrolean images, sounds, and sensations registered, tucked intentionally into my memory. I read in the Alpine air, warmed by the same sun that blessed my family at home in America.

One day, needing to stretch my legs after reading on the brightly-lit hillside, I climbed up the slope until rocky, gray outcroppings pushed themselves out of the ground. Something white flashed by as I turned my head. Homing in on the spot, surrounded by tufts of grass and moss, I knelt and touched the object. It felt like bone. Moss and dirt brushed away; a ram's skull gazed at me with empty-hole eyes and a missing jaw. I did a cursory cleaning of the skull, euphoric that God granted me such an artifact from this place. In the chalet, I rinsed away more dirt and debris. When dry, I wrapped the skull in several layers of newspaper before depositing the gem in my suitcase.

Of all the magnificent, breathtaking locations we visited, Haller am See's mountain pastures; pristine lake; and slow, steady, village life felt like my home on Earth. I moved leisurely, without being out of place, blending with the village and mountainside as naturally as a breeze passes through trees. I smiled at the locals. They smiled back, moving at my pace while accomplishing all that their lives required.

We lived in the twenty-third Psalm: "The Lord is my shepherd; I shall not want. He makes me to lie down in green pastures; He leads me beside the still waters. He restores my soul..." I could have stayed there.

Two weeks later, back in Backnang, a box of paperback books with Mom's flowing handwriting on the label waited for me. A small fortune to post, the heavy parcels appeared regularly throughout our trip—a balm for homesickness and everything else.

Not long after our return, Granny fidgeted and paced in our room. "I want to see more of Europe before September," she said.

"What do you want to see?"

"I have a list," she said reaching for a small notebook. "Venice, Monaco, and Nice on the French Riviera. Florence, Naples, Rome, Vatican City, Capri, and Switzerland," she read.

"Can we do all of that with the time we have left?"

"Ja," she said. "I find a tour company today."

That evening, Granny looked both resolute and satisfied. "I found the tour company. A bus goes from Backnang to Stuttgart. We take a train from Stuttgart and meet a tour bus in Zürich, Switzerland."

I shook my head, "All of the places you named in one tour?"
"Ach, no. All in four tours. We use *Reise mit Rouff* or Travels

with Ralph."

"When will we go, Granny?"

"In four days."

We arrived in Stuttgart early on a Monday morning. Shops surrounded the bus station. As I scanned, a camera shop jumped into view. "Granny, I need more film," I said, pointing to the shop. Once inside, with the film on the counter, Granny kept talking to the shop-keeper. "Violet, show Herr Strauss your camera and light-thing." I gave him both pieces of equipment. He examined them, nodded, and chose four different German cameras, which he placed on the glass counter.

Granny spoke again, and he chose one of the four, a Voitländer Vitomatic. Between Herr Strauss and Granny, I understood that this camera had a light meter and an automatic aperture setting. Granny must have noticed my juggling act between camera and meter. "You go slow with your camera. Try this one. You like it; tell me."

The Voitländer Vitomatic performed with easy focusing and fool-proof aperture setting. It included a leather case and lens cap. I played with the camera, using all the nearly instant setting devices; it only took five minutes. Far superior to Dad's equipment in every way, the German camera shot pictures in a fraction of the time with almost no effort.

"Oh, Granny, this camera is amazing."

Granny counted out traveler's checks—as I watched, stunned by the sum. We left the shop with a carrying case, film, and a miracle camera that would bring Europe home to my family, by way of Kodachrome. Before the camera purchase, I never imagined such giving love in Granny's nature. Yet, the entire trip screamed her understated generosity. I hugged her hard as she laughed softly and patted my face. The incredible camera only left my side when I slept.

We boarded a train for the three-plus hour ride to Zurich,

Switzerland. Rhythmic clickity-clacking and gentle swaying enhanced the colorful countryside as we sped by. I picked up my book, and by the time I helped Joe Green save Black Beauty, our train pulled into the Zurich station. We boarded a silver tour bus up to Zermatt in the Swiss Alps.

As the bus climbed, curves in the road became serpentine. Scenery plunged from top to bottom as each curve we put behind us became visible below. Nausea snuck up on me as I looked down from a dizzying height at the snaking road. Granny patted her lap. My whole family knew carsickness and I were well acquainted. I curled up on the bus seat like a cat, my head nested in Granny's lap. Napping in a horizontal position had settled my stomach by the time we reached our destination: Zermatt, where cable cars traveled high above precipitous mountain valleys to soaring, Alpine peaks. Relieved to be off the bus, I climbed aboard the suspended car with my camera ready.

Although the cable cars swayed in space above V-shaped valleys far below, I felt fine. Air, chilled by elevation, refreshed me with the indescribable scent of mountain wildness, free from pollution of any kind. My camera recorded wide, unbroken, blue sky and distant, green, mountain foliage, springing from the valley floor. Gray, jutting mountains careened upward to peaks without snow—too warm at the end of June. The Matterhorn pierced the sky in the distance, another image for my camera. We stopped at the top of the mountain, where men dressed in *Lederhosen* and women in *Dirndls* sold trinkets and souvenirs. Collectible spoons with a small, decorative rack added to our gift collection.

Once we had our fill of the picturesque mountains from our high peak, we glided back down to Zermatt the way we had come. Before dinner, we visited shops in the village at the foot of the mountain. There were *Lederhosen* and *Dirndls* in one store window.

"Granny, Dad wears shorts all summer. He might like some *Lederhosen*."

"Ja, he just might," she said, the bell tinkling as we entered the store. After selecting gray, leather shorts with traditional, embroidered suspenders, she asked to see a *Dirndl*, blouse, and apron. Holding it against me, she said, "You remember this place when you wear the *Dirndl*." Meticulously sewn of substantial, cotton material, the dress was forest green with colorful, embroidered flowers and a red apron. A puffy-sleeved, white blouse—gathered at mid-upper arm —completed the outfit. Well cut, the dress closed in front with silver crested, metal, shank buttons. Delighted, I nodded and grinned. She bought *Dirndls* for Lynney and Gay, more gifts that would be sent home ahead of us.

From Switzerland, we traveled to the French Riviera for a day at a pebbled beach, followed by a side trip to Monaco. My decency radar went off at the skimpy bathing suits that covered little of both large, small, and in-between sized men and women. Granny's and my tiny, independent church had preached modesty. These bathing suits showed everything from rolls of fat to sharp ridged backbones, unforgiving of any physical flaws. Many bikini bottoms and briefs showed the top edge of buttock clefts. Eyes averted, I played at the surf's edge, uncomfortable and puzzled by the brazen, near nudity.

In sunlit Italy, I tasted a lemon—its sweetness a surprise. The fragrant, bright-yellow fruit grew to the size of an orange. Punctual, comfortable train service—my favorite mode of transportation—took us up and down Italy's length. On an unforgettable, choppy, ferry boat trip, from Naples to the Isle of Capri, seasickness gave the fish my lunch. Once on solid ground, I recovered well enough to scamper up the hills of Capri and enjoy the bright houses and gardens.

Venice's canals, gondolas, famed architecture, and pigeons— although picturesque—smelled of stagnant water. Florence and Naples, filled with famous art, delighted my photography obsession and appreciation of sculpture. Michelangelo's massive statue of David posed for my camera. The artist had carved a set of four unfinished figures who sought to escape the remaining bonds of marble. There they remained, frozen in their discontented struggle. Painted hues of Botticelli's original *Birth of Venus* in warm, bright colors came as a surprise. Mom's dulled print in the downstairs bathroom could not compare to the original's vivid coloration. I took a picture for her.

Rome shocked me. Paper litter swirled in the breezy streets. Men wolf-whistled at me. I looked twelve years old and found it disturbing, unsettling, insulting. But the masterful architecture softened my criticism. Three coins, thrown over my shoulder into the grand Trevi Fountain, held wishes. It took several pictures to capture the massive composition.

Vatican City on a drizzly, warm day required the purchase of an umbrella. Granny—usually immune to souvenir peddlers—stopped, transfixed by a sterling silver rosary contained in a small, silver pot with a hinged lid. Though not Catholic, the rosary and its receptacle felt holy and too beautiful to leave behind. We walked over the cobbled plaza and streets, heads doing a slow-motion arc from side to side, taking in the majesty.

Granny found our next destination; the Sistine Chapel ceiling presented a unique photography challenge. Focusing my camera on the ceiling's brilliantly painted, revered figures, I lay with my back to the floor. No one questioned a child taking pictures; the adults made room for me with indulgent expressions, some with quiet laughter. My smile thanked them for their kindness.

St. Peter's Basilica—filled with lofty arches, domes, sacred paintings, and gold gilt—housed Michelangelo's most famous work. He carved the *Pieta* of highly polished, Carrara marble—alive with deep grief, acceptance, yet overwhelming sadness at the Son's death on Good Friday. The pale, greenish-tan marble of striking, uniform color shone, polished to a living luster. I soaked my spirit with the terrible, holy beauty of Mary, her dead Son held in her lap, both faces filled with peace beyond understanding. Granny had to pull me away.

I found God everywhere we visited, anywhere beauty could be seen —whether in smiling people, Michelangelo's works, or the sloping hills of Tyrol. I always knew, in my mind, He was omnipresent; now I knew it with my heart and soul. The whole world was in *His* hands.

September came without warning. I had seen enough, and the homebody within awakened. America, the beautiful, called, and I was ready to go home.

5

TRIAL BY FIRE

"Listen to Me, you who know righteousness,
You people in whose heart is My law;
Do not fear the reproach of men,
Nor be afraid of their insults."
— Isaiah 51:7

THE S.S. AMERICA lurched as towering surf roared and crashed over the hapless vessel; September's hurricane played catch with her toy. Seawater covered the cabin porthole as Granny and I tossed in our bunks. Waves the size of buildings—taller than the America, with sea troughs just as deep—forced the ocean liner up and slammed her down as she yawed in elemental battle.

My mind churned along with the sea as I faced the idea of seventh grade at Ridge High School. The thought of arriving three weeks late for classes, in a new school, drove me to stuff fear and worry down a deep rabbit hole of denial. Images of the last four-and-a-half months shielded me with pleasant distraction. I shifted in the bunk and wedged myself against the wall, a folded pillow jammed under my ribs.

The ship veered wildly, throwing me between the wall and bed railing, until I repositioned the pillow under me. Dinner hour had come and gone—not a good time to think about food. My mind wandered over the places I'd seen, the undeveloped film mailed home, and the people I'd met. After four-and-a-half months, we were nearly back home.

Sleep snuck up on me, as the surf quieted from towering waves to whitecaps slapping the ship's hull. The wind rested, pared down to a breeze.

In a few hours, seas calmed enough to go on deck. The dining room clattered with cutlery and hummed with people enjoying food once again. Our sturdy ship passed the welcoming Statue of Liberty on our return to New York Harbor where my family waited. I could no longer ignore thoughts of a new high school, where all the seventh graders had three weeks of acclamation and schoolwork under their belts. I would be the "odd man out."

Today is still here, I thought as the wind whipped my hair. *I'll deal with school tomorrow.*

———————

"Mom, you're smothering me," I exclaimed. The dock swarmed with excited people. I started saying something in German before I remembered: *We're back in the US.* Graffiti and trash in the streets screamed that we were no longer in spotless Stuttgart or her equally tidy suburbs. Mom laughed when I forgot and spoke in German, now a habit. Looking around me, I saw the same differences in the New York City port that I had seen that night we docked in Bremerhaven. People in Germany seemed more polite, a bit more formal, and much less boisterous than Americans.

City noise, dirty sidewalks, and smells of waste assaulted me. The little country girl from America had changed. My disarranged senses didn't settle until we left the city behind and our familiar home came into sight. Glad to be out of the car, Gay, Lynney, and I stood together. "I think we each grew an inch since last May," I said. They giggled in agreement.

Dinner developed into a grand affair, like Christmas, with all the gifts collected in four-and-a-half months of travel. Dad cleared the mantle, as the wood carvings, long packed, appeared like old friends. The magnificent, carved, rearing horse did not survive the journey. Once wild and proud, high on its haunches, a splintered left hind leg rendered it hopelessly lame. The sight of the rearing horse—on its side, with the shattered leg oddly displaced—made me duck into the bathroom. I wiped my eyes and regained control without being missed. I wrapped the horse in tissue, hiding its pathetic state; but my spirit remained chilled at the loss of its pristine form.

One weekend of acclamation, unpacking, speaking English, and reacquainting myself with my family rocketed by. I had experienced other countries, with other customs—people who wore anklets with sandals—as a matter of course. I had tasted different foods, heard different languages, and saw Michelangelo's masterpieces. America no longer held the unchallenged position as the only country in my world. So, on my first day at Ridge High School, when Mom dressed me in my German *Dirndl* with its red apron and fashioned my long hair into curls, my thoughts were not about what "cool" meant in seventh-grade America. I had dressed this way in Germany.

But the *Dirndl* and hair were minor compared to the major underlying problem. My stunning mother dressed herself in fine clothes—the secondhand tag a well-kept secret. No one knew she worked at night. She also kept quiet about the fact that Granny had paid my way to Europe. Mom told her friends, in her best Elizabeth Taylor style, "Violet's going to Germany and touring Europe for four and a half months with my mother." Before I arrived at Ridge High School that September morning, the word had spread, until all my seventh-grade teachers accepted my assumed status—as a *little rich girl, born with a silver spoon in her mouth*—before they ever met me.

The day I returned to school after the trip, my first hint of trouble came in second period math class. Feeling out of place and tongue-tied, I whispered to my friend that I had no math book. She raised her hand.

"Miss Arnot, Violet doesn't have a math book."

"Does Violet have a tongue?" the teacher returned sharply. Her look skewered me, taking my breath away, as her granite eyes locked on mine. At that moment, I knew this experience could rival crossing the stormy Atlantic.

Four and a half months earlier, I had enjoyed the challenging sixth-grade work and graduated elementary school by May with high grades. Following the trip to Europe, it seemed as if a fault-line in my life shifted, and high school became a fissure that could lead to a yawning chasm.

I brought the ram's skull from Austria to class as part of my seventh-grade science project. Late to retrieve it after grading, I apologized. "Sorry I'm late. I came to pick up my project. I forgot about it yesterday," I said to my science teacher.

"Yesterday was the deadline," he said, eying me like something unpleasant. "I threw it in the incinerator. Next time, you'll get here when you're supposed to." He turned and walked out of the room.

Astounded, my mind flashed back to the high, lush, green, mountain foothills in Austria where I had found the skull, hidden from any superficial glance. Half buried in dirt and moss, stark white bone, well weathered, I had claimed it as mine. Now, I returned to the present—crushed and painfully aware that I'd lost an irreplaceable treasure. And in the end, *my fault—late, as usual.* I walked down the hallway, out into the ridiculous sunny day, and boarded my bus.

My classmates didn't take long to mirror the teacher's disdain for me. Meanness multiplied with snide remarks, dirty looks, and generalized shunning.

"I'm sorry, Mrs. Rhodes, I don't understand diagramming sentences." My English teacher's explanation made no sense to me.

With an expression of disgust, she said, "Just because you were born with a silver spoon in your mouth doesn't mean I have to treat you like someone special." I received a D in grammar that report period.

The math teacher, Miss Arnot, promised help with word problems. As I came into the room, she put on her coat. "I can't stay. I have a date." With a cold look, she turned and left me standing there. She made her assessment of me clear: *stupid, not worth the time.* I received a D in math that report period.

The final blow in seventh grade fell after a science test in geology. The teacher passed out graded papers in order—the highest grade first and lowest grade last. I knew the names of all the rocks we studied. When he put the first paper face down on my desk, I smiled at him. But he turned to the class and spoke, "I had to make this test easy. Rob Shamlin has to make the football team." The class broke into laughter, their mocking faces aimed at me. I fixed my eyes on the window and went outside, in my mind, to escape the pain. Even when I did well, I couldn't win.

During the gangly, inept years of transition from tween to teen, if I opened my mouth, I managed to put my foot in it. I blathered on when I should have stayed silent with peers and teachers alike. *Pariah* described me, at the bottom of the pecking order at Ridge High School in southeastern Pennsylvania.

Why couldn't I learn like the other kids? I could hear a pin drop and become distracted. I could read with noise, if interested in the book; but I couldn't study with any noise at all. I needed perfect quiet, whereas most girls I knew played their transistor radios while doing homework. And I couldn't memorize math formulas for any length of time. My fifth-grade teacher had been right: I learned differently, and now the price of that difference claimed my last shred of dignity.

My parents dusted off the old *lazy* label, screamed their way through anything below a C, and denigrated anything below a B on my report cards. Laurels of sixth grade were forgotten.

My books helped me fly away, far from the daily onslaught. I didn't realize at the time that a book would change my life.

6

THE ROBE

"For God so loved the world that He gave His only begotten
Son, that whoever believes in Him should not perish but have
everlasting life."
— John 3:16

THROUGHOUT SEVENTH GRADE, books had helped me escape the
bonds of reality. *The Little Lame Prince* carried me away on his flying
cloak; I was as lame as he, just in a different way. *The Littlest Princess*
became a dear friend. *Heidi* took me back to Germany and up into
the Swiss Alps. If not playing sports, studying, or outdoors, my nose
pointed to a book. Arm-chair traveling, I identified with characters
who chaffed against pigeon-holes. Imperfect, picked on, demeaned,
and bypassed, they still survived with happy endings and comforted
me as I traveled, unscathed, in their good company.

During ninth grade, *The Robe*, by Lloyd C. Douglas, found its
way into my hands. Fourteen in the fall, my strong vocabulary
allowed comprehension of the thick, secondhand, paperback book,
purchased at a yard sale for twenty-five cents. The exciting back
cover primed me to read. *With Christ's robe as the main subject, Jesus*

should be a flesh-and-blood, life-like character, a living part of the Trinity, I thought. The preacher at the independent chapel didn't preach about the merciful side of God. The social club church didn't preach about the judgmental side of God. At the yard-sale that day, I thought perhaps this historical fiction could flesh out Christ in a story, with my Bible as an accuracy barometer. I scanned the yard-sale crowd; Mom finished paying for her last purchase.

By one o'clock, ensconced on the den couch, I savored the first, fall fire and opened the paperback book. As *The Robe* swept into the Roman Empire, Douglas hooked me from the first paragraph. Slavery's cruel reality, unimaginable wealth, and devastating poverty were all conjured—as love, hate, and power spiraled up from the page's well-drawn characters. I lived and walked with Demetrius, Marcellus, and Diana. Characters' experiences, the Messiah's actions, and His lasting presence among His believers seeped into my life with each page. It took two weeks to finish reading, and I thought of nothing else. The Robe had changed my life by midnight, the evening I closed the book.

They had just signed their death warrants. He took her hand and looked into her eyes, eyes that had no hint of fear although the archery field, their deadly destination, beaconed. As they walked away from the madly screaming Caligula, Marcellus whispered to Diana, who nodded and tossed the robe to old Marcipor, his father's trusted servant. The old man caught the garment as tears streamed down his cheeks. "For the Big Fisherman," she called to him. Diana saw Marcipor nod, his lined face contorted with grief. The Roman guard closed ranks and marched the two doomed, publicly avowed Christians, toward their final moments on earth.

"Go," shrieked Caligula, his face flushed and distorted. Saliva dripped from the left corner of his mouth. "Go to your God at the end of an arrow," his crazed laughter lost on Marcellus and Diana as they marched briskly toward new life with Jesus.

I changed Caligula's words from the last paragraphs of the book and added "drooling." The scene became more memorable when reading the entry in my diary later. My eyes still welled up, and my breath caught as I re-read the text.

Jesus became flesh-and-blood real, compared to the former ghostly figure associated with isolated, memorized Bible verses. Granny's independent chapel, where the pastor warned us of hellfire and damnation every Sunday, had replaced Mom's and Dad's social-club-style church. Neither church hit the mark. I wanted what Marcellus and Diana had—a belief so powerful and real, they were willing to die rather than recant. That belief could take away death's sting. I hadn't thought much about death until this book time-traveled me back into the Roman Empire with Christ.

I had never been taught about *this* Jesus. The Bible took on new meaning because of the three-dimensional descriptions in *The Robe*. Viciously treated, enduring the all- consuming rage of Jewish and Roman leaders, Jesus and His followers exemplified true courage. *Love your enemies,* I thought. *He forgave them all, even when nailed to a cross. I can be forgiven and forgive,* I thought, *but not through my own effort.*

Those words led me toward the next step, yet I hung back. The profound decision brewing needed special consideration, aided by a bit of fresh air.

Outside, I climbed the apple tree, fall foliage thinning as leaves fell. Resting in the fruit tree's embrace, I pondered. Behind my closed eyes, images of *The Robe* came to life. Scenes from the two churches, from school, from home all played in my head. *"Forgive them for they know not what they do."*

"Lord, I've always known You were there. Let me know what You want me to do," I prayed. A comfortable pause lengthened until *"Be still and know that I am God"* spoke into my spirit. Bible verses I'd once read or memorized drifted through my mind.

Suddenly, I expected to read Paul's Epistles in color instead of black and white. My choice arose, fully conscious, sure: *I wanted His salvation.* If I chose to believe in Christ, I could walk with my head held high, regardless of the barbs and jibes of my school day.

On the previous night, by *The Robe's* final page, I had believed in Jesus, *the* Savior. I believed I could forgive my school tormentors—as Jesus would forgive me, if I asked Him to. *But you must do it right, I* thought.

I remembered a tract with a special prayer in it. Back in the house, the old church pamphlet lay half hidden on my closet bookshelf, the prayer of salvation page dog-eared by the previous owner. After looking up a couple of its words in the dictionary, I wrote, revised, and prayed each word onto paper. Pieces of the pamphlet, Psalm 23, and my own words merged. Satisfied, I prayed out loud:

Thank you, Jesus, for showing me I have sinned and need your salvation for fellowship with God. Thank you for dying on the cross for me. Please forgive me for all of my failures and sins. Wash me clean for a fresh start. I believe You are the Son of God who took my sins to the cross when You had none. I believe You died and rose from the dead so we believers will enter heaven. Now, I ask You into my life as my Lord and Savior. Please, help me love You, and walk with You, all the days of my life, so I will dwell in the house of the Lord forever. Amen!

I felt His deep, loving presence like a cloak. My body tingled as His peace permeated every cell. *My life will be different with Him, I* thought, as I copied the prayer into my journal.

In the coming weeks, it became easier to curb my tongue and stay out of harm's way. Reading my Bible and daily prayer opened each of my days. My social status didn't change, but the way I handled it did. No longer upset, I looked at the person insulting me with a little smile as I prayed Jesus's prayer: *Forgive them, for they know not what they do.* The clique couldn't make me fall apart anymore; and my resilience surprised them all. I knew my experiences paled compared to Jesus's suffering for us.

I walked with Him then and, these many years later, He's still beside me now.

But, somehow, this experience of accepting Him into my life didn't prepare me for the miracle.

The paper had my name on it, along with these words:

Your Guidance counseling appointment is scheduled:
Tuesday, 11 AM.
Counselor: Mrs. Hatcher.
Room: 204.

Ninth grade's final months initiated preparation for three educational tracks in tenth grade: college prep, business/secretarial, or industrial arts. I arrived for the appointment expecting discussion, guidance. Within five minutes of meeting my guidance counselor, Mrs. Hatcher, I found myself assigned to the business/secretarial track, although I explained I wanted college prep. She promised to talk to the committee again but repeated I would be better off in the non-academic track.

At home that afternoon, Mom's face registered disbelief when I told her about the guidance meeting. "What do you mean she said you're *not college material?*"

"That's what she said. If you have any questions, she wants you to make an appointment. They're signing me up in the business/secretarial track in tenth grade unless they hear from you or Dad. I don't want to be a secretary, and I hate business math!"

Three days later, I met Mom at my homeroom. As the classes changed, we walked toward the guidance office. Some of the girls I knew from the accelerated section came toward us. Nice when they wanted to be, their self-proclaimed leader, Bonnie, took great delight in harassing me.

"Hi Beth," I said to the girl behind Bonnie. Of five girls, four of them looked down and sideways toward the lockers; but Bonnie looked straight at me. Then, with an exaggerated motion, she arced her nose away from me, toward the wall. The group passed by in silence. They had waved their true colors, like a banner, with my mother beside me.

"What was that?" Mom asked, frowning.

"Oh, something that happens every day. Like I said, that's just the way it is. I'm used to it."

Mom's face settled in grim lines. The previous night, I had told her about my life—and, in general terms, my tormenters—from first grade to present, being very specific about seventh grade. I reaped no reward from suffering in silence—not while the school was planning to steal my college dreams. Mom's thorough questioning during my confession had readied both of us for today's guidance appointment. She wrapped me in a hug when we finally finished talking, after midnight. Now she had experienced first-hand my daily degradation at school.

In the guidance counselor's office, Mom launched without preamble. "Mrs. Hatcher, Violet is certainly not at the bottom of her class. I saw firsthand on the way to your office how other students treat her. *Upset* grossly understates my feelings. From what she tells me, she has no friends, and her teachers are more adversarial than not. The one exception this year is her math teacher, Mrs. Rush. During a phone conference yesterday, she explained that Violet is *too frightened* to learn math. She knows the root of the problem, and so do I. It started in seventh grade. That year, the civics teacher dropped Violet a full grade, because she didn't raise her hand in class. The science teacher incinerated a ram's skull from Austria, because Violet came late to pick it up. Her science teacher belittled her in front of the entire class after she made the highest grade on a geology test. And I could go on! For the last three years, except for one math teacher, she has been without encouragement from anyone at Ridge High. My experience today drove home the nightmare she's been living."

To Mrs. Hatcher's credit, she seemed contrite. After asking me several questions, she replied, "The faculty committee who placed Violet in the business/secretarial track doesn't feel she's up to the academic work level for our college prep track." Mrs. Hatcher paused and looked apologetic. "Why don't you discuss this with your husband, and I'll see what I can do on my end."

On the way home, Mom and I deliberated in silence. Finally, she asked, "What would you think about private school? Kimberton Farms School is close to home. Maybe there are scholarships available. Would you like to visit?"

"Sure, Mom. I'd visit any school you want. It can't be any worse!"

Within a week, Mom and Dad "discussed" my scholastic future in every tone of voice imaginable. Dad worried about the expense of private school education. Mom worried about a business track with no college in my future. In the end, they agreed—an obvious act of God. Mom called Kimberton Farms School for a tour and assessment of my "scholastic aptitude."

Would this school be different? Would Dad actually pay for private school?

7

SECOND CHANCE

"Come and let us return to the Lord;
For He has torn but He will heal us.
He has stricken, but He will bind us up."
— Hosea 6:1

Mr. Stone

MR. STONE STOOD over six feet tall, a man of craggy features; a deep, soothing voice; and blue-gray eyes.

"Now, Violet," he said as he handed me several pages of questions. "We need to know where to place you at Kimberton, if you decide to attend the school." He must have seen me blanche, because he added, "There is no grading, just general knowledge about the subjects."

He smiled and talked softly, until I relaxed and took part in the conversation. He asked what I thought of the campus, with a slow transition into asking about my past school life. He covered most of my schooling through ninth grade, until all of my scholastic misadventures came to light. It took just over an hour. At the end, he paused, looked at the floor, then lifted his eyes.

"My dear, I cannot tell you how sorry I am that you were treated this way." He let that sink in and added, "Here at Kimberton we say, 'If the student fails to learn, the teacher fails to teach.'"

We looked at one another for a minute—me, not believing I sat in this amazing school, and Mr. Stone, face and eyes saddened by my story.

"Do you think you can work on these papers a little, or do you need a break?"

"I can do them now," I said with certainty.

"Good! I better touch base with your mother, so she doesn't worry." He smiled and left, after patting my shoulder.

That night, I thought about Kimberton, the campus which was like a dream—in lush, green Chester County. The biggest class had twenty students. I only saw teachers treat each other with respect and humor.

But the students' kindness astonished me. One told me the school motto was, "We learn with joy." Then, she quipped, "We haven't met Joy yet!" Everyone in earshot laughed or smiled at this obvious, well-used line. But I felt welcomed.

Before I went to bed that night, Mom asked me what I thought. Without any doubt in my mind, I said, "Mom, I'd scrub floors to go there!"

The next day at Ridge High, I walked with a definite spring in my step. Both Mom and Dad had their minds set on sending all three of us to private school. At the time, I didn't think about my two sisters who liked Ridge High and Amber Elementary. I only thought of my own plight.

"Violet," Mom called. "I got a call from Kimberton."

My heart started jigging in my chest. She looked serious enough to make me nervous.

"What did they say?"

"Honey, they want you tutored in math this summer. Then you'll need to repeat ninth grade. Since you started school when you were five, an extra year won't hurt. Anyway, Kimberton is ahead of Ridge High in math and English; you'll need to catch up. If you complete everything, you'll start ninth-grade in the fall."

Mom stopped and searched my face. I considered what difference it would make if I repeated ninth grade. *An extra year in a high school like that one? A gift.* At Kimberton, they incorporated art in every course. Everyone played sports, sang in the chorus, and participated in school plays. Add the chance for grade improvement and real-life friendships, and the school of my dreams stood waiting for me.

"Mom, I told you, I'd scrub floors to go there. Actually, an extra year is great!"

The month before summer break, at Ridge High, all my tormentors knew my delight with my change of schools. The last day, my bus ride home brought thoughts of finality. *I'll never forget this last day, last ride, the end of emotional and spiritual famine.*

Dad suggested "Beginners Typing" at summer school, and I pounded the keys of his manual Royal typewriter, practicing.

Math tutoring told a different story. I still blanked out when looking at math word problems or formulas. A good memory and sequencing ability, both required for math, proved the worst flaws in my brain.

Mrs. Barbor, my patient math tutor, had two children; Haley, a girl my age, attended Ridge High. After one of my tutoring sessions, Mrs. Barbor took me with her to pick up the girls. As I sat in the back seat, Haley's conversation with her mother sent shock waves through me.

"Oh, Mom, I absolutely flunked that test today!"

Without any apparent concern, her mother asked, "Did you study?"

Haley laughed. "Well, I guess not as much as I should have!"

Her mother smiled and glanced at her with affection. "You'll do better next time. It'll all average out."

When I thought of telling my parents that I had failed a test, my stomach rolled into fear-induced back-flips. The comfortable comradery about grades between my tutor and her daughter registered as alien in my world, as *unbelievable*. I knew my parents loved me. I knew they did the best they could. But this encounter with Haley and Mrs. Barbor opened up a new view.

I thought about the many good things my dad had done. He'd taught Lynney, Gay, and me gymnastics. We stood on our heads or hands and somersaulted, laughing, in the summer grass. He'd taken us "down the river" and all through the silt basins, where we'd learned which animals left tracks in the silty dust. He'd taught us names of local birds and their songs, made campfires, and roasted hot dogs wrapped in bacon. He'd taught me how to frame a picture with a camera and use a light meter.

But when it came to school and my way of traveling through life, our relationship fell into a hole.

Dad described me as: *slow poke, last rose of summer, head in the clouds, molasses in January going up a hill, daydreamer*. Quick in movement and thought, he claimed a high IQ. Slow and contemplative, I owned the high IQ, but had little to show for it—infuriating Dad. My father excelled in math and geography. He couldn't fathom my inability to master his favorite subjects. Although tempered by love, his anger and intense displeasure along with his general worldview became a mountain range. He stayed on one side, I on the other. With effort, when needed, we spoke over the peaks.

Mom's negativity to my school performance erupted less often, but hurt more because of our likenesses. My writing talent, way with words, and love of art and music mirrored her own gifts. When she hugged me, she put her whole heart into the embrace.

The opposite also held true. Her icy glare froze me in my tracks if I crossed her. Granny possessed a similar look, yet my mother seemed nothing like my grandmother in any other way. My mother's soft side surfaced easily. Yet her need for perfect manners, flawless appearance, and beauty at all costs came from a dark place in her childhood, rooted in the tragic loss of her father and her woeful relationship with my grandmother.

Granny's tough leathery side came from war's deprivation and sheer survival instinct. It kept her alive through the pain of a son with severe handicaps and the loss of her husband. It allowed her to fight through foreclosure on her home mortgage by her in-laws immediately after her husband died. But it hardened her to the point of damage. Raw survival instinct remained close to the surface, even in times of plenty.

Granny often watched Gay, Lynne, and me and prepared dinner, so Mom and Dad had dinner with us when they got home. During fifth grade, Granny prepared a dish that scented the kitchen with a remarkable, savory, fragrance. The dark stew tasted as good as it smelled—unlike anything I had eaten before.

Handing my plate back for seconds, I asked, "Granny, what is this? It's really good!"

"*Haas 'n Pfeffer*," she replied, dishing more stew onto my plate.

Dad sighed, shook his head, but kept on eating.

"Mother, you didn't!" Mom said in dismay. "Tell me you didn't!"

"What? What?" Granny responded, as she always did when chastised for good reason.

Dad excused himself, his empty plate left on the table.

"Why? What is it?" Lynne asked.

After a painful silence, as all eyes turned to Mom, she answered, "It's rabbit stew."

"You mean we're eating Hansel and Gretel?" I asked, thinking of our pet rabbits in their hutch out back.

Gay and Lynne didn't wait for an answer. They ran out of the kitchen, screaming. Tears welled in my eyes as I looked in horror at the plate of stew Granny offered me. I held my hand up in the "stop" position, slid out of my chair, ran, and slammed the back door behind me.

There had been no reason to kill the rabbits for stew. Mom had planned hoagies for dinner until Granny claimed the kitchen. Walking in the cold, night air—thick with country darkness—helped. The moon and stars still hung in the sky. Over the next week, the memory burrowed far down underground, where it remained until Gay and I were adults. Only then did we talk about our sometimes-bizarre upbringing, and she reminded me of Hansel's and Gretel's demise. Only then did I remember. No one else mentioned the butchering of our pet rabbits until Gay unearthed the memory—almost twenty years later.

The night Granny served Haas 'n Pfeffer, Dad calmly left the table before "all hell broke loose," as he often said. Downstairs in the finished basement, he shut the door and rocked in his chair with near-violent motion, not unusual for him, especially around any confrontation not caused by him. Strains of a Beethoven symphony surrounded him in the dark. When I came back inside, the haunting chords continued to drift upward, along with sounds of his creaking rocker.

I hugged Dad when he came upstairs. I would have pulled him close; but he hugged at a distance, uncomfortable and stiff. Raised by poor, immigrant parents from Czechoslovakia, he learned to speak English in first grade. His Slovak language and "foreigner" label merited him the prize of being chased through Hazleton's back alleys by kids who wanted to smash his glasses and beat him to a pulp. The experience marked him, earning him the ranks of "poor" and "different." And "different" he remained. He worked and avoided "poor" at all costs.

I believe the rabbit stew took him back to his poverty-ridden childhood. The violence of his rocking echoed deep pain forged years before.

Mom also claimed the "different" title, a family trait on both sides, in a broken sort of way. Her younger brother, Earl Jr., had cruised and toddled until a babysitter let him roll off a high table. The crash damaged his brain and spinal cord beyond repair. Unable to walk, read, write, or speak with fluency, he still understood everything; and Granny's hard edge grew.

Mom suffered under Granny's often harsh care. Earl Jr. always came first. Her father provided the love Mom craved, until he died of a heart attack—with Mom just a sweet sixteen.

Damage—layer on layer, like sedimentary rock—coats, solidifies, and binds each individual and generation. Creativity—like igneous rock—explodes, molten, slow cools, some with bubbles inside. Crystals —clear, rose, amethyst, sapphire—appear but are seen only if the geode is split open. Each of us experience metamorphosis. The stratum of damage never occurs alone.

Dad's math and logic skills, his athletic ability and love of nature, lay within his damaged matrix. Mom's gifts in language, the arts, finding secondhand treasures, and her warm hugs lay within her damaged matrix.

No one escapes change, the bad and good intertwined.

And still, I learned: the Creator of all things, a loving God, allows us free will, the ability to choose.

In my home, I had learned by third grade to keep my mouth shut and my head down. My unsuspecting parents discovered my failures from teachers and report cards. This led to raised voices and several swats of a belt as my reward.

For the most part, I survived school through ninth grade only by reaching for the hem of His garment. He never failed me, even before I truly knew Him. When my father raised the belt in discipline, my Father in heaven held my hand. God made up for the fair and understanding father I didn't have.

And now, my Father would help me get to a place I had never been—a new school, where I could be seen with fresh eyes and treated with fairness.

Mrs. Barbor succeeded in my tutoring, and after summer school— despite all the labels I'd been given and generations of trauma that preceded me—I typed fifty words a minute. Because Mom signed on as a volunteer for part of our tuition, all three of us officially enrolled in Kimberton Farms School. Although I didn't expect a miracle, the gift came anyway: God's miracle—unique, tailored just for me.

Could I succeed even there? God knew.

8

THE ACCIDENT

"But those who wait on the Lord
Shall renew their strength;
They shall mount up with wings like eagles,
They shall run and not be weary,
They shall walk and not faint."
— Isaiah 40:31

I ONLY HAD time to scream, "Mom, a Mac truck's coming, and it's going to hit us!"

The impact caught me with my neck twisted as I looked up and over my right shoulder, eyes on the massive, vertical grille, topped by a silver bulldog. Metal crunched as the little car pitched, carried forward by the tractor-and-trailer's momentum.

"Oh, my back," Mom moaned.

Mom's car door was open. The truck side-swiped us, while her left leg and foot were out of the car. With her foot planted on the sidewalk at impact, her leg and pelvis twisted to an odd angle. Mom's little gold Corvair pushed a few yards farther down a nasty stretch of road called "Mile Hill." The car remained parallel parked just past the Fashion Bug shop that had been our destination.

Mom's back pain did not stop her from asking if I had hit my nose. Six weeks before the accident, I had nasal surgery to open sinuses and reshape my wayward proboscis. At age twelve, after returning from Europe, it grew a bump at the bridge and lengthened until it hung over my upper lip when I smiled. Mom told me I fell from the apple tree and smashed it as a three-year-old. Practicing smiling in the mirror before school pictures failed to make any improvement in my homely image. With transfer to the new school set for fall, Mom suggested nasal surgery the summer before, since none of the students at Kimberton Farms School knew me. I jumped at the chance. After the cosmetic surgery, it would be a bonus to breathe easily again.

During surgery, I surfaced through the anesthesia. No pain registered. I heard a hammer impacting a chisel—rhythmic, metallic, banging, clear yet disembodied—then nothing until I awakened in my hospital bed. The night after my surgery, a nurse came in with pain medication. I wondered why, since I hadn't requested any. The next morning, I understood, with a mirror's reflection. Double shiners of black and blue circled my eyes, the whites heavily bloodshot, sinuses packed with gauze, now bloody. A dark, plum-colored vinal splint over my nose held everything together with adhesive taped from forehead to chin, extending to the edges of my face. I looked like someone beaten nearly to death.

The day nurse also asked if I wanted pain medication. "But I don't have *any* pain at all," I said. She shook her head with pleasant disbelief as I added, "I'm not going to have to practice smiling before school pictures anymore." Her eyes opened a little wider with a flash of understanding. She nodded and smiled.

In six weeks, my reflection stared back at me—*cute!* The word "homely" didn't fit me anymore, and Granny stopped telling me I needed "height" from my hair to offset my unsightly nose. New freedom mantled my shoulders. *Boys might actually look at me*—a novel, heady idea.

After missing church for a couple of recovery weeks, I stopped going altogether. The weight of the ever-present God of judgement, with no loving or merciful counterbalance in the preaching, became too heavy to bear. Light as a wisp of cloud, my image stared back at me and smiled, the mirror's reflection a rebirth.

"Violet, did you hit your nose?" Mom asked, concerned that the accident may have reversed the transformation from swan back to ugly duckling. I assured her my nose hadn't been touched. An afternoon shopping spree for the new school year at Kimberton Farms had turned into a wrecked car with injuries. By the time we got home, sparkling, multicolored lights undulated in half of my visual field. Half of Mom's face blurred with deep hues of silver, blue, violet, red and gold, pinpoint lights.

I would later come to know the otherwise beautiful sparkles as an "aura." Within twenty minutes, a blinding headache raged. Neck and jaw muscles clenched—a bass drum beat in my head, each beat coupled with a shot of pain. Light hurt. Sound hurt. I ran to the bathroom and vomited.

Mom's original back injury had come from a car accident eleven years earlier. I was five years old at the time, when our car stopped with other cars for a red light. A drunk teen driver and his passenger slammed a little MG into the line of cars. There were no skid marks, according to the police. My chipped bottom tooth and mild concussion in that accident seemed minor compared to the horror and mayhem behind our car. Our vehicle's placement, fifth from the rear in line, saved our lives. People died in every car behind us. Later, police estimated the MG's speed at over one hundred miles per hour.

It had been a close call, made closer by what had happened in the car before the chain-collision accident. My father's parents, Baba and Dzedo, lived in Fairfax, Virginia, and we were on our way to visit them. Ten minutes away from their house, Mom called to Lynne and me, "Come on, girls. We're almost there." My sister and I climbed from the way-back of the station wagon into the backseat. Minutes later, the rear compartment—where we slept most of the four-and-a-half-hour trip—flattened, accordion style, flush with the backseat.

I had felt sick after the chain-reaction crash. But my symptoms after the next accident when the truck hit us years later went far beyond the concussion from the first accident. Severe, debilitating headaches continued.

Our family doctor sent me to a neurologist for assessment of "migraine headaches." The neurologist never touched my spasming neck and shoulders. He pronounced my "cervical and upper extremity range of motion and strength" as "normal." He handed Mom a container of phenobarbital tablets and a prescription for physical therapy. "Schedule a follow-up appointment in one month with my receptionist," he said.

"Phenobarbital is an antiseizure medication," the drug insert read. I read the informative brochure with a warning about possible addiction and flushed the pills down the toilet. Mom never scheduled another neurology appointment, but physical therapy changed the course of my life—all because of a car accident.

Mom slowly recovered, until her back and leg returned to their usual tenuous state, determined by her activities. Lifting or twisting sent her to the osteopath. With manipulation, her back and leg normalized.

My complex problems required more time and effort. Migraine headaches demanded a dark room, no noise, and lying down without motion. Otherwise, the nausea progressed until I retched, head over the soup pot by my bed.

Physical therapy treatments began, twice a week. Miss Conley, registered physical therapist (RPT), treated me with moist heat, ultrasound, massage, and gentle exercises. She examined how far my head could move in all directions. She "palpated"—or probed—my neck and shoulder blade muscles. "You have severe muscle spasms of the cervical and upper thoracic spine," she said before teaching me exactly what that meant.

After six weeks of treatment, I gained new vocabulary, and an elementary understanding of muscle spasm, range of motion, strength, and exercises. The treatment began relaxing clenched, over-worked muscles. Severe migraines became fewer and less severe—a good start, but the unpredictable headaches didn't resolve.

Mom suggested a visit to her osteopath, Dr. Lefko. He probed and prodded the bones and muscles of my neck, placing his hands about my head and rotating it in all directions.

"Do you trust me?" he asked.

"Yes," I said.

"Then, let me have your head."

Without difficulty, I felt myself relax as he moved my head about in a slow, rhythmic way. A sudden sharp motion—chin to the right, head to the left, and nose toward the ceiling—resulted in a loud, reverberating "POP!" The weight of the universe lifted from my head and shoulders, bringing a lightness compared to the terrible heaviness held by taut, steel-band muscles.

Slowly, I turned my head with freedom, then hugged him in amazement. His smile of acknowledgement told me he understood.

A blaze of scintillating lights attacked if I read with my head down, let my head and shoulders slouch forward, worked with my arms overhead, or became stressed. Later, medication stopped each headache before it passed the aura stage. By tenth grade, I no longer missed school for headaches. I taught myself to "crack" my neck as the osteopath had done. As my learning curve continued, correcting muscle and bone alignment, I learned through ongoing trial and error to avoid migraines without meds.

"All things work together for good to those who love God" — *Romans* 8:28. I didn't understand the depth of Paul's Scripture at the time, but even this early on, I recognized good things could come from difficult times.

Life became sweeter as Kimberton Farms School welcomed me. My math teacher, Mr. Stone, often taught through storytelling or everyday examples to make lessons come to life. With his teaching, I completed algebra one and two, and geometry and trigonometry, a far cry from business math.

Of all my classes, art and English freed my creative expression. At Kimberton, poetry, prose, clay sculpture, geometric drawing, and color pencil shading lived at my delighted fingertips. My first year, I sculpted a Lipizzaner stallion and his rider performing the "Levade." In this exquisite, equine, ballet position, the gleaming, white horse froze in a half rearing pose, head and shoulders balanced over hind legs and tail. The rider, clad in scarlet coat and black hat, sank deep in the saddle, ramrod straight, yet still fluid. My art teacher helped me mount the fired piece with a supporting copper rod, which connected the horse to a walnut base, carved and sanded in shop class.

Even before my art teacher entered the Lipizzaner in a high school art contest, the sculpture and all that it symbolized pleased me to my core. The contest entry surprised me; I didn't think myself gifted enough.

Within a week, my ceramic horse and rider returned from the juried art show. Mrs. Harvey exclaimed with angry passion as she read the note attached, "They've rejected your entry! The committee members claimed *a ninth grader could not have completed such a complicated piece!*"

My eyes widened, viewing my kind and patient art teacher's unusual wrath.

"Mrs. Harvey," I said after a pause, "I guess we have to take this as a great compliment! I'm just happy, sculpting in clay and creating artwork I enjoy! This school, especially this class, encourages me every day. Kimberton helps me accomplish things, like sculpting the Lipizzaner, that I never could have imagined at my other school. Don't even think twice about that contest!"

She smiled. "Have you thought about taking art in college?"

"I'm not talented enough to make a living with art, but I love being creative. Art is a serious hobby for me, but I want a profession in some form of medicine. Maybe I'll become a nurse or doctor," I replied.

Lynne's and Gay's experience at Kimberton proved the opposite of mine. Dad started comparing my honor roll report card to Lynne's C average. "Why can't you get grades like Violet?" he asked her. I had no idea how much she hated Kimberton, or how our relationship would corrode. Oblivious in my joyful world, sudden understanding came the hard way. Mom's praise of my horse sculpture the afternoon I brought the statue home reached the entire family. Mom placed the Lipizzaner and red-coated rider in a place of honor on a table in the den. I never saw what happened, only the results; but I heard it—a terrible, shattering, crash. I jumped down the three steps from kitchen to den. My horse and rider lay shattered on the den floor. Nothing else seemed disturbed.

The sculpture's heavy, clay structure could only move with help. It had to have been lifted high and thrown down with violence. Wounded, with pain radiating through my spirit, I stayed silent. But I knew who had done it.

Lynne allowed no discussion of her feelings with anyone. Her intense dislike of Kimberton, hidden from Mom and Dad, sealed her attendance at the school through graduation.

Voicing my sadness and concern for Lynne's unhappiness fell on her deaf ears, only resulting in anger. Although I had good times with Lynne—like singing together, accompanied by my guitar—in a small, local venue, the path of eggshells remained between us ever after.

Kimberton Farms School rated *just this side of heaven*, in my estimation. To say that I thrived was almost an understatement. My Ridge High seventh-grade best friend called me—a surprise, since I hadn't seen her for a year. She invited me to a Ridge High School dance "for old time's sake." With newfound confidence and a pleasing reflection in the mirror, I accepted. A feeling of strangeness enveloped me, as I entered the familiar building with a new persona and look. I stopped by the lavatory before entering the gymnasium. As I washed my hands, a familiar voice came from the other stall.

"How's your nose, Violet?" Bonnie asked in her best mocking voice.

I laughed. "Just fine, Bonnie. How's yours?" She came out of the stall and looked at me—dumbfounded, mouth agape. I smiled, making eye contact. "I love my current school. I'm doing great and have lots of friends there. Enjoy your evening, Bonnie." Her look never changed, as I left her gaping in the bathroom.

My old civics teacher stood in the gym, surrounded by adoring students.

"Well," he exclaimed, catching sight of me. "So, you missed us after all—coming back to see us at last!"

I grinned, looked directly into his eyes, and shook my head to contradict his assessment. "Oh, no," I said with a small laugh. "I'm making straight As and Bs and have good friends at Kimberton. I'm planning for college now, probably something in *medicine*."

His stunned expression remained worth a thousand words.

The summer after tenth grade, I worked as a nurse's aide in a tiny, local hospital. I tried my best to help the understaffed nurses and aides. I removed spent IVs, gave complete bed baths to both men and women, and documented vital signs—while enjoying both patients and staff. The job clarified *medicine* as my future profession.

Nurses, I observed, seemed relegated to the medication cart, which did not enamor me with the profession. With such limited knowledge, I assumed a nurse's job centered around medication rather than actual patient care, a mistake that eliminated nursing from my personal career choices.

Looking back, God knew His plan fit my life perfectly; and He knew the "mistakes" I would make. *Life is a three-dimensional puzzle, and He knows where every piece fits.*

PRELUDE

"Children, obey your parents in the Lord, for this is right.
'Honor your father and mother,' which is the first command-
ment with promise: 'that it may be well with you and you may
live long on the earth.'
And you, fathers, do not provoke your children to wrath, but
bring them up in the training and admonition of the Lord."
— Ephesians 6:1-4

"Shh!" My mother nudged Dad, who closed his mouth in mid-sentence. In the 1960s when I was fifteen years old, an unusual closeness developed between Mom and Dad. They stopped speaking or changed the subject whenever one of us came in ear shot. More distracted than usual, like something disturbing occupied their minds, I assumed the blame. Between my new boyfriend and anti-Vietnam War views, I had been driving them crazy.

But that wasn't it. The real reason came to light when accountants discovered missing funds at the Lutheran church my parents had helped found.

"Have you heard anything new about the church funds?" Mom

asked Dad. His mournful face fell further as he shook his head. Visibly upset, they talked openly but had no in-depth information.

A week went by. The back door slammed, and Dad charged up the hall steps into the kitchen. "Violet," he called my mother as he brushed past me.

Mom appeared around the corner. "What happened, Rudy?" she asked.

"Look," he said, thrusting the *Times Herald* into her hand. The pastor's mug shot appeared as first-page news: "CHURCH EMBEZ-ZLEMENT!" the headline screamed.

"We've decided to leave the church, girls," Dad said.

"Where will we go?" I asked.

"We haven't thought that far ahead," Mom explained.

"I don't know if we'll go anywhere," Dad finished.

Neither Mom nor Dad recovered from the blow after giving their all to the church. Both founding members, Dad was the treasurer—and Mom played piano for the services, worked in the nursery, and organized the choir.

They left the church and never made any attempt to search for another. Sunday became nothing more special than an extra day off.

Granny and I still attended the independent chapel. One summer day, the pastor came to "save" my parents. A simple man versed in a "hellfire and damnation" view of the Bible, he rarely mentioned mercy or grace—and never mentioned secular history. My father's love of history and grasp of events and historical figures made him knowledgeable in the subject. As the pastor moved into his salvation message, Dad began asking questions. "So, Pastor Reign, what about Buddha and Confucius? Where do they fit into history?"

"Jesus is the Son of God. Their history is unimportant after Jesus's gospel."

"But they are founders of world religions," Dad continued.

"After Jesus," the pastor stated.

"What do you mean *after?*" Dad asked.

"They were *after* Christ. He is the one Son of God."

My father looked with amazement at Pastor Reign. "Christ came after Confucius and Buddha," he said with finality.

"Oh," said the pastor. "But it is Christ who brought salvation through His sacrifice for us. Without him, we are damned to hell. Belief in Him brings everlasting life!"

"Well, consider the Buddha," Dad continued. "He believed in peace and encouraged that long before Jesus came on the scene. Confucius's sayings were filled with wisdom, long before Christ."

"I don't know about that. I only know..."

"If you don't have a well-rounded *knowledge*, how can you be objective in your assessment of the *messages?*" Dad gestured, his palms turned up.

Dad always asked intellectual questions, since in my family, intelligence reigned over all else, close to God in importance. Calling someone "stupid" amounted to the lowest form of insult.

Hidden from view, I listened to my well-versed father make the pastor appear unlearned and foolish, especially when the unfortunate man didn't know that Christ came chronologically after Confucius and Buddha. No one in our family heard the message of salvation he attempted to give. The pastor—judged only on his knowledge of history and stuttering, verbal attempts—left knowing that he had failed.

But there were other repercussions of that event.

For me, at the ripe age of sixteen, Pastor Reign's utter failure served as a final blow. Chafing under constraints of legalistic Christianity, I jettisoned the pastor and his church—and questioned the Bible's message as well. Both my parents leaned toward a popular philosophy: *many paths to God.* As "intelligent people," they did not believe in the Bible as "the inerrant Word of God." Beaten down, diluted thin by "rational" discussion, the message of Jesus Christ's role as Savior deteriorated to "great teacher." Their jaundiced view of church and its suspect message launched questions about the Christian Gospel, with Jesus Christ as the *only* path to salvation.

Trained up as "intelligent," I sought truth with *my* thoughts. Pride—in my perky mirror image and honor roll performance—killed any vestige of my previous homely, wallflower failure. After my church experiences, I found that my morals and biblical guiding principles followed my ugly duck existence down the drain. Even my parents' mores seemed antiquated and superficial; I kept some and threw out the rest.

Despite my distaste for much of what I had seen in church, my relationship with God remained unwavering. He would always be close, since the day I had prayed the Salvation Prayer and strove to forgive those who had bullied me. I could learn to forgive the church too, in time, but that wasn't my top priority, since I didn't think I needed them.

In the weeks and months following tenth grade, I concentrated on which college I would attend—and what profession could yield a good and satisfying livelihood. Because of my experience with Dad's total control of household finances, I vowed never to be totally dependent on my husband. I *would* have a profession and be self-sustaining.

I watched Mom scrape by with late-night, part-time jobs. She eventually found a good full-time job in real estate, which gave her collateral for a car loan. The little, gold Corvair and her salary meant freedom for her—a freedom she hadn't known before. Mom's natural gift in sales allowed her to sell 75 percent of the houses in her company's new development.

A lover of all things French, she began using the name "Violette" in her own decorating business, Interior Moods, during the 1960s and 1970s. A bit of a joke between us, I teased her and called her, "Violette, the *Frrrrench* violet." My name, Violet, represented the American woods violet.

"Mom, there's a package for you," I called.

"I've been waiting for this," she said as I tossed the little, brown, paper-wrapped parcel to her. Paper fell away, revealing a white business card box with her new card pasted on top. *Interior Moods by Violette* was printed on the outside, with an explanation of her services on the inside in purple writing. The life-like image of a purple-flowered, woods violet with well-drawn green leaves accented the folding, business card's front under Mom's French-inspired name. "Oh, they're just like I imagined they would look!" she exclaimed.

When she finished her examination of the package, I opened the box to take a look; five hundred cards filled the inside. "May I take some to give away at school?" I asked.

"Of course," she said, pleasure shining in her eyes.

After she sold a house, she helped the new owners through her own business: Interior Moods, an interior decorating service that branched out beyond home decorating into antiques, bisque dolls, antique doll clothing, and home content valuation for those downsizing or selling estates. The confidence she gained changed her. Mom no longer took Dad's belittling remarks submissively. He soon learned to control his tongue—or have it nailed to the wall. No match in verbal skills, Dad became the pitiable partner in their marriage. Yet the mask remained intact in public, where they still had "the perfect marriage."

I searched for a profession, while living lies, both old and new—lies woven into my subconscious, like pretending that Mom's and Dad's marriage was fine, secondhand clothes were new, and petty theft wasn't a problem. Sedimentary layers formed about my matrix.

A deficiency in math skills limited my career in the sciences. Geometry, planes, and angles—which I could visualize—brought me straight As. Mr. Stone's nurturing, tutoring, and extra credit produced Bs in algebra I, II, and trigonometry. I knew I couldn't expect that level of care in college math, so any profession with a calculus requirement transferred to the "impossible dream" list.

Thinking back to treatment after my second car accident, physical therapy stood out as a good professional fit—with no calculus requirement. As requested, brochures about the field began arriving in the mail. Job availability and a good, starting salary ranked PT high in choice professions. I thought back to my mother's and father's bitter arguments over money. A profession in physical therapy epitomized job independence, as a single woman or an equal financial partner in marriage. As I researched, physical therapy became my top profession contender.

A run-in with Dad placed the final seal on my professional choice. "Dad, why don't we have a dishwasher?"

He replied with a laugh, "I have three of them," indicating his three daughters. Teeth gritted, I let this demeaning remark go by; but the fuse glowed.

A week later, I showed Dad some schools in the college guide I'd received. His first question for each school related to price: room, board, books, incidentals. "You know," he said after hearing about the three schools, "you *could* be a secretary."

Years of accepting his male chauvinism boiled over. I would not be silent. "That would suit you, wouldn't it, Dad? You wouldn't have to pay for college. How dare you even suggest secretarial work to me, when you degrade your own secretary every time you talk about her! I don't want a boss like you, looking down his nose at me. I'm going to choose a profession where I can eventually *be* the boss."

Uncharacteristically, Dad walked away without commenting.

Appointments for college visits began popping up on my calendar. My short list included two schools. Although too early for interviews to matter, I made appointments with University of Pennsylvania and Temple University. My parents also insisted on Ursinus and Cedar Crest appointments and applications. They wanted me situated on a campus in the middle of nowhere or "safe" at home as a commuter. The first "love of my life," Mark, who I was dating at the time, had *not* met with their approval. They wanted to severely limit my ability to leave campus, thus avoiding getting into "trouble" with him—and anyone else I might meet later.

University of Pennsylvania lay in traffic-filled, West Philadelphia

—alien to the nature sounds and stillness I cherished at home. After informing me that I didn't meet their standards in the math SATs, the interviewer chatted, without giving me information about physical therapy—making the conversation a waste of my time.

Both Cedar Crest and Ursinus had only pre-physical therapy programs. Assured I could transfer elsewhere in my junior year, I had no interest. Once accepted, I wanted to grow my roots in one school environment without quibbling over transferred credits.

Another of my main criteria: easy access to public transportation. Mark and I expected to spend weekends together. Self-absorption grew, as I turned more and more toward Mark. I still sent dart-like prayers, many times a day, to the Lover of my soul; but I wasn't "walking the walk." My secular life became more important to me, since I had made Mark the focus of my world.

Looking back, I still had faith in God—in His nature and in His guardianship of my life. I trusted Him, all the while going my own way. My relationship with Him became unconscious. I always felt protected by Him, even though I gave little back and broke commandments.

Under duress, I applied to Ursinus in Collegeville, and then turned down their offer of early admission. I discussed my decision only with Mark.

Having turned away from Christ while still expecting the benefits of His capacity as Savior, I stored more rope. It would be just enough to hang me, in a metaphorical sense.

10

EVIL AND GOOD

"Watch and pray, lest you enter into temptation. The spirit indeed is willing, but the flesh is weak."
— Mark 13:48

MARK CAME into my life when he needed a date for his high school senior prom. I was a junior. One of my Kimberton classmates gave him my phone number. Mark and I agreed to meet before the prom to prevent unpleasant surprises.

"Do you smoke?" I asked on our first date.

"No," he replied, head down. He peered at me with bright, brown eyes—his straight, sandy forelock falling just to his eyebrows. "Do you?"

"No," I said. "And I won't date anyone who does."

He smiled. "Disgusting habit."

I agreed. "How old are you?" I asked.

"Seventeen."

"Me too."

He looked at me with a question in his eyes. "What do you want to ask me?"

70

"If you're seventeen, how come you're a junior, and I'm a year ahead of you?"

I shook my head and laughed. "That's a long, sad story. The bottom line is simple. I was miserable and headed for the secretarial course in public school. I repeated ninth grade to get into Kimberton Farms School where I'm a junior now." That seemed to put him at ease, and we talked for an hour. His prom went well. Conversation never lagged yet he seemed inexperienced in a social setting. He had applied to Makefield College, an upper crust, Main Line school.

The boy I had been dating stumbled out of my life. Good looking and my introduction to "parking," he lied to me, left me home on a Saturday night and went to a dance. My girlfriend caught wind of his duplicity. She and I schemed and went to the same dance. I smiled and waved at him. He never called me again. I enjoyed beating him at his own game. Mark seemed refreshing and honest compared to the slick, handsome guy who introduced me to the dating scene. I began dating Mark sporadically.

Makefield College not only accepted Mark, but they offered him a full scholarship. Initially nervous, almost timid in my company, he took me to Makefield. In the dark, we walked the tree-studded, fairyland campus, dotted with faux gas lamps. His hand warmed mine, as he told me of his early acceptance for the next fall. In a humble, self-effacing way, the reason for his acceptance came to light.

"I won first prize with an important science project. My guidance counselor told me it placed me in the *genius* category." He looked almost embarrassed. "Then my IQ score came back that way too." He shrugged, with a half-smile, "Straight As—with a C in French and gym—didn't hurt." My attraction to his sweet, quiet ways grew each time we met.

The Makefield admissions committee seemed sure they had ample proof of an ideal scholarship candidate; I thought I had proof of a good boyfriend candidate. Everything was good to go—for our relationship, and his college plans. Mark accepted admission to Makefield.

At first, my parents thought of Mark as "a fine boy"—bright, motivated, a good conversationalist. Once Mark entered Makefield and I entered my senior year at Kimberton, I found his circle of friends in the dorms shone with intelligence and good manners. They became my friends too.

One evening, Mark and I came into the common room. His roommates and friends called us into their circle.

"You have to try this! It's mind blowing!" Ed's hair had grown from close cropped to shaggy over the past two months. As I looked around the group, none of them looked clean cut any longer. Ed passed me a hand-rolled, white paper cigarette of sorts.

"No thanks, Ed. I don't smoke."

"You mean *cigarettes*. Neither do I. This is a *joint—Mary Jane, hooch*." When I still looked confused, Ed said, "Marijuana!"

Mark asked, "What makes this stuff so special?"

"You get high!" Ed rolled his eyes, and the whole group cackled with laughter. "You've got to try it. There's no way to explain how cool it is!"

"Yeah, man, very cool, far out," other voices affirmed the "weed's" results.

With all of his friends proclaiming good times, Mark took the joint and puffed on it.

"No, no, no!" Ed took it away and demonstrated. "You take a toke and hold it in, see?"

"Sure." Mark followed suit and offered it to me.

The heavy, acrid smoke choked me. I passed the joint on. I did better when it came around again.

"Man, am I hungry... Oh wow, look at the lava lamp... I'm stoned, man... cool." Quiet laughter erupted here and there, as each of our worlds warped, slowed, and mellowed.

The next morning seemed normal. I didn't know what to expect, *maybe a hangover?* I had never been truly drunk, just mildly high and happy with liquor. This was different; I didn't know how I felt about it yet.

Mark made a rapid ascent in the drug-using pack. He and his friends branched out to hashish and "mind expanding" hallucinogens. I dabbled, using small amounts of each. Time passed for my assessment of "the drug culture." I found lethargy increased with use. Motivation suffered. I liked being "straight" better than the drug-altered state. With Mark taking a leadership role in the drug scene, my unpopular straight side never came out in the open. I used drugs in small amounts as I wished, surreptitiously not inhaling or only pretending to take a hallucinogen tab, while enjoying Mark and my friends.

Mark had excelled with little or no work in his small, country high school. At Makefield, he began failing or receiving poor grades in the accelerated classes of a near-Ivy-League-level college. "I'm *the expert*," he said of his increasing drug expertise. "I can get good deals for the guys in the dorm." His significant intellect paved the way to score exceptional marijuana, hash, and "clean, good quality" hallucinogens. He portrayed himself widely as knowledgeable about drugs and became disdainful of anyone with less of an intellect than he claimed for himself. Everyone at Makefield bought drugs from Mark.

My parents sensed Mark's new, conceited attitude with disapproval. But the defining moment in their relationship came by surprise.

My cousin from Virginia, a year older than me, and her fiancé visited my parents. Mark offered them tickets to a rock concert for Saturday night. Dad suggested we use the family Pontiac to go to the concert for a more comfortable ride. Mark's vintage 1941 Pontiac, weathered to a mottled grape purple instead of its original blue, stayed at Makefield.

When we arrived, the parking lot was jammed. Even outside, the music resounded. Inside the venue, hard rock blared to headache-volume. A crush of people packed together, like in a rush-hour train, added to the discomfort and drove us back outside.

Mark managed to separate me from my cousin, so he and I could smoke a joint. When we found them again, their long faces and hunched shoulders spoke dissatisfaction at being abandoned in the ear-shattering din. Coming back slightly stoned couldn't have helped. Their disapproval obvious, they seemed more like our parent's age, except for the birth control pills I had seen in their bathroom medicine cabinet next to the guest bedroom.

"Would you like to leave?" I shouted above the music. They nodded.

"Pooh, keep me awake," Mark whispered.

Nearly home, I nodded off for a few seconds. The car's motion felt strange, forcing my eyes open.

"Mark!" I screamed. His head shot up. A telephone pole stood dead center ahead of us. Mark jerked the wheel. The bang and crunch of metal spelled damage. We had sideswiped the pole, one eighth of a mile from home.

No injuries and minimal damage to the car meant nothing after Mark made light of the car accident, and began badgering Dad about seeing me again.

The lack of responsibility coupled with Mark's inability to read my father's well displayed body language proved a turning point. After that night, my parents lost all respect for him. Dad said he couldn't understand how someone so smart could pester him about a date with his daughter right after a car accident with *his* car. He concluded that Mark had no common sense. Although Dad had assessed the situation correctly, I stayed blind. Mom just stayed angry.

Mark dealt drugs to all the student users on the High Council, Makefield's ruling student body, which made them impotent at curbing his behavior in any way. Along with the drug use, I heard more and more frequently, "The professors are out to get me. They mark test questions wrong when the math is actually right."

"Mark, ask for help with the math. You weren't prepared for this kind of high-level work at your high school."

"I'm good at other things," he replied.

"What about the science award in high school? Didn't that require this kind of math?"

Stoned and not thinking, he replied, "I cheated and copied that part. No one found out."

Shaken, I realized his scholastic aptitude did not match the school's demands. *What will sophomore year bring?* He seemed in denial about the reality of his situation.

My subsequent denial—of his fatal flaws—kept me loyal and by his side every weekend. At this point, I wasn't considering God's point of view; although He protected me at every turn as things went from bad to worse.

The year before my college acceptance, I had no idea of physical therapy's scope, other than from personal experience being treated by a PT. Originally, I made the Temple University appointment at the end of my junior year at Kimberton to evaluate my interest in this city-bound school located in a terrible, North Philadelphia neighborhood. The newest program at Temple, the PT school, would graduate their first class a year ahead of my college graduation date. After two years of college requirements, applicants reapplied for admission to the College of Allied Health Professions and graduated with a bachelor of science in physical therapy.

The day before my Temple appointment, I retrieved the mail and found a pamphlet about physical therapy. Excited, I took it to my bedroom upstairs and sat cross-legged on the bed.

"Physical therapy includes the use of musculoskeletal and neurological assessment, pain-relieving modalities comprised of heat, light, water, electricity, and massage. Restorative modalities include gait training, activities of daily living, body mechanics instruction, and therapeutic exercise," I read. Over the next day, I memorized the simplified definition. A whisper said it would be *helpful*.

Temple University stood out as a well-constructed campus, pleasing to the eye, until coming to its boundary. Being used to open country and small-town America, or Center City Philly at Christmas with Granny and Lynne, I had no experience with "slums." Surrounding Temple, much of the North Philadelphia culture did not consider throwing trash on streets a problem. Dwellings squatted together row on row, in dirty disrepair. Occasionally, clean, tidy homes speckled the landscape and showed a different standard of living amidst the squalor. But overall, I found the slums unsightly and off key.

Mr. Hiram Dershowitz, director of the Physical Therapy School at Temple University, held the deciding cards in his hand.

I dressed in my favorite outfit: a purple wool miniskirt, matching purple sweater, and handsome, secondhand, suede boots. I can only imagine what Mr. Dershowitz thought about this "teeny-bopper" eleventh grader with a Pixie haircut and mid-thigh-high skirt. He hinted at his impressions of me with his opening remarks.

"So, I guess you want to work with *children*." He drew out the word, so it sounded like *cheeeldren*.

"No," I said, puzzled. "I like working with people of all ages." The sarcasm of his question left me unfazed. I had survived bullies, including my father, most of my young life. Since coming to Kimberton, instead of retreating, they brought out boldness, a "make my day" kind of response. And yet, in spite of his tone, I felt something good in this man that kept me from snarling. Although he started in an adversarial fashion, something deep within led me to give him an honest rather than armored response. I trusted the leading and waited to see where he would steer the interview.

He inspected me as if looking at a small, crawling creature. Cocking his head, and with the hint of a sneer, he asked, "Are you squeamish around blood?"

"No, not at all," I said with a smile, as I looked into his probing, dark eyes.

Without taking a breath, he asked, "Has anyone ever vomited on you?"

Puzzle solved! He had looked at me as *a prissy, little girl who never got her hands dirty.* This time I laughed openly, enjoying his look of surprise. "You don't know me at all," I said. "At sixteen, I worked as a nurse's aide and gave full bed baths to both men and women. I disconnected IVs—they were short staffed. It was a small, private hospital. At home, if I accidentally ran over a toad with the lawn mower, I looked at its anatomy to see if I could identify any organs. I'm not squeamish. I don't faint at the sight of blood. Actually, blood versus vomit? I'll take blood, any day. I hate the smell of vomit!"

His face no longer registered distain. A glimmer of hope appeared when he continued his questioning. "So, what *is* physical therapy?"

I confidently parroted my memorized definition from the previous day. "Physical therapy includes the use of musculoskeletal and neurological assessment, pain-relieving modalities comprised of heat, light, water, electricity, and massage. Restorative modalities include gait training, activities of daily living, body mechanics instruction, and therapeutic exercise."

His face relaxed, eyes softened; his mouth turned up in a smile. *He's finally viewing me as a worthy candidate for admission,* I thought. I found out—much later after graduation, pending satisfactory completion of prerequisite courses—that he had chosen me, at that interview, for the short list in Temple's second graduating PT class.

Preparation and timing are only miracles seen when looking back at events. When I finally recognized His exquisite, dovetailed workmanship in my life, the Lord became personal, beautiful, and awe inspiring, without measure. And with each passing year, that recognition and appreciation increases.

11

GOD IS NOT DEAD

*"And immediately Jesus stretched out His hand and caught
him, and said to him, 'O you of little faith, why did you doubt?'
And when they got into the boat, the wind ceased."*
— *Matthew 14:31–32*

THE LETTER CAME LATE in February, emblazoned with a red return address from Temple University. I raced into the house, yelling for my mother and father as I waved the cream-colored envelope in the air.

The family ran from all corners, as I tore the envelope open and snatched the letter into the light.

"It is with pleasure that I inform you of your admission to Temple University..." I read with a crescendo that rose to a near scream. Joined in by everyone, the family celebration cut short as I dashed to phone Mark.

"That's great," he said. "You can stay with me every weekend, unless they make you commute."

"We'll see about that," I said. "I want to stay on campus. Which train will I take to go to Makefield from Temple?"

"The Makefield Local," he said. "The train station is walking distance to the college. But I don't think your parents will give up that easily. I don't see them letting you stay anywhere but home—or in the middle of nowhere."

I nodded, though he couldn't see me. "I'll make it work, so I can live on campus," I said as I heard truth in Mark's words.

After graduation from Kimberton, the subject of room and board remained out of view, like a child playing hide and seek. Only hints and innuendo bubbled up in conversation with my parents, both sides avoiding explosion. The taboo nature of the topic didn't last. As I passed Dad in the kitchen one evening, he said, "I'm sending in your school tuition."

"Don't forget my room and board too," I added as Mom came through the doorway. Both my parents turned in unison.

"You *will* be commuting. Dorm space is limited and only for those who live too far to commute," Mom stated. "We're only an hour away at the most. You have a car, so there's no problem."

"There *is* a *big* problem. I will not stay at home and commute so you can control my every move—including whether I see Mark or not." *There,* I thought, *truth finally out!*

"Well, that's another thing," my mother said glaring. "Until you can be respectful, you're grounded."

Adamant, Mom and Dad refused to discuss the situation. *Commute or nothing.* They left, and I ran for the phone in tears.

"I told you they wouldn't give up easily. We can write long letters in Elvish," Mark said, referring to Elf language in *Lord of the Rings.*" And we can plan what you'll do until you're not grounded. You can do it, Pooh Bear!" Two prison-like weeks went by—tense, monosyllabic, the monotony broken only when two letters came from Mark, written in Elvish. Usually, I camped by the phone when my next call with Mark was scheduled to begin. The phone rang; but, this time, Dad picked it up. I knew it was Mark. By the time I got there, he hung up.

"Dad, why did you hang up?"

"Wrong number," he said.

"No, it wasn't! Mark's supposed to call me now."

"I don't want you talking to him."

The phone rang again, and I grabbed it.

"I just tried to call you," Mark complained.

"Dad hung up the pho—" a hand grabbed the receiver and tried to wrench it free from my fist. I hung on, as the phone hit my head in the fray. Held captive, instinct took over, and I bit the offending hand. Dad yelped in pain, let go, and backed off. Then, looking deflated and hurt, he faced me.

"You *bite the hand that feeds you!*" he said.

"Mark," I said into the lifeless receiver. No reply. I saw the cord swing free, no longer attached to the phone's base.

While Dad gathered his wits, I dodged him, ran upstairs to my grandmother's apartment, and locked myself in the bathroom. Later that afternoon, while my parents were out, I called Mark.

"My mother says you should come live with us," he offered. "You can work, and we can be together."

Still in a cloud of anger, I didn't hesitate. "Okay," I said and wrote a poem to my parents.

Dear Mom and Dad,

A sad, dark day this is for me
You've turned away my urgent plea
And forced my hand to leave this house
Since I will never play the mouse.

Childish things I have outgrown
Your control now overblown
So, though I've found my heart's desire
Your rejection lights the fire.

A fire that burns the bonds of love

And forces lies to rise above
The usual forms of subterfuge
And in our house, the lying's huge!

You reject my plain, plumed bird
And I reject all lying words
That trample real life and give
A mask instead of life that's lived

I thank you for the care you gave
For many years you made the save
When beaten down and so bereft
You helped when I had nothing left.

But now I'm grown, you need to know
The time has come for me to go
To my new life where truth abides
With no more masks and no more lies.

I packed a few things and said goodbye to my sisters. Mark picked me up.

His mother spoke in excitement as soon as I arrived. She had everything planned. I could work, maybe secretarial, and help put Mark through school while I lived with Mark's family. Apparently, *my* plans for college didn't count.

Mom became quiet when I relayed these suggested plans to her the next day by phone. There was no mention of my note—or my reason for leaving. Neither of us wanted my college admission scrapped. I knew Dad didn't either.

"Let me see what I can do," Mom said. "I'll call Temple and see if we can get you into the dorm."

That September, I moved into William's Hall on campus.

My parents drove thirty-four miles to Temple in December to surprise me for my birthday. I had signed out in the dorm log to

Makefield College for the weekend.

Freshman year, my room—a "triple"—was on the third floor of a dorm slated to be torn down the next year. I had a fire escape window beside my single bed. Opposite, bunk beds stood by tall windows in the spacious, bright room under the eaves. Mink—my Siamese kitten from a friend's litter—snuggled, purred, and adored, her face expressive with slightly crossed, blue eyes. She slept on my chest or curled up in my arms. Mink diluted the brutal course work: seventeen-and-a-half credits with a course in probability for prerequisite math and Chemistry 1 my prerequisite science. I managed math, but chemistry lost me in the weeds—a different language, foreign, unintelligible.

Chemistry 1 had three parts: lecture, an auditorium of floor-to-ceiling students; lab and recitation, smaller groups for practical teaching; and testing. As a grad student, lab and recitation teacher Barry Gelernt tutored me, prepped me for tests, and worked to raise my grade from a D average. He watched me struggle and listened as I explained I would never need chemistry again if I passed this required course. Barry went above and beyond to help me.

The night before my final exam, destined for failure, I hurled the chemistry book across the room and cried myself to sleep. At 7:45 the next morning, I prayed and headed for the 8:00 a.m. exam, nearly hopeless. God's mercy would be a long shot.

We opened our tests at the proctor's instructions. I took a surprised, deep breath. The only scenario that could give me a fighting chance lay facing me on the test: *multiple-choice*. Informed before starting that the exam questions required no written work, only an answer—and after a final prayer, partially in gratitude—I took the exam.

It would be weeks before my grades came. I had one more weekend before my dorm closed. Scheduled next fall to stay in the only on-campus housing in Hardwick Hall, I toured the new dorm.

Each room proved a tight, sterile, two-person rectangle in a high-rise setting—*claustrophobia up close and personal.* Sharing a room the size of an anchovy tin with a stranger and no privacy made me cringe.

My sophomore year's fee schedule for room and board sported a $100 hike over freshman year's costs. The expensive room and board, coupled with typical college food, germinated a seed of thought. With some research, I found an apartment priced $500 dollars less per year; but the deal would require a roommate.

Dad, open for discussion with the $500 price tag, met me for dinner at Kelley's Seafood House. I sold my idea over a bucket of steamed clams; high room and board prices made the apartment an excellent deal. Money talked, an easy sell, to my delight. Dad agreed to pay me a set amount for room and board each month.

My apartment search launched at the perfect time; everyone had gone home for summer. I took an apartment across Broad Street from Temple's main campus on a month-to-month lease with two room-mates: two mistakes in a row. The girls promised to send me money for escrow and the first month's rent within two weeks.

I moved into the slum unit, complete with dirty walls and cock-roaches that scattered in all directions if I turned on the kitchen light after dark. The creatures crunched underfoot when I walked over the bubbled, linoleum floor.

Out the front door, four lanes of Broad Street traffic either crawled or flew past the row house's front windows and littered curbs. Cracked, concrete steps matched the sidewalk. Going out after dark in North Philly rivaled a game of Russian roulette with gangs on the prowl. But I could walk to school, the only plus on the scorecard. I sifted through the mail each day, but no money arrived. My prospective roommates broke their promises.

I looked around my bug-infested surroundings one bright day, took a walk, and bought a newspaper. A Center City apartment was advertised for $50 less per month than what I was paying for a dump. Fifteenth and Spruce—a much safer, city center address—boasted a spacious one-bedroom apartment with a dining room. I signed the lease for a year and advertised for a roommate.

The large dining room partitioned into a roomy, second bedroom, arranged so that a five-foot tall, free-standing cabinet blocked my bed from view. Within a week, I had a nice roommate. Mark and Dad seemed happy; Mom seemed resigned. While Dad's thoughts were about money, Mom's concerns were about Mark in my life—a "problem" that still wasn't resolved, in her mind.

Now, only my chemistry grade remained outstanding. Anything below a C would end my dream of a physical therapy career.

When my grades came, Mark watched as I unfolded the single sheet of paper. Under *Chemistry 1 lab and recitation*, both had bold, capital Cs next to them. Tears of joy welled up, as Mark gave me half a smile and left the room.

He passed freshman year with a warning that his scholarship would be terminated without significant scholastic improvement. I thought that explained his tepid response to my success, which made no difference in my state of bliss. I still claimed the status of *physical therapy major*.

Only God, alive and well, could see me through my inability to master chemistry. My angelic recitation teacher had given me a grade of C, even while simple addition proved my grade point average a D. Angels surrounded the C on my final exam.

But, still using simple addition, *this* many angels equaled a miracle.

12

DON'T GO!

"You shall not steal."
— *Exodus* 20:15 (*the eighth Commandment*)

THE STYLISH CUP and saucer disappeared into my grandmother's voluminous pocketbook. The remaining rolls, wrapped in a napkin, followed the cup and saucer. Then all of the sugar packets dropped into the bag. Soft metallic clicking of silverware and muted conversation drifted by in the dim dining room of the diner as Granny surveyed the table.

"Mother," Mom whispered. Granny looked up from her activities.

"What? What?" she asked. "They won't miss a thing. They're rich," she sniffed.

Scenarios like this occurred on a regular basis throughout my childhood and teen years. At the time, I didn't think much about "stealing." I certainly didn't consider my Granny a thief. But the definition fit. Mom fit into the same category. I learned at a young age to keep quiet about this aberrant family habit. Even before my preteens, I knew we shouldn't steal.

"Mom, the cashier gave you $5 too much!" I said when I could count change.

"Shh!" Mom lowered her head and arched her eyebrows at me. "That's her problem. She didn't pay attention." Young enough to avoid argument, I didn't pursue the subject further.

By junior year of high school, after wearing secondhand clothes as long as I could remember, I yearned for new dresses, just for me.

"Oh, my gosh! That's my plaid skirt from last year!" My class-mate fingered the bright, red, plaid wool. I smiled, shrugged, and said nothing. *No use denying it.* It probably had been her skirt recycled to a used clothing shop. I never wore the plaid skirt again. In response to my increasing distaste for secondhand clothes, I developed new skills: I became an adept shoplifter. I had my favorite stores, including several popular clothing shops. *They can afford it. They're rich,* I ratio-nalized. I stole often: clothes, books—and in college, groceries, targeting the expensive cuts of meat.

Mark thought it funny and made no move to discourage me. It became a game to see how much I could get away with in my counter-culture rebellion.

One day, on the way to visit Mark, it rained. I carried Mink, my petite Siamese cat, in a basket with a lid and a few extra clothes in my oversized purse. Without an umbrella or raincoat, the rain left its mark on me. Mink and I made regular use of the train from Philly to Makefield. The conductor always joked with me about paying only one fare, as I petted the purring cat curled up in my lap. On this day, he also teased about how wet I looked compared to the unmarked cat.

"Well, I'll just have to get a raincoat," I pronounced, smiling up at his familiar face. And so, the hunt began. I walked up and down Chestnut Street and searched for a raincoat that I liked. Of course, I found it in the most expensive, exclusive clothing store on the street: Papa's Shop, top drawer. The coat I wanted was draped over a mannequin in the window. I planned a special trip to get it the next day.

On a bustling, summer Saturday in Center City, I wore my favorite sandals and carried my usual, oversized bag—summer shopping gear. On cooler days, my wool cape hid many items that became part of my household. For some reason, something in the back of my mind told me not to go. But I didn't listen.

Three blocks from Papa's Shop, my sandal strap broke. *Don't go! pause, don't go!* My broken sandal strap let the sole hit my foot and the pavement in a rhythm with extra beats. A block away, I secured the strap with a stray piece of string so I wouldn't attract attention in the store. I nodded to the shopkeeper and climbed to the second floor. Three of the same raincoats in three different sizes hung on the rack. All of them came into the fitting room with me. I chose the size six after trying it on: perfect and very chic. Carefully, I folded the coat, so no bulge showed in my bag. I replaced the other two coats and went downstairs as the shopkeeper came up. I smiled, nodded, and kept going. As I neared the door, I heard rapid footsteps on the stairs. I reached for the handle.

"STOP," her angry voice commanded.

One step away from freedom, where I could have blended in with the Saturday crowd, I stopped. My feet wouldn't move. Then, a hand grabbed my shoulder. She had nicely styled blonde hair and wore stylish clothes from her shop. She led me, without protest, to her office where she pointed to a chair facing her desk.

"I own this shop," she said. "I know my merchandise. I work hard to pay for all the goods so I can sell fashionable clothing to the public. And I know my size-six Misty Harbor raincoat is missing." She looked at me in expectation.

Guilty as charged, reluctant, I reached for my bag and drew out the coat. She took it and put it aside. Examining me with her hazel eyes, she asked, "Why did you take the coat?"

"I don't have a raincoat," I said.

Her expression hardened slightly. "I need a phone number for your mother or father."

Until this new development, nothing about the situation seriously concerned me. Now I panicked. I couldn't remember Mom's number at the real estate business where she worked; I told the shop owner.

"Where does your father work?"

"At the IRS on Broad and Spring Garden," I said, feeling weak.

She picked up the phone book and found the number.

Red-hot fear heated my face, melted my innards, glued me to the chair. Dad would be furious and take the theft as a personal affront. I took a deep breath as if submerging under water. Then, suddenly, my mind went still, quiet, almost peaceful. Mom's phone number came to me—clear, miraculous.

"Please, I just remembered my mother's number. Could you call her instead?"

The store owner paused and looked into my pleading eyes. "All right," she said and took the number down. She dialed, then spoke for a moment or two and handed me the phone. "Your mother would like to speak to you."

"Hi, Mom," I said in a small, sad voice. "I'm sorry."

"Why didn't you ask me for a raincoat? I would have gotten you one!"

"I know, Mom. And it would have been secondhand. I wanted, uh, I really wanted something new that no one had ever worn before. I wanted a new raincoat that I actually liked."

After a silence filled with unspoken words, Mom said, "Stay right there. The owner gave me a choice of coming to get you or calling the police. I'll be there in an hour. Let me talk to her again. We're going to deal with this together."

What does she mean by dealing with this together? After a brief exchange, the trim, blonde owner hung up the phone and turned to me.

"You can stay right there until your mother comes. I want you to understand that each item in this store was bought with money out of my own pocket. Do you know that I have to make the cost back for each item I buy, plus pay for shop rent, phone, electricity, cleaning products, and sales help?" She waited for me to respond.

"No. I never thought about it."

"There are other young women besides you who come in here and never think about what their thieving does to me, either. Now that you know, I hope it makes a difference. Where're you going to school, and what're you studying?"

"I'll be a sophomore in the fall at Temple University. I'm taking pre-requisite courses for physical therapy."

"You will be helping people. You can also help people by not stealing. Does that make any sense to you?"

"Yes, it does make sense. I'm so sorry! I won't steal again now that I know it really hurts people." I knew I shouldn't steal; but I wanted things I couldn't afford. I didn't think my thieving caused harm. Her explanation changed everything.

As the bell over the door jingled, the owner rose with a look that said: *Stay still and be quiet.* I nodded at her. She waited on the new customer. This repeated for an hour, with Saturday shoppers. The sparse, off-white, back office spoke of work with no time for decoration—*utilitarian.* The public shop areas painted in pleasant pastels gave a background for merchandise arranged with artistic care. Two display windows that had brought me into the shop advertised their wares using stylish, color-coordinated outfits and matching accessories. I pictured the owner on a fashion buying trip, followed by all the activities required, so that each piece would beg to be tried on and bought. *No wonder she was angry.*

The bell jingled. I heard Mom talking. Then she appeared in the doorway—her face neutral, the lack of anger puzzling, unexpected.

After introductions, Mom asked to speak privately to the owner. Five minutes later, she went upstairs, and Mom had me to herself.

"Mom, I'm so sorry," I repeated.

"Mrs. Travis, the owner, told me what you two discussed. I'm so glad she took the time to educate you about the cost of shoplifting. Tell me again why you did it."

I kept my eyes on the floor. "Most of my clothes are someone else's hand-me-downs. I don't have a choice of style, or color. They're perfectly serviceable, but the other kids don't have to get their clothes that way. I guess it's selfish. Some kids have so much less. But it's the way I feel, especially since Dad won't wear secondhand clothes. Remember the big fight the day you brought that handsome, blue suit home? He wouldn't even try it on. He said he's *the bread winner*—like you don't do anything, and my sisters and I don't count. It made me so mad! It's like being a girl is second class." I glanced up as Mom tried to hide the tears in her eyes. "That day, we found out how ridiculous Dad's double standard was. It was such a handsome suit— still with the price tags on it. I thought if it had never been worn, it would count as new."

She nodded and said, "Let's go. We have some things to do on the way home."

When we turned into the Plaza Mall, I wondered why we were there; but I kept my mouth shut after my earlier disgrace. Mom parked facing Wanamaker's Department Store.

"Let's go," she said.

"Mom, what are we doing here?"

"Something I should have done a long time ago."

I followed her without asking any more questions. She approached the customer service desk.

"I would like a Wanamaker's credit card. I'd like to use it today," she stated. The clerk handed her a pen and forms that Mom filled out, with Dad as the "payor/head of household." With the Wanamaker's credit card approved, she ushered me to the women's petite department. I moved in a state of shock. I had overheard Dad in the past as he lectured her on credit cards.

"*Rich people* can afford them," he said. "We're not rich. They're for people who have money to burn."

Mom broke into my unpleasant reflection over that prior situation. "I can't fix the past," she said, "but let's settle this now. You will have new clothes in the future. They won't all be new, but you will have clothes you want. There will be *no reason for you to steal*."

This turn of events made me giddy. I expected to be grounded forever, screamed at, berated, persona non grata; *and instead we were shopping?* I almost ran to keep up with my mission-driven mother. Reflecting, I already knew that money posed a deeply-rooted problem for my Dad. He constantly told us we didn't have enough money. I thought about Mom's and Dad's relationship; their arguments always revolved around money.

Looking at our past, as Mom became more self-sufficient with her own car and a good paying job, Dad never changed his "not enough money" tirade. Although she contributed to the household finances, she received no credit for her work. Dad married Mom but treated her more like a servant, unless they were in public. There, he would call her "honey," open doors, pull out her chair, and help with her coat.

I looked at my mother's resolute face in a department store—that was previously deemed too expensive for our family's pocketbook—and saw liberation evolving before me. It took no imagination to picture our family in the future. There would be repercussions. Dad had just lost his iron grip on the home finances.

I followed Mom all over Wanamaker's. We looked at a magnificent, black maxi-coat; a lovely, belted, black raincoat; a light, wool jacket that flattered my lithe shape; and a new pair of black boots. They all fit, and she bought every one of them.

Back in the car, I wondered how Dad would handle this change. *Mom set a new course today.* This could bring on open war, instead of the armed truce under which we lived at home. But maybe that would be better than living a lie.

When I was at home, Dad never brought up the credit card or our Wanamaker purchases within my earshot. True to Mom's promise, I had new clothes that I liked—and secondhand clothes that comprised about three quarters of my wardrobe, which I didn't mind.

Mom and Dad's relationship changed. The war had started, via a quiet undercurrent.

At that time, I thought it overdue.

God's intervention—with conscience in the shape of a broken sandal, and the divine memory of Mom's work phone number—confirmed God's presence. It confirmed His care for a thief, who He loved anyway.

Family picture 1968.

13

THE PRECIPICE

"He has delivered us from the power of darkness and conveyed us into the kingdom of the Son of His love, in whom we have redemption through His blood, the forgiveness of sins."
— Colossians 1:13–14

NEAR THE END of freshman year at Temple and my stay at the 15th and Spruce Street apartment, I found myself half asleep from studying late into the night for a final. My eyes jerked open. Overhead, two sets of pounding feet sounded like the ceiling might come down. Our new upstairs neighbors had two children, who galloped about at all hours just above our heads.

I had a young roommate who worked with me at Occidental Insurance Company. During evening shift, we typed letters and sorted customers' insurance paperwork. Horatio managed our crew of three: Sarah, John, and me. Horatio—a slight, kind man with a ready smile—had immigrated to the US from the Philippines. John—an intelligent, sweet man of color—worked evenings for his school tuition. He often stayed at our apartment late into the evening to be with Sarah.

Sarah had left her Ohio home after an unhappy break-up with a boyfriend. She told me she was eighteen. After we lived and worked together companionably for several months, I noticed her gaining weight, but I said nothing. She mentioned she had met someone who she described as *a friend*. He took her out twice.

One afternoon after work, she brought him to meet me and visit. Unusually quiet, almost secretive, he had strange eyes—with pinpoint pupils. I'd never seen anything like them. He expressed great interest in my twelve-string Elger guitar and admired my songs and poetry. He liked the way my tiny chess set opened; as one drawer pushed open, the other opened simultaneously. Each drawer—cleverly hidden on opposite sides of the little six- inch, square box—held the chess pieces. Handcrafted in Tyrol, one of the treasures from my trip to Germany, it remained a close favorite to my Voitländer Vitomatic camera. He smiled in an odd sort of way.

"How nice," he said.

I didn't understand his interest in my items until I came home from school two days later and found the apartment door ajar. My camera, guitar, silver dollar collection, tiny travel chess set, and all my jewelry had been stolen. Within half an hour, Sarah rushed into the apartment. Tears smeared her eyeliner. Too late, we found out morphine constricts eye pupils to pinpoint size. She said she couldn't remember where he dropped her off before he doubled back to rob me.

Sarah had nothing to take. All of my belongings would pay for his next morphine fix.

Inconsolable and truly apologetic, Sarah came with me to the police precinct and filed a complaint. The officer's bored looks and lack of true interest made it obvious my treasures would remain gone for good. I suggested pawn shops would be likely places for my stolen items. I received amused looks and laughter in return. No murder committed, no armed robbery. Just a petty theft statistic.

That night, two men in plain clothes knocked on our door. They had police badges, and one stated he needed to ask Sarah some additional questions. Although I considered 9:30 at night late and unusual for a visit like this, they came in. I explained that Sarah went to bed early, but the first officer led me to the living room couch, while the second called to Sarah that he had come to discuss her statement. I heard her say he could come in.

The officer sitting opposite me on the couch tapped his foot on the carpet—silent, shifting position, nervous. He asked me a few questions but wrote nothing down. Twenty minutes went by.

"Please, let me alone!" I heard Sarah's voice, vibrating with fear—the male voice low, soothing, too soft to hear.

"No! Please, stop!" I heard Sara crying.

I jumped up. "You," I pointed at the cop with me. "Get your coat." I ran to Sarah's room.

The second officer sat on the bed, leaning over her, his hand under the covers where she cowered.

"I don't know what you think you're doing, but you better get out of here right now," I said, my voice strident with anger.

His partner came from the living room, coat over his arm, and bustled him out of the apartment. We never saw them or any of my belongings again. I had to put the theft behind me.

The drama with Sarah didn't end there. A few months later, she came home from a doctor's appointment, her face ashen.

"What's wrong?" I asked.

"The doctor said I'm eight months pregnant," she said in a strangled voice.

"Holy Toledo! That's why you've been gaining weight! I know this is a surprise, but what are you going to do?"

"I can't go home, that's for sure. I'll have the baby here and have it adopted. I'd like to stay in Philly," she said. Sarah looked at me, her head tipped sideways. "Could you stand to keep me on as your roommate?" she asked.

"I think that sounds great! Now, we need to talk about your eating habits. You have a baby to keep healthy!" It felt good to laugh together.

About a month later, relaxing after school, I answered the phone. "We have Sarah Long in labor and delivery at Graduate Hospital. We need a next of kin to give permission for an emergency C-section, since she is underage for surgical consent. She's been in labor for over twenty hours, and the baby's in distress."

"You'll have to phone her parents. All I know is they're in Ohio."

For the next two days, I called, trying to find out Sarah's condition. Only a close a relative could receive any information, they said.

A week later, insistent banging on the front door brought me on the run.

"Who is it?"

"Victoria Long, Sarah's mother," a woman's voice said—cold, clipped. "I've come to get Sarah's things."

When I opened the door, a well-dressed woman of medium build pushed past me. "Where is Sarah's room?" she asked with an accusing look and tone.

I showed her Sarah's bedroom.

"How is Sarah? Is the baby okay?" I asked.

"Sarah will be better when I get her home," she said, her words cut short. In half an hour, she strode out of the apartment without a backward glance.

A few days later, I cleaned the room that had been Sarah's, as I contemplated how to deal with the roommate situation. At that time, things were up in the air with Mark and Makefield. If he left, he would expect to live with me. Then, there were the girls in the apartment next door, Mary and Jo. They may be up for a move. I liked both of them, but Jo talked about moving back to Illinois. Mary would be the one.

As I mopped under the bed, I heard a scraping sound. I reached under, and my fingers wrapped around a spiral bound notebook—Sarah's address book. I found her parents' phone number and address.

I dialed the number, pleasantly surprised when Sarah answered.

"Hi, Sarah! It's Violet! How are you? I had to call to see how you're doing and find out how the baby did!"

"I can't believe you're calling me here, after all I did to you—the robbery and now this. I'm so embarrassed," she said in a distant way. "I don't have much time. My mother can't know you called," she said, her voice rushed, flat. The lack of warmth felt disconcerting after the connection we had forged during six months as roommates.

"Why? What did I do?" I asked.

"It's not you. There's too much to explain. They wouldn't take the baby for adoption in Philly after the long labor and delivery. His APGAR score was low right after he was born. We took him home on the plane, and he already has a family lined up that's been waiting three years for a baby. He's fine." Sarah gave a deep sigh that turned into a sob. "I want to forget this ever happened," she said, crying. She blew her nose. "Please don't call me again. It reminds me of this whole, horrible mess." After a sniffling pause, she mumbled, "I've got to go." I inhaled to speak, but the phone clicked in my ear. Sarah had disconnected.

I took a moment, puzzling, before I hung up. *The Sarah I knew didn't feel like the Sarah who hung up on a friend and turned a relationship to ashes in one phone call.* Stung, I mailed the little book to her parents' address. Sarah placed herself firmly in my past. I had forgiven her, but it seemed she hadn't forgiven herself. I wondered if she ever would.

With my Spruce Street roommate melodrama still fresh and the lease about to expire, I went apartment hunting mid-summer before my sophomore year at Temple University. A narrow street behind Graduate Hospital seemed on the other side of the city, or so I thought. Mary, my next-door neighbor at the Spruce Street apartment, came with me on the hunt for a new place. On a late summer day, we stood looking at a handsome townhouse on Naudain Street.

"It's a great location for me," I said. "I can go to work through the hospital ER entrance now that I changed jobs. I never liked secretarial type work, and that's all I did at Occidental."

"It's good for me too," she answered. "Now that my roommate is moving back to Illinois, I can't afford the Spruce Street apartment. This is perfect with two bedrooms."

"Well, you know my story. I'd need another roommate too. Even though the 15th and Spruce address is a good location, this is so much nicer in every way. Shall I sign the lease?" I asked.

"I think so. It's near my theater company too. It'll be a great place to live!"

Mary and I moved to Naudain Street, one-half block away from Graduate Hospital, where I worked as a nurse's aide. Living in next-door apartments at 15th and Spruce, Mary and I had become close friends. Our new place—a three-story townhouse—sat on a quiet, one-way street, almost cockroach-free. Mary's boyfriend, Randy, stayed with her most of the time—more good company.

Mark left Makefield College, his scholarship revoked. He moved in with me, for one-third of the rent.

The mail slot clicked shut as a batch of mail hit the living room floor. I raced downstairs to see if my Temple letter arrived. I had to reapply at the end of sophomore year for the physical therapy program, junior and senior year. A cream-colored envelope with a red lettered, return address for Temple University leapt out at me. The second line said, "College of Allied Health Professions, School of Physical Therapy, Philadelphia, Pennsylvania." The stairs flew under my feet, two at a time going up.

In the bedroom, Mark measured nickel and dime bags of marijuana. All his friends from Makefield and its sister college, Baron Crest, bought their drugs from him. His supplier, Ron, lived in New York City. Mark received phone calls when new shipments came in. He took the train or drove to New York every couple of months, or more often, and replenished his supply of marijuana, hashish, and a limited quantity of hallucinogens. Mark's "designer" named marijuana became his specialty—different strains of marijuana had names like Panama Red, Blue Dream, Indigo Bay, etc. On his last trip, he brought home "good quality" cocaine, now in great demand.

His shirt drawer camouflaged the baggie of white powder. I focused on my studies and kept my head buried in the sand as much as possible.

Nearing the top landing, I crowed, "It's here!"

"What's here?" Mark asked without looking up.

"My admission letter from the School of Physical Therapy!"

He grunted, still not taking his eyes off the measuring process as he filled baggies with "Panama Red" from a two-pound garbage bag.

I didn't wait for Mark to show interest. The letter opened and unfolded in seconds. It stated, "Welcome to the College of Allied Health Professions, School of Physical Therapy. With acceptance of this position, you will be admitted to the second Physical Therapy Class, scheduled to graduate in 1972."

Too excited to jump around or even speak, I silently dropped the letter in front of Mark, who stopped his task with an expression of impatience.

"I knew you'd get in," he said.

"Do you know the competition I faced?"

He looked at me with a bored expression and said, "Duh, they picked *me* up off the street and put me in Temple University."

Speechless at his meanness with the implication that Temple University admitted the lower-intellect students, the irony of the situation could not be ignored. Mark really believed people were inferior to him, including me. I walked out of the room and called my parents with the good news. They celebrated on the phone with me. Dad asked how much I thought books would cost. Laughing, I told him, "Plenty. But you'll have a physical therapist in the family!" Both he and Mom chuckled. The pride and warmth in their voices went to my heart. Mary and Randy shared my delight as well. In spite of Mark's attitude, I celebrated success— and future promise.

"Violet," Mark said, coming toward me later that afternoon. "Sorry I didn't get excited about your acceptance. This last trip to New York turned out more expensive than I expected. Ron got me a Mettler scale for the coke and some really good product..."

I cut him off. "Yeah. Well, coke is more than I bargained for." He gave me a derisive look and turned away.

His comment about the competition for PT school admission still echoed in my head. *Hurt* didn't begin to touch my feelings. Disgusted and angry, the incident left a deadly shadow that grew with each negative remark, slight, and illegal sale. Not willing to dissect the situation, I only knew Mark had changed—his lifestyle and mine, diverging. I pushed that thought back, collected our wash, and headed for the laundromat. I wanted a distraction.

By Sunday afternoon, my acceptance into the PT program began to feel real. I sat in my favorite stuffed chair and looked at my kitchen and living room—which constituted the whole downstairs in the townhome's open layout. I remembered all the hours of work put into making the little townhouse a pleasant, comfortable place to live. Hours with a paintbrush created walls of cheerful apricot with a pink blush. Café curtains in cream with pale blue and apricot accents allowed the natural light in with our privacy intact. An Indian, brass table stood centered in front of the living room couch.

I basked in the restful, pleasant, well-appointed, open space —*mine* to live in. It made me smile, even with the emotional roller coaster and school stresses.

14

THE TOWNHOUSE

"I will have mercy on whomever I will have mercy, and I will have compassion on whomever I will have compassion."
— Romans 9:15a

AFTER MOVING to the Naudain Street townhouse, everything began falling into place, even though I knew two years of PT school wouldn't be a cakewalk. I had no inkling that school would be the least of my problems.

I blinked and became a junior in the Physical Therapy School of the College of Allied Health Professions. The first semester opened my eyes with Gross Anatomy. In lecture, I took notes—spelling the unknown, anatomical, and medical vocabulary phonetically. *Cadaver lab.* Mown-over, mangled toads looked much different than embalmed human tissue. Dissection lab smelled of formaldehyde. Scheduled late in the afternoon, we took turns dissecting with one cadaver shared by four students. Dr. Kraft, witty and nimble, moved through the massive amount of required material with his own brand of humor. His personality and skill guaranteed a dedicated following of loyal students.

By late afternoon, my stomach growled with hunger. The apple in my bag called, even through the smell of embalmed bodies. I took off my surgical gloves. As I took a crunching bite, three sets of eyes looked at me with disgust.

"Oh, how can you eat in here?" asked one of the two women with a grimace.

I smiled. "With no problem at all!" They turned back to the dissection in progress. I finished my apple and donned another pair of gloves.

Though the work proved difficult, I enjoyed cadaver lab; anatomy fascinated me.

At the same time, my memory had never been an asset. I knew I could look up things later that required memorization in the short term. Though my flawed memory wouldn't affect my skill as a therapist, it denied me high grades in school. At this point, I cared only about earning my degree, since I knew I'd be successful once in my role as a physical therapist.

In amazement, I realized my junior year had flown. I was halfway through my Bachelor of Science in Physical Therapy degree.

Mark continued bringing in money by dealing drugs out of the townhouse. He had clients all over the city and surrounding suburbs. One of his clients was Ken, a violinist from Curtis Institute of Music, who practiced so long and hard that he raised a thick, red, calloused patch of skin where his jaw rested on the violin's chinrest. He seemed a nervous sort, not anxious to talk when I met him buying a nickel bag of marijuana. *Odd*, I thought.

Increasingly distant, Mark's new identity hardened like a stony shell around him. He covered his inadequacies, always appearing in control. As I buried myself in PT studies, his clients fawned over him, asking if they could "taste" the latest, newly-named product. He spoke like a professor, rarely asking about anyone personally, just talking about his product.

As I progressed through PT school, senior year required "affiliations"—a clinic or hospital physical therapy department that allowed students to gain experience in a supervised, live setting. All the techniques learned in class waited in my head for a patient's benefit. Encouraging grades, complimentary instructors, and love of my chosen profession gave no excuse for my stabbing feelings of unhappiness. By senior year, I began losing weight. Always lean, it didn't take much to make me look hat-rack thin.

The physical therapy curriculum posed no significant problem, until the senior year statistics course threatened to sabotage my efforts. By the end of September, the same weeds that surrounded chemistry plagued me with statistics—and I don't mean the weed that Mark sold. Statistics theory posed no problem. The math, *insurmountable*. Never good with formulas and word problems, I blanked out completely when taking a test. I earned perfect scores on the theory portion of quizzes—and zeros on the math. Worst of all, I had a statistics paper due by the end of the year.

I mentioned the paper to Mark. I had to formulate a research study with a valid hypothesis. Quantifying outcomes and proving theorems utilized statistics.

"Don't worry about it. I'll write your paper," Mark said in an offhanded way. *He can't be serious.*

"Mark, it's like speaking a different language. I've become fluent in medical and anatomy terms with two-and-a-half semesters of learning under my belt. This is really specialized."

"How hard could it be? I can do it, so don't worry," he said.

I knew he couldn't write my paper. Now, I also knew that he considered me an idiot and my schooling simplistic. Although irrational, and perhaps because it *was* so irrational, I cried myself to sleep.

I called Mom the night before Thanksgiving and asked what I could bring for dinner. I told her Mark would drop me off and go on to his parent's house.

"Do you have any powdered sugar?" she asked.

"Yup! How much do you need?"

"No more than a cup, hon'. How are you doing?"

"Hanging in there. Statistics is killing me! I'm going to have to ask my prof for extra help. We use computers, but I can't remember the formulas to plug into the darn thing!"

"Well, you've managed so far, and you'll beat this too. Come home and forget about school for the day. It's been a while!"

"Thanks, Mom. I can use a vote of confidence right about now." We talked a little longer before I put a baggie of powdered sugar in my pocketbook for Thanksgiving dinner.

With Mark at his parents' and me with mine, we each enjoyed Thanksgiving. Mom's and Dad's warmth and interest in my course work drew me closer to them. Catching up with my sisters started mending my fractured sense of family.

I still felt odd seeing Granny's chair empty. She had passed away suddenly two years before. At age seventy-two, mowing the lawn on a hot day, she fell over dead. I hoped my death would be like that. My sister, Gay, found her. The memorial service faded from my memory, except the part where I played Edelweiss on my guitar and sang—bolstered just enough by an anti-anxiety pill from Mom.

Thanksgiving night, back in the townhouse, I dropped the baggie of leftover powdered sugar on my nightstand and fell into bed, pleasantly exhausted.

Giving thanks to God *with* my family gave me hope in mending differences. *With God, all things are possible.*

But the morning would come earlier than I expected. And there would be no joy in it.

15

BUSTED

"What will you say when He punishes you?"
— *Jeremiah* 13:21

AT DAWN, I awakened to pounding on the front door. Our German shepherd barked a deep, bass alarm. I scrambled out of bed, ran, and secured Sergeant with his leash.

"Who is it?" I asked, stroking the dog to calm him.

"Police. Open up. We have a search warrant."

My heart flipped over and sank. Mark had a massive shipment of hash and marijuana in the bedroom closet. The new Mettler balance scale for the cocaine in his shirt drawer sat in the open on the dresser.

Two uniformed police officers with badges clearly displayed marched through the open door. The older, seasoned veteran glanced at the neat surroundings. He looked to be in his fifties—disdainful, hungry for a big drug bust. The younger officer's sympathetic eyes gave a polite cast to his face, which he kept neutral. A twenty-some-thing "youngster"—probably fresh from Vietnam—he moved with deliberation, calm.

"Upstairs," the senior officer barked at the younger man. Sergeant led me up the steps, as I pushed ahead of the invading force.

"Connors, you search the second-floor bedroom. I'll get the third floor."

"Yes, Sir, Captain Mulder."

"That's my room," I said, patting the dog who looked at me with questioning eyes. "It's all right," I soothed the shepherd. "It's going to be all right."

"My roommate, Mary, and Randy are upstairs," I said to Captain Mulder. He smirked, moving up the steps.

Through the open bedroom door, Mink—blue Siamese eyes inquisitive—perched on the bed. Mark, dressed in pants, moved toward the dresser. He had no time to get into his shirt drawer. Pale, face tight with fear, his sandy-colored hair fell, uncombed, over his eyebrows.

"This is officer Connors," I told Mark. "They have a search warrant." I had no doubt he had heard already. Silently, he nodded, opened a drawer, and pulled out a T-shirt.

"Sit on the bed and keep your dog secure," Connors commanded, but without the rancor that characterized Mulder's demeanor. Connors started with the closet, which yielded five pounds of Panama Red marijuana and seventeen pounds of hashish. Captain Mulder came in and spied the small baggie of white powder on my bedside table.

"What do we have here?" he asked with a knowing smile. "Powdered sugar from Thanksgiving dinner," I replied.

"Ha! You expect me to believe that?" he laughed.

"Taste it."

He opened the bag, licked a finger, and drew it through the white powder. His eyes bugged open in surprise, as the sweetness hit his taste buds and registered in his brain. He closed the bag and threw it back on the table.

"Keep searching here. I'm going downstairs," Mulder said as if nothing had happened. Connors nodded, but I saw the smile he hid a second too late.

Sergeant wined, then gave a short, sharp bark. "He has to go out," I said.

"Downstairs, both of you."

We trooped downstairs. Connors spoke for a moment with Mulder, then motioned Sergeant and me outside. Mark sat on the couch under Mulder's watchful eye.

Sergeant didn't need long, but it gave me time with Connors. He seemed about my age and affirmed he had just returned from Vietnam.

"You have a really nice place here. It's not what we usually find," he said.

"Thanks. I'm going to Temple University for physical therapy. I'm a senior."

"I had physical therapy after I got home from Nam. It got me fit enough, after my wounds, to get into the police academy."

"Now that you have the job, do you like it?"

"Yes," he said without hesitation. "I like it most of the time." Briefly, with no pretense, he appraised me. "Whose drugs did I find in that closet?"

"Mary and Randy have nothing to do with the drugs, and I'm a full-time student." He nodded, understanding.

"Tell me, coming from Vietnam, that you *haven't* smoked marijuana," I asked, peering into his gray-blue eyes. Though he only half smiled, his eyes told me what I wanted to know.

We returned to the townhouse. I accompanied Officer Connors back upstairs to the bedroom, where he impounded the scale, marijuana, and hash and searched the dresser. When he got to Mark's shirt drawer, I saw him move the little baggie of cocaine to his pants pocket. He asked for the bathroom, and I pointed. A minute later, I heard the toilet flush.

The arraignment finished in a blur. After our fingerprints and mug shots, a guard separated me from Mary. Bail, set at $5,000 each, sounded insurmountable. During arraignment, I met Mark's lawyer, kept on retainer for situations like this. He screamed at the judge, pacing back and forth while looking maniacal through the entire process. I didn't trust him.

When they read the charges, Officer Mulder claimed we had one hundred pounds of hashish and fifty pounds of marijuana; but he made no mention of cocaine. Now, fear settled in. Knotted with dread at Mulder's lie about the massive drug quantity, I felt sick. My single, painful, phone call went as well as could be expected. Dad answered the phone. Considering the circumstances, I admired his control. I knew Mark's drug dealing had never entered Mom or Dad's minds.

I was stuck in detention until Monday. Mark and I had some time before we were separated again.

"Mark, your lawyer's crazy! This is the guy you trust? And now the cops are lying about how much stuff you had!"

"He's fine. Everyone knows him, and he works with them all. Don't worry. I called my mom, and she's getting our bail money. She was a little shocked, but she'll come get us."

I didn't really listen to Mark. I went on, "I talked to my dad. Because it's Friday night and all the banks are closed, I'll have to stay until Monday when the banks open and he can get the money."

Separated once again, time passed in the sterile holding room. Finally, I curled up on the bench and closed my eyes. The door banged, startling me awake. "Get up and follow me," a new guard demanded. She led me to a large room with lockers and shelves filled with detainees' belongings. She searched, found, and handed me my purse and jacket. "Your bail was posted," she said. I signed a receipt for my personal effects.

I could see Mark and his mother through the wire-reinforced window. *She must have posted my bail.* A strange sense of weightlessness came over me as I exited the building. Cold, night air refreshed me after detention's stale atmosphere. Then, I hugged Mark's mom. I thanked her, several times, for posting my bond; but I expected to be with Mary. I felt guilty at my desertion of her but had no choice.

"Well, let's get you two home. I have to get some sleep," Mark's mom said. Mark and I sat in the backseat, wrapped in a state of unreality, as she drove us to Naudain Street. Sergeant barked a happy greeting.

Waking up in the townhouse, the surreal fog from the night before remained, dense and numbing. Arrested the day after Thanksgiving, nothing about it appeared in any newspapers—my parents spared the embarrassment of explaining any news articles about their wayward daughter. *I will not desert Mark. I'm no fair-weather friend,* I thought. Mary and Randy didn't come home until Sunday.

"You've got to get out of here," Mary said as she gripped my shoulders. "We can take you home."

"I can't leave now. It's not right! I've been with Mark for five-and-a-half years. That's got to count for something!"

Mary shook her head and squinted at me. "You have a good job ahead of you. Mark has no future at all, because of who he is by choice. Get out! Now!"

I twisted away from her and locked myself in the bathroom until I heard her go downstairs.

When I went back to the bedroom, Mark said, "You know, we can always get married."

"Married?" I said. "Why now?"

"Husbands and wives can't be forced to testify against each other," he said with a calculating smile. *Devious. An earth-shaking omen.*

He didn't stay for my response or further discussion. I knew what he thought of my intellect and Temple University; but this coldhearted proposal for legal, ulterior motives shredded my last molecule of love. *Only loyalty remained. The surreal fog thickened.*

Mary tried to talk to me; but nothing made sense. I told her we would talk tomorrow.

I had to find the horizon to my inverted world.

Half an hour later, Mark found out who had turned him in to the police. He roared into the bedroom, red-faced, veins in his neck protruding.

"It was Ken! His mother found the nickel bag under his pillow, and the coward told her where he got it!"

"What are you going to do about it? Ken isn't really the problem. How are you planning to make a legal living?"

"He ruined my life," he said, raising his voice a little more with each word. He repeated this phrase three times before I left the room.

He hadn't seen or heard me. I went downstairs and sat in my comfortable, apricot and peach-blush living room. *What would happen now?* The phone rang once and quit. Mark must have picked it up. I opened my journal; this entry would be a doozy. Writing always clarified things for me.

Ten minutes later, Mark appeared on the stairs and stopped midway down. "I know what I might do. I could take a contract out on his life."

My world stopped as I heard those words. Something that had been submerged inside—held down for a long time—arose and shook me. *My schooling prepares me for the art and science of healing, while Mark talks about killing someone over a drug deal. How does my life and purpose juxtapose with his?* My topsy-turvy world suddenly gained a horizon. I focused, possibly for the first time in years, on the reality of my situation—as if I finally saw Mark with clarity.

Near dusk, he told me not to expect him until late and drove off in the car. Mary begged me to go home again as soon as he left. The fragile, focused horizon from the afternoon disappeared as I refused to leave. I let my mind go, closed my eyes, and sank deeper into the chair. Evening crept forward; I sat motionless as a decision formed—one not made of glass, but steel. It welled up, straightened my spine, and sent all the warning bells I ever owned into alarm mode. For the first time in five years, I consciously recognized Mark as a bad character. *Oh my God, I must get out of here!* As I looked back over my years with him, his comments repeated in my head. I visualized his disdainful expression, recognizing my vulnerability; my loyalty had saddled me with my current situation.

"Mary," I called, standing at the bottom of the steps. Mary's face appeared over the top railing. "I've got to get out of here!" Desperation sounded in my voice. I could not face Mark yet, but I could put distance between us and let the molten steel harden into true resolve, a real backbone. My guardian angels, still working overtime, finally gained some ground.

"Randy, Randy! We've got to get her out of here, *now!*" Mary hollered.

I called my mother. She said two words, "Come home!" Although the relationship between Mom and Dad was brimming with emotional turmoil, given my situation, her words created a life raft.

I had my grandmother's apartment to myself. After Mom and I had a frank discussion about drugs and Mark, she gave me an ultimatum. She insisted that I visit the psychiatrist who had helped unscramble her world when my father attempted to have her committed for profound depression.

Mom had told me the story when I was a junior in high school and started dating. The act of trying to commit her typified Dad's lack of understanding of Mom's needs as a wife and a mother.

The present impact of that story became clear, as I began a post-mortem of my relationship with Mark. I realized Dad's and Mark's insecurities turned into a need to be controlling, powerful, and someone everybody turned to. As a family, we turned to Dad for money. People turned to Mark for drugs. I turned to Mark for a man's love; but Mark didn't know how to care for me any more than Dad knew how to care for Mom.

I still have a picture of my family at that time; Gay was about six years old. Mom's eyes look dead, her face cracked by an attempted smile. This family portrait shows the lowest ebb in the tide of her life, the beginning of Mom finding herself, developing the steel to stand straight and fight instead of giving up.

Now, with my youngest sister fifteen years old, Mom had to be sure she could trust me with Gay in the house, since I would be moving home and commuting to school.

An average looking man, the psychiatrist's unremarkable visage belied a depth of wisdom rarely found. We discussed school, my views on drugs (I omitted my minimal use of psychedelics), the Vietnam War, my parents' relationship, and my relationship with Mark. In one hour, I admired and appreciated this man—who held the keys to my future.

The psychiatrist called Mom into the office and helped us lay ground rules for our conduct. I promised I would not lead my younger sister into the drug world or astray. Mom promised not to hold my past against me. *I still have a home.*

Over a year before the demise of my Naudain Street life, I had started growing my hair long to suit Mark. All through high school, I had worn it in an ultra-short pixie cut to control its unruly, curly texture. As it grew, I wore a wig until the disheveled, in-between stage grew out. My hair, straightened by a hot blow-dryer, now fell to my shoulders.

Here at home, the mirror's reflection showed the busted *pleaser.* I wanted *independence.* Scissors flashed and cut off great hands full of hair, until I achieved pixie length once again. It felt light, free, delicious.

I smiled. The mirror smiled back. So did my guardian angels.

16

MOVING ON

"If the Lord should mark iniquities, O Lord, who could stand?
But there is forgiveness with You, That You may be feared."
— Psalm 130:3–4

DURING THE DRUG BUST DEBACLE, I missed a week of school. At Mom's request, my PT school advisor, Miss Jeanne, traveled from Philadelphia to visit me. I had to catch up and get back to school, or I would forfeit my degree.

I thanked Miss Jeanne for coming as she hugged me. "Violet, your mother filled me in on the situation. I've been worried about you. You seemed so lost and unhappy. I watched you lose weight; you're so thin! I didn't know what to do," she said. "Right now, you're failing statistics. You have good grades in everything else. What can we do about that?"

"I talked to Dad, and he's going to rent the same computer we use in statistics class so I can practice," I said. "Mr. Dershowitz and Mr. Brody were both trying to help me before I got into trouble."

"How soon can you come back to classes?" Miss Jeanne inquired.

Mom joined the conversation. "Monday. Violet, you can commute. The white Pontiac will be yours to use. Oh, and we have to move all your things home."

"Thanks, Mom. That would be great. I'm ready to get back on track," I said with a heartfelt smile. Anticipation and the first hint of excitement surfaced. It had been a long time.

Miss Jeanne touched my shoulder and said, "I haven't heard you excited or seen you smile in months! I'm so glad!"

"I'll see you at school Monday," I said. Mom nodded in agreement.

After Miss Jeanne left, Mom reminded me that Dad and I had an appointment with a lawyer on Wednesday, the next week.

Just before lunch, I called Mary. She told me Mark wouldn't get back to the townhouse until evening. "Thanks so much for keeping at me, Mary! I don't know what I would have done without you and Randy. Mom, Dad, and I will be down in about an hour to pick up my stuff." We talked as best friends, and she shared her experience of being in the detention center. I told her how terrible I felt leaving her there, even though the choice hadn't been mine. "I know," she said. "If I never see Mark again, it'll be too soon. I'm so glad you're out of here!"

"I know, Mary. And thanks again. I'm sending you a hug over the phone." Mary's laughter cut away the last vestige of guilt. "I'll see you in a little while."

I wrote a note to Mark explaining that he would be responsible for my bail money. He should be the one to repay his mother.

The weather turned mild that early December afternoon when Mom, Dad, and I caravanned into Philadelphia for all of my earthly belongings. Since I had signed the lease, I called the realtor about ending it. While Mom and Dad loaded my things into the cars, I set the utilities and water shut-off date for Monday, a week away. Dad and I moved my ugly-but- functional chest of drawers home and left it in the garage to freeze any hitchhiking cockroaches. All of my clothes, on hangers, hung in the garage to keep the chest of drawers company.

The next morning, dead cockroaches littered the garage floor underneath the hanging clothes. I emptied the drawers, shook the clothes outside, and threw them into a hot dryer. The infested chest of drawers went to the burning pile.

Things went well with the realtor when I spoke to him during the move. After the first year, the lease became month to month, which gave Mary and Randy time to move before Christmas. I talked to Mary. She and Randy would live with Randy's parents until they could find a place of their own. I let her know the utilities and water shut-off date. Finally, I delivered the note to Mark's dresser, explaining about the bail money and utility shut-off date.

Mom, Dad, and I moved everything out six days after the drug bust. The next morning, Mom came to me, her face darkened with suppressed anger.

"Mark's on the phone. I can tell him to call you later, or that you don't want to talk to him. What do you want me to do?"

"I'll talk to him and get this over with right now," I said firmly. "Mom, stay there. I want you to hear what I'm going to say." No longer under Mark's spell, I realized he had no understanding of "love." Newly hardened steel in my resolution went beyond distancing myself from him. My backbone hardened, straight, and strong. I knew I would stand firm.

Mark tried to talk me into coming back. Mom nodded in approval as she listened to me tell Mark I would *not* be seeing him again. Although I left him a note, I made sure he understood it was his responsibility to pay his mother back for my bail money since he owned the drugs. I told him about the keys and leaving the house in order. The shut-off date for phone and utilities didn't make him happy. He took a minute or two to understand I would not be using his lawyer.

After that, there was nothing more to say. I told him so and hung up. Mark was still talking.

That was the last conversation we had, until years later at a mutual friend's party.

I wrote a poem called "In Memory of Good Times."

So many years gone by
Those times when we were happy:
Sharing a little single bed
Listening to the Grateful Dead
Wondering if we'd ever get my Mother off our backs...

But all of that is in past tense
I've grown up now; I've got more sense
Than to make my life an experiment
Of such a volatile nature.
Of course, you're in the latest scene
You've found the newest rap.
You said you'd die before you were thirty
But I want more than that.

Your life became too crowded for me
And then that last whole year:
I never really smiled at you
Only laughed or frowned
When I was just too low to care
Or too happy to be down.

A close friend of the family recommended a lawyer. Dad and I went for the 2:30 p.m. appointment with Carson Slade, Esq. When Dad introduced me, I sensed that Mr. Slade's opinion of me reached lower than sea level. I explained about the drug quantity being terribly inflated by the police. His expression registered disbelief. He spoke to Dad rather than me, although I asked all the questions.

I had called a close friend in law school, Amy, about the case against Mark and me. She told me we had to get the cases separated. Otherwise, I would be held as responsible for the drugs as Mark.

When I mentioned Amy's instructions to Mr. Slade, he huffed.

"I'd be laughed out of court," he said. The longer I talked to him, the more obvious it became that Mr. Slade would not lose any sleep if he lost the case and I went to jail.

I called Amy back when I got home.

"Violet, you need a lawyer who's familiar with drug cases. I recommend you see someone at Segal, Aaron, and Naphtali—a law firm in Philadelphia. I know Rick Aaron. I'll call him and see if you can see him ASAP."

"Thanks, Amy! You're the best!"

Amy phoned back fifteen minutes later. "You have an appointment tomorrow morning. Rick Aron is coming in on a Saturday to see you and discuss the case."

I thanked her profusely and phoned Carson Slade, Esq. I thanked him for his time, but told him I would be retaining other counsel. He seemed shocked that I turned him down as my lawyer. My suspicion, that he would have sold me down the river, remained.

I went downstairs to explain to Dad why I couldn't use Carson Slade.

"Dad, I want to thank you for taking me to see him. I'm sure he's a fine lawyer for things other than drugs. But Amy, my friend in law school, said this is a specialized type of law, and the cases must be separated. Mr. Slade wouldn't even consider that. I'm going to an appointment with Rick Aaron tomorrow. If you want me to pay for it, I will pay you back."

Dad looked uncomfortable. "What am I going to tell Ralph? He's the one who gave me Slade's name."

"Tell him how much you appreciate his kindness, but we need a specialist for this particular case." That seemed to satisfy Dad, who offered to pay for the new lawyer. I hugged him hard, buried my face in his shoulder, and sighed, "Thank you."

I traveled the Schuylkill Expressway to Philly, alone, for the appointment with Rick Aaron, Esq. He and another lawyer listened and asked questions for a solid hour. At the end of the appointment, Rick said, "I'm going to put a motion before the court to separate your case from Mark's. Your friend, Amy, is right. It's the only way you will get a fair shake. Otherwise, they have to try you for the drugs along with Mark. I'm not worried about being laughed out of court. You cannot be acquitted otherwise, unless something crazy happens!"

Rick got the cases separated. He was not laughed out of court, and I started commuting to Temple on Route 76 east, from Valley Forge. When the case finally came before a judge, his decision read "Not guilty." Rick had my record expunged.

But later I learned any sentence would have been reversed for "lack of evidence." That made no sense to me. I called Rick. He chuckled when I asked about the "lack of evidence."

"Remember me saying you couldn't be acquitted without the cases being separated, unless something crazy happened? Well, this is pretty crazy. Captain Mulder got caught stealing pornography from the evidence room. They fired him. Any evidence given by him would have been inadmissible. The Vietnam vet, Officer Connors, testified it was clear the drugs were not yours, but Mark's. So, it's over! And don't worry about a paper trail. I burned all the records."

Rick Aaron hadn't asked my permission. I wanted to read my "record", but it made no difference now. There had been many meetings in that Philadelphia law office, some with Mom, more with me alone. The meetings were informal yet professional. Although Rick and I felt comfortable in each other's company, his role as lawyer disallowed anything beyond a professional relationship. But Mom told me later, after the acquittal, "Violet, Rick said if you had been Jewish, he probably would have married you."

"Really?" I said and smiled. There had been something there that could have grown with that very special man.

As promised, Dad rented the special computer to help me with statistics. I practiced the formulas, learning theory by heart. Mr. Brody and Mr. Dershowitz both spent time with me, trying to get past the math block and memory issues. All attempts to master the math portion of the subject failed. By the time the final came around, I had great grades for extra credit and the theory portion on quizzes; but I couldn't do the math. I had to get a decent mark on the final for a grade of C in the course. Nothing below a C was acceptable in the physical therapy curriculum.

I took the final exam. I knew every question in the theory portion. I left the math section blank. My empty head gave me nothing to write down. Mr. Brody corrected my test immediately: one hundred percent on theory, zero on math. He squinted and handed the paper to me.

"Take this home and study. You're taking a retest tomorrow."

At home, I did all the math problems and got them right, with the help of the rented computer. I had to look at the formulas, but once I did that, with no pressure, I knew how to use them. I practiced the final, over and over with the same numbers, then with different numbers to make the formulas stick in my brain. I memorized the numbers and formula sequences on the final. There was nothing more I could do.

The next day, Mr. Brody showed me into an empty classroom and handed me the make-up final. He left the room. I looked at the test questions. Then I looked at them again. He gave me the same test I had taken home and memorized! I emptied my mind onto the paper, as my fingers skimmed over the computer keys that plugged in formulas needed for the right answers. Re-reading the questions, I knew I had them right; *all* of them were right.

"Mr. Brody, it's the same test," I said as if he didn't know.

His eyes sparked with amusement. "I know," he said, giving me a pat.

My final grades displayed a C in statistics.

God and my angels smiled in heaven. I walked on safer ground, as they aimed me toward the path God had in mind—the path that followed Jesus's footsteps. It took a while to see the path; but there were two sets of footprints in the sand, once again.

17

TRANSITIONS

"The Lord is not slack concerning His promise, as some count slackness, but is longsuffering toward us, not willing that any should perish but that all should come to repentance."
— 2 Peter 3:9

THE WIND HOWLED—WHIPPING heavy, pelting rain sideways against the car windows. Pummeled by hurricane-force winds, the white Pontiac rocked with each gust. Hurricane Agnes raged up the Susquehanna River, wreaking havoc.

"I wonder if they'll let us cross the bridge?" Elena asked. She was one of eighteen in my PT class who carpooled with me, to our first affiliation. Elena paid me for driving in gas for the car.

I shrugged as we approached the Susquehanna. The river churned, leapt, and rose to new heights; overflowed its banks; smashed and pillaged. Yellow-slickered police and firefighters patrolled the bridge, stopping each car until the one before crossed over the roaring water to the other side. I stopped, my car next in line, as the car in front of me proceeded slowly to the opposite riverbank. Townspeople filled and stacked sandbags on the river's edge. A hint

VIOLET BATEJAN

of guilt surfaced at our planned escape from the town and terrible weather; but both of us wanted to get home for the weekend and relax. It had been a hectic week of putting two years of book knowledge into practice—both exciting, and exhausting.

"Ma'am, I'm going to have to turn you back," hollered the patrolman above the screeching wind.

"Officer," I screamed, "Please! There're only two more cars behind me. Let us go across, please!" Rain blowing through the open window drenched me. The officer took a second, then turned to his partner.

"Hey, Harvey, let these three cross. Block it now so we get ahead of traffic!" He waved us across one-by-one.

Wind buffeted the car even harder as we traversed the bridge. I gripped the wheel forging ahead. *Get us home safely, Lord. Protect us, please.* My fellow PT student and I slogged our way east to our respective parents' homes, late Friday afternoon, for the weekend.

On Sunday afternoon, rested and ready, Elena and I returned over the calm waters—to a changed town, mangled and water-logged. The first Temple PT affiliations started in May; for Elena and me, Williamsport Hospital in Pennsylvania became home for six weeks. Flood waters and winds that hurled their way through the town of Williamsport created an influx of patients injured during the terrible storm. Many needed physical therapy. Extra hands made a difference. Satisfaction at being needed and able to help warmed my being.

After positive reports from Williamsport, I started my second affiliation—a pediatrics hospital in Wilmington, Delaware—opened my eyes to the all-inclusivity of disease, trauma, and bodies gone wrong. Children—missing limbs, in wheelchairs, on crutches, with canes or bedridden—resided there for medical reasons, and in some case, medical tragedies. During my introductory tour of the facility, while in a ward of children, I watched with amazement as a ten-year-old girl in halo traction laughed and chattered with a teen in the bed next to her.

"Hey, Bonnie," the young girl called as she lifted her head off the bed with her "halo," a stainless-steel ring screwed into her skull and attached to weights. She grabbed the device with both hands and turned so she could see her friend.

"Dawn, you're going to twist your head off with that thing!" Bonnie said grinning. "What do you want?"

Bonnie and Dawn chatted amicably, as Bonnie shifted her left leg, skewered with pins through the long bones below the knee, which attached to stainless steel bars—a "Hoffman Device" to stabilize fractures.

Dawn giggled. "My halo looks bad, but it doesn't hurt any. Your leg is just as bad as my head, but you can cover it up." She pulled the sheet over her head. "Oh, look! I can too!" Both girls guffawed, as the sheet clearly outlined the draped halo.

"Violet?" asked a slight woman in her late twenties. "I'm Carla Falcone, your supervisor for this affiliation. Let me go over the three patients you'll be seeing this week. Have you had the tour?"

I nodded, and we jumped right into the psychological ability of children and teens to cultivate an upbeat emotional state. Carla explained it wasn't unusual to have a depressed child. Yet, when grouped together in wards, they seemed to enjoy their neighbors and benefit from their shared physical, and sometimes mental, limitations.

A spunky, seven-year-old girl with spinal cancer stood out and wrapped herself around my heart. My second week at the hospital, Carrie had surgery scheduled to remove the cancer-ridden portion of her spinal cord. The neurosurgeon and orthopedic surgeon discussed her case in a team meeting I attended. Her prognosis sounded grave. They had no idea if her cancer had spread far enough to limit the use of her arms. Invited to observe the surgery, I eagerly accepted.

"Miss V, tell me about your parakeet again," Carrie asked as a ploy to further postpone her strengthening exercises.

"Ah, that's a nice story. Pixie was a green parakeet with blue across his nose, which means he was a boy parakeet. Our neighbor found him in Valley Forge Park whistling 'Yankee Doodle' as he walked on the sidewalk. He jumped on her finger, and she took him home; but her own parakeet and Pixie fought. So, Pixie came to live with us. He talked, rode on our shoulders, and loved pizza. Now, let's do your arm exercises!"

A sweet, well-spoken, little girl with short, auburn hair; deep, blue eyes; and a generous laugh; Carrie made everyone smile. I didn't expect to be affected by this special attachment to Carrie, as a student in a medical profession.

The day of her surgery dawned with a sense of concern. *How much of her spinal cord would they have to remove?* I worried she would be a "quad," someone without full use of their arms, trunk, or legs. *Please, God, let her at least have the use of her arms and hands. Bless the surgical teams with wisdom and skill!* I dressed in green scrubs after strict instructions not to touch anything in the OR, since my gloves weren't sterile. The ventilator hissed and puffed as it breathed for her prone, anesthetized body. I watched as the nurses finished preparing the sterile field and readied the still, little body for a surgery that would both save her life and permanently disable her at the same time.

The scalpel cut sure and deep. Blood welled up around the incision, staunched by the assisting OR nurse. A chilly, 68 degrees Fahrenheit registered on the thermostat in the green-tinted, tiled OR; but I began to perspire. My vision, no longer crisp and clear, plus a strange woozy feeling in my head, registered warning. I read the physical signs of faintness and, face reddened with embarrassment, left the OR before I fell.

The surgery took five hours, giving me plenty of time for thought. Carla had to be told what happened to me in the OR.

"You have to give yourself credit," she said. "You got out of the OR before you created a problem. What do you think happened? You were looking forward to observing the surgery."

"I've never had to watch someone I cared for have surgery that would leave them unable to walk. Carrie walked, ran, and jumped up to the day of her surgery. The surgeons weren't even sure she would have function in her arms afterward!" I rolled my eyes and shrugged.

"Well, Violet, now you understand why family members should never treat or operate on other family members. They can't be objective, because they care too much. They're personally involved. You've only been treating Carrie for two weeks. But in that time, you became attached to her."

It made sense, and I nodded at Carla. I had no practice at setting aside emotion for the priority of cutting out cancer. I had become too involved in the hand that life had dealt the small, adorable patient and her family. With the first cut of the scalpel and the welling of blood, I lost what little objectivity I had. Had she been a stranger, the surgical procedure and anatomy of the cancerous invasion would have been my main interest.

Carrie changed after her surgery. She used a prone cart to prevent any pressure on her incision. It saddened me to see her once ebullient personality become subdued by the drastic changes in her physical capabilities. Although she would never walk again, Carrie had the use of her arms. I still wonder if she survived the cancer; and if she survived, what did she do with her life?

I never worked in pediatrics after my affiliation at A. I. duPont Hospital for Children. Yet this invaluable experience gave me answers for many adult patients struggling with the "poor me" or "why me?" mindsets. Stories of brave kids and their parents helped some of my patients come to terms with their own disabilities. That six-week affiliation gave me sufficient stories to last an entire career.

My search for a job began in late spring of 1972. Temple PT school instructors recommended we start with a general hospital (acute care) for a broad experience, with a transition to rehabilitation for more specialized skills. I searched for PT jobs in large general hospitals and found a listing in the newspaper for Graduate Hospital in Philadelphia. An acute general hospital, it provided the type of general physical therapy experience I would need for every job in the fore-seeable future.

My interview at Graduate fell on a Friday afternoon in June. I came home early from my affiliation at A. I. DuPont with their blessings, smiles, and best wishes. I chose a conservative, bright, yellow summer dress and my favorite tan, chunky heels. Jack Robards, PT, chief of physical therapy, met me at the secretary's desk. A handsome black man in his thirties with a smooth, pleasant voice, he handed me the job application forms before my interview. A standard form for employment started out with the question: "Have you ever been convicted of a felony?" It required a yes or no question—with no "almost" category.

My mind rewound the last year. *What might have happened if Mark's case and mine had not been separated. What if I trusted the lawyer my dad's friend recommended? What if Mulder had not stolen the pornographic material and been caught?*

Breathe. Pray. Be still, and thank God it didn't go that way. Move on! I filled out the form and handed it to the department secretary. After waiting briefly, she showed me to Mr. Robards's office. A one-hour interview gave me a taste of the man who would be my boss, if offered the job. He seemed knowledgeable, friendly, well-spoken, and respectful. Quite a pleasing interview.

My feelings must have mirrored his; I received a job offer the next day, which I accepted without hesitation. My first day of work fell on my sister, Gay's, birthday at the end of July, after my last affiliation ended. I had just enough time to find an apartment and move before starting work.

Apartment hunting solved itself, when the complex across the street from Graduate Hospital had a vacancy for mid-July, less than two weeks before I would start my new job. I took Mom to see the apartment.

"It does have an odd layout, but the location's perfect. It's across the street from your new job, and where else would you get a parking space with your apartment, if you decided to get a car?"

"Location, location, location," I said, "even though the kitchen and dining areas are dark like a downstairs cellar."

"How much time will you spend downstairs anyway? The upstairs is a good size and sunny. What do you think?"

I prayed over the decision a little longer to find peace—longer than my usual dart-like prayers that flowed naturally through my life's circumstances. The lease ran a year in length; the decision had to be a sound one. I signed the lease and started moving things in over a weekend. Made of block glass, the upstairs windows faced 19th Street at eye level. Pedestrian traffic passed by my bedroom window. Each floor held one large room. The brightly lit, top floor faced south at the 19th and Lombard Street bus stop. I could hear busses and passengers come and go, a foreign city sound compared to *country quiet*—or even *backstreet Philly quiet*.

Creating my first home on my own became the next priority. Mom gave me an antique Dutch table and benches that once sat in our kitchen breakfast nook at home. We carted the table downstairs and planted it opposite the galley kitchen. Large and basement-like, the kitchen/dining room craved light. Goodwill furnished a yellow rose, upholstered chair, and side table that held a tall, three-way bulb lamp, a great reading spot.

Upstairs, an Indian, carved, wood screen separated my bedroom from the living room. Dad gave me three-inch-thick boards from a downed oak tree at home. On a cloudless summer day, I sanded the bright oak slabs, coated them with polyurethane, and created bookshelves in arm's reach of my box spring and mattress.

Granny's old, single bed and fold-out love seat completed the living room. It looked inviting—reupholstered in white, textured vinyl—installed with end tables and lamps on either side. A little chest of drawers faced the love seat with another lamp. Complete with accenting candles and pictures on the walls, my comfortable, pleasant apartment sparked a prayer of thanksgiving.

Dear Lord,

Thank You for Your loving care
Of infinitesimal me
A flake of snow, unique, it dares,
Flaunts individuality.

And though it's tiny when compared
To my own form and style,
You made it beautiful and shared
With it and me, creation's smile.

You care for me and this small flake;
You placed us both on earth.
You gave us each a place to take,
And raised us up from birth.

The end from the beginning
Is only Yours to know;
But what You give, Lord, makes me sing
And grateful for Your help below.

I thank You for this place to dwell
That You designed with me;
So I may rest from work as well
As find delight in all I see.

I find delight in work and leisure
In this life with friends so true
For You are love, and my great treasure,
Lord and King, my all for You.

After the frightful chaos of last year, this place of peace and comfort in the city sang of the Lord's mercy and love.

18

NEW BEGINNINGS

"The labor of the righteous leads to life, the wages of the wicked to sin."
— *Proverbs 10:16*

IN ONE SHORT walk across the street, my new career became real. On July 28, decked out in a fashionable, short, white uniform, I pinned on the blue name tag, proud of the "P.T." after my name. The brilliant, hot morning outside became cool and fluorescent lit as I headed inside. The elevator opened at the physical therapy department on the third floor.

Four people staffed the Graduate Hospital PT department: two other therapists, the secretary, and Jack Robards, the chief. I started the same day as another new hire, an aide named Michael Batejan. Other than a cursory glance at him and brief greeting, my mind homed in on Jack Robards's method of patient care, the location of supplies, and general department routine. After a couple of days, I began to feel more confident—at home in my first paid position.

The first week, I followed everyone downstairs to the hospital cafeteria—everyone except Michael, the new aide who ate his brown, bagged lunch alone. He seemed a quiet man, around my age, with wavy, dark-brown hair and a mustache. Well-built and taller than me, he had a pleasant, angular face with serious, brownish eyes. His quiet, gentle manner with patients impressed me more than anything else.

Cafeteria prices wrecked my budget in a week. Limp, yellow broccoli and other wilted vegetables revised my meal plan. I hoofed home for lunch.

A few days later, as our chief turned out the lights for lunch break and left with me not far behind, I glanced into the daylit room. There, on one of the tall, treatment tables with a backdrop of sunny windows, Michael sat alone. Without thinking, I called to him.

"Michael, why don't you come to my place for lunch? At least you could have a can of hot soup with your sandwich. It's just across the street."

He closed the bag. "All right," he said and followed me downstairs, across Lombard Street.

While he selected a can of tomato soup, I showed him where the utensils and saucepans were kept. We worked companionably alongside each other and carried our food to the wood Dutch table and benches. After a few bites, I asked him why he had chosen the PT aide job.

"I considered physical therapy, but West Chester didn't have a program. I did all right with health and phys ed until student teaching. I found you don't have a lot of control over what you teach. Then, I student-taught at a Southern Chester County High School in farm country. Students went on vacation during hunting season and had time off for the harvest. The last thing they were interested in was anything I said in front of the class. It was a long semester!" He laughed and glanced at me. "I knew I wanted to work in PT even before that, but I wanted to finish my teaching degree." He took a couple of bites before he continued. "I saw this job in the paper and figured I'd get paid and knock off the PT experience requirement at the same time. I turned down a teaching position at Neshaminy High School for this job. I hope I made the right decision."

Smart, I thought, as he ate with efficient grace. *Oh, wait. His eyes aren't brown. They're hazel!* A rich hazel, varied brown—shot with green—living art. I looked away so he wouldn't see me staring. I agreed with what he said and focused on listening to his words—a quick mind, thoughts in concise, comprehensive language. This quiet guy had brains and a quirky sense of humor that made me laugh. We talked about jobs, politics, likes and dislikes. His conversation and warm, low laugh made the hour disappear. We decided lunch at my place seemed like a good arrangement: same time, same place tomorrow.

I'd been involved with some real losers, which made comparison simple. Knowing him only a week, Michael put them all to shame. My last loser, Harry, left without even saying goodbye.

Prior to graduation, I had dated Harry—a handsome Jewish boy about my age. If marriage had been predicated on his family, I would have married Harry in a second. But Harry only had eyes for my girl-friend, Jenny—the one who wanted *me* to go out with him. A petite, five-foot, one-inch beauty with deep, burnt-sienna eyes and lustrous, walnut hair that fell below her waist, Jenny didn't love Harry. With her quiet manner—compared to my more boisterous style—blue eyes, and curly, seal-brown hair, the word *opposites* came to mind. One day at Harry's apartment, I led him over to the window and pointed, three stories down. My white Pontiac Tempest gleamed, washed little more than an hour ago. I expected some sort of a positive response.

He grasped my shoulders, turned me to him, and scrutinized my face for interminable seconds. "You're just *not* what I expected," he said. He wagged his head with a puzzled expression on his face. I shook his hands from my shoulders and backed away. His face spoke of discontent, not love. My mother's assessment, after she invited Harry and me to dinner, drifted through my mind.

"What do you think of Harry, Mom?" I asked.

"He's nice for now," she said in a soft tone, her words hemmed in finality.

I thought about her words. My *touchy-feely* nature opposed Harry in every way. In fact, it annoyed him. We dated exclusively for over a year. Then, suddenly, he disappeared— without a letter or phone call. Mentally reviewing our relationship, mostly one-sided on my part, an obvious conclusion surfaced: *Harry didn't love me enough to call or write. Instead of prolonging a wrong match, he did me a favor. Mean? Perhaps. But my heart survived, unbroken.*

During the first week of having lunch together, Michael and I had just started downstairs when a knock at my door stopped us.

"Are you expecting anyone?" he asked.

"No," I said, turning to answer the door.

"Who is it?" I peered through the peephole and winced.

"It's Harry."

I opened the door, and Harry spied Michael behind me.

"Oh, I guess I should have called," he said.

"We just came here for lunch. This is Michael Batejan. We started work at Graduate Hospital the same day." Michael and Harry shook hands. "Where have you been?" I asked.

"In Ohio at Case Western Reserve University," he said, as if I should have known.

Mentally, my brain screamed, *WHAT? You left for college in another state and never told me, never called, never wrote?* "Surprised"—too anemic a word. Recovering quickly, I shrugged one shoulder, "I only have an hour for lunch."

"Oh, sure. I'll call you." Harry backed out of the door. "Nice meeting you." He nodded politely to Michael.

I felt slightly unbalanced as we trotted downstairs.

"I'm really sorry I put you in such an awkward position," Michael said.

"Why?" I asked. "I haven't heard from him since August of last year! My head is still spinning!" His smile warmed me. Without much time wasted, we disposed of Harry and moved on to more interesting topics.

Over the next weeks, I discovered Michael stood five-feet, eight-inches tall. His lean, well-muscled body and kind personality attracted me enough for an experimental kiss. And then a second. He kissed with soft, moist longing. Passion and sweetness combined with exploration and discovery. Patient and unhurried, he and I melded, more certain with each embrace.

I never dated anyone else. And neither did he. His presence satisfied, and a lonely space stayed behind when he went home to his parents' place at night, an hour away in Feasterville.

Violet and Michael, 1972

Soft-spoken ease, honesty, strength, and kindness marked Michael's actions as we dealt with all kinds of people who needed PT. His hour commute often waited until after dinner together. Gradually, there were nights he didn't go home. I didn't tell him I loved him—*he would run like a deer chased by hunters.* But I knew if he asked me to marry him, I would say yes. *Nourishing something so precious takes time. Love, like a unique flower, needs to be fed and nurtured with patience.*

I called Harry a week after his impromptu visit. Gallant Michael offered to phone him for me; but Harry was *my* problem. I explained that such a length of time had passed with no word from him, I assumed he had moved on and began seeing other people. Harry asked, "Is it the guy I met at your apartment?"

"Yes," I answered. With that, Harry bowed out of my life.

Physical therapy requires a state license to practice the profession. In Pennsylvania, the State Board assigned me to the Harrisburg site. I arrived at the hotel early so I could settle, sleep well, and take my time the morning of the exam, since I'm *not* a morning person.

A platoon of desk chairs stood waiting in the test room, lined up in military precision. Retrieving a pen and pencil from my pocket, I listened to pre-test instructions for this professional, life-or-death exam. With the "begin now" command, silent prayer rose as I focused on the paper before me. A deep breath, a glance through the test questions, an exhale: I knew most of them! Just as important, *all* multiple choice questions. *It doesn't get any better than this*, I thought as my pen began to fly over the blank answer sheet. Like the much-feared chemistry final of freshman year, multiple choice placed the odds in my favor. But *this* time, unlike in Chemistry, I actually *knew* the answers.

The final question stared back at me. As I filled in the last circle on the computerized form, I knew: *I passed.*

Six weeks later, I held the official letter of proof in my hand: my license. Michael and I danced around the living room. We ate dinner at Happy Gardens in Chinatown, where the scent of authentic Chinese food enveloped us as we chose our favorite table. Clumsy with chopsticks, the fun of making them lift food to my mouth trumped a fork. Egg rolls, green tea, and wonton soup—pork lo mein and the spicy bite of General Tso's chicken—all delicious with left-overs for tomorrow. *But best of all, Michael celebrating with me.*

Later, a delicious lobster gave its life in my honor at Old Original Bookbinders, where Mom and Dad toasted my achievement with champagne. They beamed with delight through dinner and dessert in such honest celebration they almost looked happy together—a statement of their love for me, a sweet gift from God in addition to my profession.

19

FAMILY

"Oh, that men would give thanks to the Lord for His goodness,
And for His wonderful works to the children of men!
For He satisfies the longing soul,
And fills the hungry soul with goodness."
— Psalm 107:8-9

MICHAEL OWNED A FADED, 1964, light blue Chevelle. We joked about the non-existent chance of his car being stolen. He could park it in any neighborhood, and no one would give it a second look.

As he drove to my parents' home, I nestled close to him on the bench seat, content. Mom and Dad invited us to dinner to meet Michael for the first time, October of 1972. I wanted them to meet the man who was glued to my side much of my present-day life. When I thought about his family, I wondered how he would react to a home full of antiques decorated by my artistic mother.

Mom Batejan, Michael's mother, baked Romanian cakes and cookies called *kiefla*. Whether flakey, crispy or jam filled, kiefla melted their many flavors in your mouth. They were completely different from any other confection I had ever tasted. A typical

Eastern European mother, she said, "*Menka, menka*, Violet," Romanian for "Eat, eat," as she placed a plate of food in front of me. She called me "skinny," like Granny used to, in an endearing way.

But it was Dad Batejan who lived in the soft spot of my heart. He and Michael were a good deal alike, although Michael had his mother's restless energy. Dad Batejan enjoyed his self-built, custom rancher with a breezeway that led to the garage. The quarter acre he purchased in Feasterville had allowed him to live and raise his boys in the country. He planted a nice-sized garden with a grape arbor in the backyard and flowers in the front. Uncluttered and spotlessly clean, the small but pleasant home saw four boys raised—Michael designated "number three," according to Dad Batejan.

Mom Batejan had no time for knickknacks. Her practical, general rule stated each item had a function. It simplified housekeeping in a minimalist way I had never experienced.

Home décor at my mom's house, in contrast, involved decorative objects. Artful ornaments and glassware glowed with varied colors, part of a beautiful environment, pretty—but certainly not functional alone or easy to keep. Michael had no idea what he would find in my family home at dinner: artistic, elegant, and secretly secondhand.

The dinner occurred late on a clear, crisp, autumn day. Colored glass and ornaments sparkled with sunlight on glass shelves in the dining room. The French Provincial table had an individual plate design for each place setting. Some commemorative plates came from Valley Forge, local churches, Lower Providence Township, or various national locations and events. Others had simple decorative merit, like my favorite with black-eyed Susans around the rim. Each plate, unique in color and design, set a stylish table. The glasses, a complete set of twelve, came from an old estate—fine crystal, found in one of five or six secondhand shops, which Mom gleaned on a regular basis. A large fruit centerpiece moved aside to allow the standing prime rib center stage. Mom had decorated a magnificent table and crafted a sumptuous dinner. I introduced her to Michael with the pride she had earned.

Presented with this rarefied milieu, Michael's expression remained his usual: honest, unflappable, and friendly. He had never lived with oriental rugs, French Provincial dining room furniture, picture windows, or a stained-glass window—rescued from a wrecking ball—set in the wall between dining room and living room. He looked at the table and complimented my mother on her artistry in an easy yet deferential way. Conversation never flagged, and my father talked to Michael with none of his usual social self-consciousness.

After the apparent smashing success, I caught Mom alone in the kitchen. "So, what do you think of Michael?"

She gave me a smile but paused. My heart ricocheted in my chest as the silence lengthened. Everything stopped until she spoke. "I think he's the one," she said with a certainty that made me giggle in delight. I grinned at her and took a quick breath, since I hadn't breathed for a bit. At the kitchen table, Coco, our rescued standard poodle, laid his head on my lap and looked up at me with adoring brown eyes. I realized how much I missed him. Sighing with satisfaction, I stroked Coco's head as he closed his eyes in pleasure.

After seeing Coco again, I wanted a dog. Instead, I added a $15 kitten to the household to torture four-year-old Mink, my diminutive, cross-eyed Siamese. The last little Siamese kitten for sale—left in a large cardboard box, too cute to leave behind—I couldn't abandon him. The kitten with seal-point markings, like Mink, sat quietly in my lap, as my friends and I drank *sake* with our lunch. The piquant, warm rice wine went down easily, as the kitten peered up at me—blue eyes wide, curious, unafraid. "*Sake*, is that your name?" My friends laughed and agreed. He became Sake, but spelled with an *i* instead of an *e*. After several days of Mink and Saki pawing at each other under the door, I let him have the run of the apartment. He took great delight in sneaking up and jumping on Mink's back whenever possible. Mink's blood-curdling scream sounded deadly; but they always came away without a scratch. Saki hugged me, one paw on either side of my neck, and his kitten head tucked under my chin. He melted Michael with this little maneuver.

My menagerie still needed a dog. With the big, tiled floor downstairs, puppy accidents presented no problem during housebreaking. After some research, I decided on an Airedale. Michael liked the idea and leafed through newspaper pet ads looking for Airedale pups. "Let's go see this litter. They're in Huntingdon Valley, a nice drive," he said. Within a week, we sat on the floor playing with four Airedale puppies. The owner told us she wouldn't sell the little female I liked; she planned on breeding her. But that puppy wouldn't leave us alone. She loved on both of us equally. In the end, when the breeder called her and she wouldn't leave our sides, we bought the puppy not for sale. I named her Shani after Chani, a main character in Frank Herbert's sci-fi novel, *Dune*.

Shani and Saki sniffed noses, back in the apartment. The kitten flipped onto his back, Shani's nose in the fur of his underbelly. They played, until Shani flopped down on a blanket with Saki curled up against her chest. Mink needed more space; she wacked the surprised puppy on the nose a few times until Shani learned respect.

The little Airedale learned we couldn't stand hearing her cry downstairs at bedtime. Everyone ended up snuggled, contented in the queen-sized bed. *Mission accomplished; family complete for now.*

A few weeks later, Michael greeted me with a surprise. "Guess what?"

I shrugged. "What?"

"I'm moving to Penndel with Joe. We found an apartment by Flannery's. It won't take me much longer to get to town, and it's walking distance to the train station in Langhorne." Michael fetched my coat. "Come on. I want you to see it."

Flannery's Restaurant and Cocktail Lounge, an old DC7 airplane, rested on concrete pillars above the ground. Red beacon lights flashed day and night, giving the new apartment's big living room window an interesting view. The reputation of mediocre food delegated the landmark to a conversation piece. Circa 1960s, the two-bedroom apartment had orange, shag, wall-to-wall carpet in the living room, a little kitchen, and a full bath.

"It's perfect," I said, hugging him as Shani sniffed new smells. We split our time between the two apartments. Shani trundled back and forth with us between Philly and Penndel, happy for the car rides and company of her favorite people. We had a lovely life.

Mom told me about the fight. Dad made a negative comment about a few dishes left in the sink, and the final war ignited. Soon after the October dinner with Michael and my family, Dad moved into a hotel. I went out of my way to encourage him. *Life had to be better for him without a wife who despised him, regardless of just cause.* He worked in Philadelphia, and I offered company, good conversation, and a home-cooked meal once in a while.

While it wasn't a topic that I typically faced head-on, Mom's and Dad's mismatched relationship had spread toxic fumes throughout the household all of my life at home. When I was a child, Mom seemed beaten down, with the last straw being her third pregnancy. Physical abuse never entered the picture, but the ravages of emotional abuse coupled with both parents having perfectionistic tendencies made the pair of them grate on each other, until Mom found who she could be in the world outside of the home. Her job, compliments on her good performance, freedom of her own car and money became intertwined with the effects of her abuse as a child— and her ongoing situation living with my dad. She became bitter.

I once told a psychologist during attempted family counseling that when a dog is beaten, it either gives up and dies, or bites and savages the one doing the beating. Although she submitted for many years trying to be a *good wife* despite lacking the nurturing she deserved, Mom never gave up.

Her psychologist, speaking off the record, told Mom to divorce Dad.

In the early years, Dad had the upstairs apartment built for his mother and father. Mom, pregnant with Lynne, two months after birthing me, endured Baba's condescension, as she and Dad spoke Slovak without including Mom in their dialogue. Baba dictated kitchen organization and meals. Mom endorsed Dad's paychecks for their joint account, while Dad hid the amount. She never knew if there was money in the bank and had no access to the checkbook without him handing it to her. Dad did all the banking.

When Dad came home from work, he went upstairs to greet Baba before coming in to Mom. Before the first trimester of pregnancy passed, Mom began vomiting when she heard Baba come down the steps to the kitchen. This continued, until her family doctor gave Dad an ultimatum: lose the baby, or have his parents move out. They returned to Fairfax, Virginia, since Dad's sister was ready to have her first and only child.

Eventually, Granny moved into the upstairs apartment. At some point in time, Granny sold the house her husband had built to Dad for $1.00.

My parents lived a lie as long as I can remember. Our lives seemed perfect on the surface to Mom's "friends" and the world; but it was a world of walking on eggshells. When I was little and they argued, I stood between them until they went to separate rooms.

So when they finally separated, I kept reassuring Dad: life had to be better without the verbal abuse from Mom's resentment of him. A divorce ensued for irreconcilable differences.

My immense, overwhelming relief attuned me to the stress I felt as their designated peacekeeper, even though I lived in my own place. Now, I no longer felt responsible to referee. I prayed they could move on and live in peace.

Within two months, Dad rented an apartment in my complex across from Graduate Hospital and began dating the pretty, blonde manager. It didn't last. He met a petite, buxom brunette with a home in Wilmington, Delaware. Widowed, she had a grown daughter around my age. Later, he ran into the blonde manager again in another awkward meeting on the sidewalk and started looking for another apartment complex.

The phone rang after Dad hit the three-month mark at our complex. "Honey, I'm moving! There's brand new apartment building with a pool starting to rent at 1500 Locust Street. I can walk to visit you and swim every day before and after work."

"That sounds fantastic! Why don't you come over for dinner tonight," I said.

"Okay, honey. I'll see you about six."

After dinner that night, Dad relaxed in my downstairs reading chair. I sat on a stool at his feet with my guitar.

"I wrote a song for you, Dad."

"You did? Let's hear it," he said.

"It's called, 'Can't You Be a Lady.'" It was based on a theme throughout my time with Dad at home. I strummed the guitar and sang:

Hi Dad, it's been a long time
We're almost thinking along the same line.
But I can clearly recall,
Those mixed-up ideas when I was still small.

Can't you be a lady, can't you act like a girl
Look at those dirty blue jeans
Can't you be a lady, get down from that tree!
You're going to be the death of me.

Tree climbing, horse riding, can't you wear a dress
You smell like the whole barn yard
From this occupation I need a vacation
Is raising girls supposed to be so hard?

Can't you be a lady, can't you act like a girl
Look at those dirty blue jeans

Can't you be a lady, put that snake down!
You're going to be the death of me.

I thought I'd go crazy if he said it one more time
I'll never be a "femme fatale";
I'm just not the type to sit still without a gripe
And oh, how my dad would howl,

Can't you be a lady can't you act like a girl
Look at those dirty blue jeans.
Can't you be a lady, let that frog go!
You're going to be the death of me.

Thank God that's behind us, there's mutual respect
But my jeans are still dirty blue;
I still collect animals and ride every week
And I even climb a tree or two.

Thank God I'm a Lady, I've the best of two worlds;
It's good to be a woman today.
Thank God I'm a Lady, I do what I like
And, don't you know, now it's okay!

As I finished, Dad shifted toward me, a little smile on his face. "I'm glad you got your mother's English talents and voice. But you *did* get my guitar playing ability! That was really good!"

Moments of connection like these gave encouragement in the face of all the other teeth-clenching times that made me regret I had the indelible stamp of Dad's concave, great toenails—a mark of heredity, undeniably his progeny. More often, our visits degenerated into Dad blaming Mom for leaving him. This revisionist history brought up dark events from my past. As I sat in my apartment with him, my mind wandered to some of these situations. By the time I had reached my teens, deep anger at Dad's unfairness became volcanic.

At fourteen, my love of horses led me to find a stable where I could work for a ride and teach summer camp. I brought oats and hay home to feed my guinea pig. "Dad, there's a horse show this weekend. You've never seen me ride. Would you come?"

"Why don't you find something practical to do instead of waste time on a rich man's sport?" Dad returned to reading a history book. Discussion ended.

My youngest sister loved horses as much as I did. Gay took some of the oats and hay to bed her plastic horses down in the middle of the cellar floor. Her horse farm sprawled over to my guinea pig, who lived behind the finished basement. I kept the area neat with a broom, dustpan, and brush. I hadn't finished the sweeping, when Dad came in and saw my little sister's horse scene.

"Clean this mess up," he ordered in his best Lieutenant Colonel, Army Reserve voice.

"It's not my mess," I said, still sweeping.

"I said clean it up!" he raised his voice.

I stopped sweeping. His flushed face foretold the future. *But it wasn't my mess.*

"Dad, call Gay. These are her horses, and she's using my guinea pig bedding and food." Dad came toward me, the flat of his hand raised—punishment for disrespect. My eyes fastened on his. Steeled, I lofted the rectangular headed broom over my right shoulder, like a baseball bat. His hard eyes dissolved to shocked surprise. A sturdy weapon of self-defense, the broom felt solid in my hands. Dad's face dissolved into hurt as he turned away; but I did not get hit that day. And I did not clean up my little sister's mess.

Mom forced me to say I was sorry. Mostly obedient, I had lied. *I wasn't sorry for refusing to clean up Gay's horses.* I wasn't even being disrespectful—just angry *at the* unfairness that lit the fuse.

Years later, after I married, Dad asked me why Mom left him. Although Dad physically left the house first, Mom had already left my father, in spirit, years earlier. Pent-up anger flared between them multiple times each month; but anger never degenerated to physical violence. He asserted up to his death that *she was his one true love.* He simply had no aptitude for showing love in practical, endearing ways that create closeness, bonding. Dad didn't forge bonds of love— but of control, by demand, and without any credit given.

His control disappeared when Mom gained her financial independence with the real estate job. But the marriage had died long before he left, because Mom was already emotionally gone.

"Why did your mother leave me?" he asked, his voice sounding sad, puzzled over the phone. "Remember that two-carat, heart-shaped, amethyst ring I gave her for Valentine's Day? She threw it at me!"

"Okay, let's start back at the beginning," I said, feeling my way along. "Before I was born, Mom said you wouldn't give her money to buy a cradle. You said, 'Babies can be happy in a drawer.' That's an early example; but it sounds like you treated her like a queen during courtship—and like a scullery maid afterward." I paused. Dad didn't deny what I said. "Did you give Mom credit for working when you told everyone you did all the pick-and-shovel work, and she was *the artiste?*" Silence. "Can you see how it sounded in public like you did all the work, and Mom played the piano and decorated?" Sounds of a body shifting position registered from the other end of the phone. "Did you ever tell her what *a good job* she did in the house, finding secondhand furniture and making a beautiful home with it?"

"I never thought about it that way."

"I know, Dad. Money played a major role in the marriage's break-up."

"I made pretty good money for that time. You kids had everything you needed."

"Dad, most of our clothes came from secondhand shops, because you never gave Mom enough money for new clothes. She brought home two secondhand suits in perfect condition in your size. Do you remember what you said to her?" Dad cleared his throat. "You yelled that *you brought home the paycheck and wouldn't wear anyone else's clothes*. Your attitude sent a message to us about a woman's worth. One amethyst ring didn't make up for the rest of the time, Dad."

"Hmmm, I get the picture," he said.

"I'm not bringing these things up to hurt you. But Dad, you asked. Do you want me to go on?"

"No thanks, honey. That's all I needed. I, uh, I understand now. I see what you mean."

Grateful that God finishes what He starts, I thanked Him for the guidance and ability to forgive. *The Son forgives us—His forgiveness, free, with belief in His gift of eternity. My life reflected His mercy, grace, and immeasurable love* and I smiled at His gift.

20

SEERS AND FORBIDDEN THINGS

"In Him we have redemption through His blood, the forgive-
ness of sins, according to the riches of His grace which He
made to abound toward us in all wisdom and prudence."
— Ephesians 1:7–8

I HAD FALLEN, and fallen hard, for the second time in my life; I was in love. I knew two weeks after I met him but didn't say anything. Michael liked his apartment and time to himself. He often left after dinner and took the last train home. One evening, after he was gone, my feelings overflowed onto paper.

Missing You

When you leave me alone at night,
I miss you.
I hear the street noises,
My neighbor practicing opera;
I make dinner and read,
Talk to the dog and cats;

And the whole time, I miss you.

I see you all day at work,
Watch you move, talk, instruct,
Kiss you in the back room
When no one is looking.
I wish you were with me now.
I don't feel neglected or unloved;
I just miss you.

I wonder if I will still miss you
When we are apart during the day
And together in the evening?
It won't be the same;
I want to miss you enough
To write poems, songs and thoughts for you;
I want to miss you, occasionally, always.

Tonight, Michael boarded the last train home. Peaceful, quiet, the stillness echoed with emptiness and set me to cleaning, just for something to do. My desk came under scrutiny first, the top drawer crammed with memorabilia and assorted junk. Something colorful near the back of the drawer caught my attention. A rectangular box slid out of its space: a deck of Tarot cards and, with it, a riot of memories. Divination had fascinated me throughout my childhood and teen years. My family dabbled with a Ouija board, especially Lynne and me, in our early teens. My parents gave us the "game" for Christmas one year. I graduated to tarot cards, the very deck I held in my hands. At Kimberton, one of the teachers read palms at our school fair. No sermons, in my hearing, ever addressed divination—or any connection with the dark realm showing a paucity of biblical knowledge. I had no idea the occult included divination, one of the forbidden activities in Scripture. I even took my mother to a fortune teller in Audubon as a gift in 1972. I had met Michael a few months before our appointment.

The "seer's" modest home looked normal from the outside—no neon sign or yard advertising. Mom went in first, after she took off her engagement and wedding rings—*no clues*. In a half-hour, Mom smiled and said, "It was interesting; but nothing really clicked."

I walked through the doorway and saw a pleasant looking woman, fortyish, plainly dressed behind an old, oak desk. She looked at me with a quizzical expression as I sat down.

"You're going to have to explain something to me," she said. "When you walked in, I saw a large teddy bear and a basketball. Does that mean anything to you?"

Caught off guard, I thought, *Spooky*. "Yes," I said. "It's actually pretty clear to me. I've been dating a really nice guy. He was a basketball star in high school, and I call him my Huggy Bear."

She smiled and nodded, "Well, that seems to fit the bill!"

"Is he the man I'll marry?" I asked.

She took out a deck of playing cards, laid nine cards face up on the desk, and studied them. "That isn't clear." Pausing, she looked at the cards again. "It seems promising, though."

"Will I be happy?"

Studying me for a minute, she cocked her head slightly. "If you let yourself be."

She continued for another fifteen minutes, but nothing else sparked my interest or rang true. I left money in the donation basket on a living room cabinet, as I headed for the car.

On the way home, Mom told me nothing the fortune teller said had meant anything to her.

"But what did she say?" I asked.

"She got charged up the minute she saw me." Mom began imitating the seer. "She said, 'Oh, my dear, divorce him! You are going to marry the most wonderful man! And you know him! He has a boat beside his garage. You'll know him, because there will be sparkles all over the room!'" Mom rolled her eyes. "I don't know anyone like that!"

I thought no more about Mom's experience, until I received an excited phone call from her a couple of weeks later.

"Violet, you will never believe what happened!"

"Mom? Are you okay?"

"Al Fell called me last week. He wanted to donate a Paul Revere, sterling silver plate to the Questers in honor of Lyda Mae." Lyda Mae—Albert Fell's wife, and Mom's best friend—belonged to the Questers, a woman's antique group. As president, Lyda Mae collaborated closely with Mom, the vice president of the local chapter. Lyda Mae and Albert, whom everyone called Fell, qualified as experts in sterling silver. Mom, known for her bisque dolls, had a more eclectic assortment of antique items garnered from many secondhand shops, flea markets, and estate sales under her own company name, "Interior Moods by Violette."

"Paul Revere? Wow, that's really amazing!"

One day in June 1970, Lyda Mae had a massive heart attack. At the hospital, after all attempts to save her, only machinery kept her breathing. Once disconnected from the ventilator, she died.

Everyone who knew Lyda Mae reacted with stunned disbelief. Devastated, her daughter, Leigh, and Fell grieved Lyda Mae's sudden death—the loss of someone beautiful in so many ways. Now, time had passed, and Fell wanted to donate the Revere sterling plate in her memory.

"So, what did Uncle Fell want from you?" Not truly an uncle, my sisters and I used the term as an affectionate title.

Mom continued, "Fell wanted to present me with the plate, since I took over the Quester Presidency after Lyda Mae's death. But first he wanted it engraved. He said I'd never find the engraver by myself. So, he invited me to lunch to talk about old times after we had the plate engraved."

"Did you go already?" I asked.

"Yesterday. The engraver did a beautiful job, and we had a lovely

149

luncheon. We both still miss Lyda Mae. It was wonderful to reminisce."

"Oh, Mom! I'm so glad! What a nice day for you."

"That was only the beginning. On the way home, Fell spotted an antique store. Neither of us ever saw it before. He asked me if I had time to take a look. Of course, I agreed. The shop had a large interior, full of beautiful, old collectibles. We browsed in different directions, and then, he called me. He was standing by a glass jewelry case. He said, 'Look at this ring! I guarantee Lyda Mae would have walked out with it on her finger. Let me see what it looks like on a woman's hand. Will you try it on?' It slid onto my finger. I turned my hand so he could see." Mom gave a little gasp, "Violet, rainbow sparkles danced all over the room, as sunlight hit diamonds around the big sapphire."

"No! You've got to be kidding me, Mom!"

"I kid you not! I was speechless!"

"I can only imagine! What did you say?"

"I told him Lyda Mae would definitely have walked out of the shop with that ring on her finger."

"I'm sure you're right. He treated her like a queen, and she loved him back, just as much."

"You know, I've never told anyone about the impending divorce with your father; not even my closest friends know. But on the way home, Fell said, 'I guess you and Rudy will be starting to travel, since your youngest is fifteen now.'"

"What did you say, Mom?"

"I said I planned to divorce your father. I just needed a lawyer. Suddenly, he pulled the car off the road. I asked him if he hit something. He said, 'Tell me what you just said, again.' I said, 'You mean about divorcing my husband?' You know, honey, I still can't believe this even happened."

"What, Mom?"

"What he said next..." I heard her suck in another breath. "He said, 'Because you're the only other woman *on the face of this earth* I would consider marrying.' And then he told me he has a very good lawyer!"

"Holy smoke! What did you say?"

"Nothing! But after he started driving again, we talked. I'm still in a state of shock," she said, her voice ringing like a clear bell.

At that moment, I knew I would have an incredible stepfather and wonderful stepsister.

God uses all things, even evil things, to bring good to life. The occult is not to be used to see or to foretell the future. It is plainly forbidden in Scripture. Yet He allowed it for good, this time. God works in mysterious ways, but His plans are always good, since He knows the end from the beginning.

> *"There shall not be found among you anyone who makes his son or his daughter pass through the fire, or one who practices witchcraft, or a soothsayer, or one who interprets omens, or a sorcerer, or one who conjures up spells, or a medium, or a spiritualist, or one who calls up the dead. For all who do these things are an abomination to the Lord, and because of these abominations the Lord your God drives them out from before you."*
> *— Deuteronomy 18:10-12*

Nearly two years passed at Graduate Hospital before I sought a physical therapy job with greater complexity. I joined the staff at Magee Memorial Hospital, specializing in rehabilitation, per my Temple advisor's instructions: *Work in an acute general hospital for at least a year, where you'll see every kind of malady known to man. Then work in a rehabilitation hospital for a solid base in the more specialized practice of physical therapy.*

Before I left Graduate, Michael whispered to me, "Do you know what I like best about this job at Graduate?"

"No. What?"

"Watching you leaning over the Hubbard tank in your short skirt." He took my hand. Shadowed in the back room, one more shared, heady kiss; intoxicating, covert embrace; exhilarating and promise filled; he bonded us further.

Looking back, God's hand moved in my life little by little. A pattern of dovetailed "circumstances" leading up to our meeting, rose to consciousness. A time came when "coincidences" became statistically impossible. The idea of random events gave way to the discovery of God's unique plan for my life—me, a miniscule part of His magnificent, unfathomable design.

21

LIFE AND DEATH

*"For we know that if our earthly house, this tent, is destroyed,
we have a building from God, a house not made with hands,
eternal in the heavens."*
— *2 Corinthians 5:1*

I TREATED ALMOST every malady at Graduate: I debrided burns and
wounds. There were outpatients with low back pain and debilitated
inpatients with strokes, broken bones, prolonged bed rest, and post-
surgical cases. I remember one burn patient in particular. He came to
PT for debridement of his face and arms.

"I would rather have you do this than the doctor," he said. I took a
scalpel in my sterile gloved hand and, with conscious care, removed
some grayish tissue from his forearm as it soaked in the Hubbard
tank.

"Why?" I asked.

His burn-encrusted face distorted into a crooked smile; his eyes
filled with life.

"Besides you being better looking," he paused as I laughed. "It's more than that, you know? You take your time, and it doesn't hurt near as much. The docs are all in a big rush."

The doctors' crush of patients and limited hours created a small window of time with each person. I understood *medicalese*, medical language frequently used by doctors, often beyond the patient's understanding. If I took the time, I could bridge that gap in understanding and reduce pain.

Later in my career, a patient handed me an X-ray report with a look of confusion. "I don't understand any of this! My doctor told me I need physical therapy, but I don't understand why," she said.

"Let's see if we can understand this report. Your prescription says you have sciatica, right?"

"Yes," she said, "but why does my leg hurt?"

"It hurts because the sciatic nerve runs all the way down your leg from your low back. Look here." I pulled my chair next to hers. "Your X-ray explains that you have some arthritis where nerves come out of your backbone. If we can give you a little more space there, take the pressure off nerves and strengthen your core muscles, your pain should improve or even go away." I showed her the nerves exiting the spine in my anatomy atlas.

"How are we going to make more space?"

"That's why I went to school for PT," I said, winking.

After the second visit, her sciatic pain improved by fifty percent, with muscle energy technique (MET), one of many continuing education courses, guiding my treatment. Another of my former patients, a Christian of deep faith, became a dear friend, after her discharge from PT. Between meetings for lunch, we wrote letters. Diagnosed with schizophrenia, Barbara controlled her symptoms with medication. "You know, my friend, you help me trim my sails and skim along better when we're in touch. I miss you," she wrote.

Years into our relationship, Barbara began having symptoms of weakness and pain. Her diagnosis, delayed by her pre-existing schizophrenia, turned out to be brain cancer. A tumor took up space in her head, compressed her brain, and caused her symptoms. One of her family members let me know her new address at a local nursing home.

The hardest of all medical conversations is the end-of-life discussion. Few doctors of medicine, reared and trained to heal people, become comfortable with discussions about death. I found purpose in comforting, explaining, handholding. My last two visits with Barbara at the nursing home proved such a time as this.

"I can't remember," Barbara exclaimed, her voice and eyes registering fear.

"Well, you remembered me," I said chuckling. That made her smile and nod.

"Will you call my daughter, Tara? My doctors aren't telling me anything." She remembered where Tara's phone number was written. I promised her I would.

"Violet, she has brain cancer. She's in the terminal stages now," Tara sniffled. I could feel her tears through the phone.

"Has anyone explained her diagnosis to her?" I asked. "I think she's frightened."

"I thought the doctor had; but I'm not sure," she said.

"You're her power of attorney, right, Tara?"

"Yes. I'm still going through all the things in her apartment." She sighed. "I don't know how to handle this."

"Would it help if I talked to her and explained what's going on? She and I have the kind of relationship, with our faith, that I can talk about dying as the gate to heaven."

"Oh, would you? I can't tell you how much I'd appreciate your help!"

"Yes. Thanks for explaining the situation. I'll go tomorrow and see if I can answer her questions. Not knowing what's happening can be frightening. Would you like me to call you after I see her?"

"Yes, please. And thank you so much." Grateful to understand the situation, I looked forward to easing Barbara's mind.

Barbara seemed peaceful, asleep when I arrived. Her nurse whispered a warning about Barbara's confusion and bizarre actions: she had attempted to put her pajama bottoms on over her head. I sat quietly and prayed. Barbara lived and breathed as a born-again Christian who loved to discuss her faith and encourage mine. She watched my relationship with Christ develop over the life of our friendship until "born-again" described my beliefs as well. Curled on her side in bed, her weight loss became obvious, as I studied her sleeping form. It had only been four days since I saw her, but the transition struck me hard: the shadow of death surrounded her. Giving myself a little shake, I focused on what Barbara needed. And the list did not include me getting misty now.

"Need sit," she said, swinging her legs over the edge of the bed, wide awake.

"Hey, sweetie," I said. "How are you doing?"

"Hall lamp," she said, then shook her head in frustration, sitting on the bedside. Extending her right hand toward me, she raised her eyebrows. I took her hand and sat beside her.

"You're having some trouble talking." Barbara nodded.

"Nnn remembering..." she said. She tapped her head with her right hand and sent an intense look in my direction.

"Can you understand what I'm saying?" Her energetic, affirmative nod answered my question. Reading her facial expressions and hand gestures, I gradually understood what she wanted. "You want to know what's wrong with your head?" I asked. She nodded affirmation again.

"Angel," she said, pointing to me. "What's wrong?"

"You're getting better speaking with a little practice, Barb." She motioned that she felt crazy, index finger pointing to her head and circling. "No, you're not crazy." Barbara turned her palms up and shrugged with a questioning look on her face. I put an arm around her and leaned in. "Barb, you have brain cancer. You're getting ready to go home."

Her eyes widened and teared, along with mine. The quiet grieving lasted a few minutes, then turned into celebration as her profound faith took over. Home meant *being with Jesus*. We smiled and hugged each other, still crying between bouts of low laughter. Pointing a finger at me, she commanded, "Don't you cry!" She made a few more attempts before she came out with, "Promise!"

"I promise, because I'll see you later, and we'll have eternity to enjoy each other's company!" Leaving her there, I smiled through the hurt—so bittersweet. I knew I'd never see her alive again.

I called Tara when I got home. We cried together; but, in the Bible, believers are promised, "joy in the morning." I finished the conversation with Tara, smiling at that thought.

Barbara's funeral filled the room to capacity with all the lives she had touched in her ministry and family. I met her Sunday School class, there in force. She once told me, with a hint of pride, that they had nicknamed her "Feisty Greisty." Tara and I embraced—long, quiet, full of love for my dear friend and her mom. As I told Tara, "We will meet again."

"The valley of the shadow of death" can be a dark place or a place of amazing transition, depending on the spiritual state of the dying and those at the bedside. All human beings are neatly wrapped packages of mind, body, and spirit. The living, dying, and injured, all had emotional needs I filled with comfort, conversation and hugs, only through God at the helm, and a little bit of extra time.

2 2

LOVE'S SPECTRUM

*"But the fruit of the Spirit is love, joy, peace, longsuffering,
kindness, goodness, faithfulness, gentleness, self-control.
Against such there is no law."*
— *Galatians 5:22-23*

MICHAEL HAD MOVED. He enjoyed his apartment and time to himself. Pleased for him, his move came with no burden; we complemented each other so completely, worry about the distance never took hold.

"You know there are eight flights of steps to this apartment," Michael said with a droll look.

"I'm well aware," I panted, hoisting the chest of drawers high enough to miss the step as we puffed our way to the top. "But it's a great apartment once you get up here."

With Michael's help, I moved in 1973 to a fourth-floor walk-up on Walnut Street near 20th. Closer to my new job, my apartment sat high above incessant street noise and an ever-present parade of people. The front door opened to a long hall with the single bedroom immediately to the right of the entrance. A sunny galley kitchen lay straight ahead at the hall's end with the living room/dining room a right turn at the kitchen's entrance. Kitchen and living room faced Walnut Street, where golden sunlight streamed through the brownstone's tall windows. I had a locked parking area out back.

The dark, extended hallway provided a perfect stretch to hang laundry. A red-faced Sears delivery man climbed two flights of stairs per floor with a new, sink-hook-up washing machine, in tow. Heavy and awkward, he bumped it up, one step at a time. "Lady," he said, breathing hard on the top landing, "Next time, please buy your appliances from another store!"

With the new apartment located five-and-a-half blocks from Magee Rahab, I rarely made it there on time at a walk. My internal clock always ran a half-hour slow. I arrived at a dead run to meet the 8:00 a.m. clock-in time. Stowing my pocketbook in the locker room, I glanced up and down the hall, all clear of the chief, Garnet Schiller.

The chief—a smart, blonde PT—had a sharp edge; but she also knew how to hire top notch staff for her department. Eight or more PTs staffed Magee Physical Therapy, plus the chief and assistant chief. Each therapist had a particular diagnostic predilection, from amputations and multiple fractures to spinal cord injuries and cerebral vascular accidents/strokes. Every diagnosis had its own unique knowledge base. When medical challenges changed people's lives, my problem-solving skills kicked in. My professional capabilities hung on the framework of these skills.

A bent, broken, mangled body with parallel emotional trauma posed the ultimate challenge: *how much of the person's previous life could we reconstruct as a rehab team?* Special equipment, physical training, family teaching, education, sweat included, planted a seedling, new life. A different life, but productive if the patient moved ahead rather than looking back. The team—occupational and speech therapists, psychologists, physiatrists (doctors of physical medicine), social workers and physical therapists—worked with a full picture of each patient's needs, capabilities, and probabilities. We helped the patient build a sense of what could be and how to get there.

Margo Baylor, assistant chief of physical therapy, spoke in a clear, level voice with accents of her Eastern European upbringing. Blue-eyed, well-proportioned, to-the-point yet compassionate, her superior knowledge in her specialty, hemiplegia—cerebral vascular accident (CVA)—made me take notice. One of the more complex diagnoses, CVA interfered with brain function, where all human activities originate. I liked complex. Like all the therapists at Magee, I learned to treat all types of patients. As I learned, hemiplegia became my choice of specialty, and Margo became my mentor.

Garnet and Margo assigned new patients to therapists. They looked for a broad range of experience for each therapist and the best treatment for the patient. Margo flagged me down one afternoon.

"Violet, there's a new patient with multiple fractures. Her husband died in the car accident. I think you and she would be a good fit."

"Sure," I said. More straightforward than other injuries and diseases, fractures needed healing time. Every activity that placed weight through the break required the physiatrist's approval. X-rays measured bone growth at the fracture site. Overactivity could mean longer healing time, if the broken bones moved before a solid union formed.

Aqua water in the glassed-in therapeutic pool shimmered at the center of a rectangle of four walkways. Entrances to the secretarial, gym, work, and staff areas extended from each, open, airy walkway.

I took the elevator to the second floor, read Maria's chart, and scheduled her for PT later in the day with her nurse.

"Such a tragic case," the nurse said. "She has two children."

"How's she doing?" I asked.

"She's amazing. I haven't heard her say a negative word since she's been here."

Maria waited for me in her wheelchair. Multiple fractures included her pelvis, femur or thigh bone—with a stabilizing intramedullary rod—and right radius, or large bone of the forearm, stabilized with a plate and screw fixation. Her chart history told a terrible story. The other driver crossed the center line—causing a head-on collision, killing Maria's husband instantly.

Her calm, brown eyes and ready smile greeted me. She looked younger than thirty- two and needed her hair washed; post-surgical wounds did not allow a shower.

"Oh, please excuse me," she said. "I haven't been able to wash my hair since the accident." Her steady gaze punctuated with a wince, she continued, "I'm happy the nurses promised it would be washed in the next couple of days."

"You'll feel much better after that. How are you getting from the wheelchair to the bed?" I asked, beginning her evaluation for treatment.

"I need a lot of help. I'm so tired, because I can't get comfortable at night. I can't move without pain, and I'm afraid I'll do something to hurt the broken bones." No complaint lay hidden in her melodic voice. She stated facts.

"That will change quickly. I'll teach you how to transfer safely from the bed to your wheelchair and how to roll in bed. We can work on positions of comfort so you can sleep better." I watched her expressive face. She seemed comfortable with me. "How are you doing psychologically?" I asked in a quiet voice.

"You know I lost my husband, Joe, in the accident." Her sad expression eased; our eyes stayed connected. "But my children are fine! It will be hard without him. We loved each other. But how can I stay sad when my children could have been killed too? *Such a gift!*" Her face lit up with inexpressible gratitude. "I'll work hard to get home and be with them. They're with my mother and father right now. I have so much to be thankful for, to God!"

Maria earned her discharge in six weeks. With a walker and some help from her parents, she returned home to her children. Her smile shone from her heart, even when she told me stories about Joe.

Paul, a jovial, mildly overweight fellow, had both legs amputated —one above the knee, the other below.

"What happened?" I asked, although I had read his chart already.

"I'm an electrical lineman who lost an argument with lightning." He showed me the scar—a dot-shaped, wheal on his right palm. "Here's where the lightning went in. He looked up. "It went up my arm, down my trunk, and blew my legs off."

"Wow, and you're still here to tell the story!"

"Yup," he said, with a glint in his eye. "I just can't say I landed on my feet!" After I finished laughing, he added, "But I have you and this place, so I'll walk again."

Paul followed Maria's pattern of success. He regained his independence over the next several months. Both Paul and Maria exemplified positive attitudes with inner strength, a sure combination for success. They represented the pleasant cases.

Carol turned seventeen a month before her admission to rehab— an elfin, thin, wispy-haired girl with a paralyzed right side, hemiplegia from a left cerebrovascular accident—in her case, a brain blood clot, probably caused by birth control pills. Her brain damage from the clot and resulting lack of oxygen affected muscle function and speech. Carol had a one-word vocabulary—"my"—but she repeated it over and over, with inflection, as if speaking in normal sentences. Youthful ebullience and self-confidence vanished, as Carol's stroke affected her ability to reason and problem-solve in addition to stealing control of her right arm and leg. Her limp arm stayed in a sling, while her ankle and knee needed the support of a brace.

One morning, Carol's swollen eyes left no doubt she had been crying. A nurse told me her boyfriend broke up with her the night before, after only two weeks of rehab. A pretty girl with a slight build, blonde hair, and brown eyes, the lost waif of a teenager never recovered her speech, or anything else. Her discharge home came due to lack of improvement. Despite intensive rehab and all of her effort, independence lay beyond Carol's ability. Her parents learned safe ways to help her in everyday activities that had once been taken for granted. They rarely smiled; but occasionally, pain and anguish escaped from their eyes, before they regained control. Carol would never leave home, go to college, have a husband and family. Her brain remained damaged beyond help—her one gift: loving parents who would take care of her for life.

Patients came from every circumstance, every social class, some with devastating disabilities, who "made it" in the world after their medical problems occurred. One young saxophone player, on tour with a band, had traveled by camper from gig to gig. Ned was sleeping in the bunk over the cab when another vehicle plowed into the camper. Thrown to the floor, he landed on his head, severing the spinal cord high in his neck—instant quadriplegia. A brilliant musician who also played flute and harmonica, Ned lost use of his hands, arms, trunk, legs, bowel, and bladder. He learned to manage his losses with training and help, grounded in an absolute Christian faith rarely seen. He married, became a successful composer, and chaired the music department in a well-known city university. I felt privileged to be his physical therapist.

It still felt like an amazing honor to have physical therapy as my profession. Each patient I met and treated seemed to be in the right place at the right time, for themselves and me—*His divine plan?* With each person and event, I could see God's weavings in my life and other's lives as well. Each time I witnessed people with a strong faith that sustained them, each time I witnessed God's hand at work, my faith grew in strength and sustenance. Three years spent at Magee Memorial Hospital proved the formative years of my professional life. *God had a plan. And I liked it.*

My apartment door opened and closed softly on a warm April afternoon in 1973. I heard Michael's footsteps in the hall. "Hi!" I called.

"Hi, Violet," he said as he appeared in the living room doorway.

A letter in his hand dangled by his side. "I didn't get into Penn's physical therapy program."

"Aw, hon', I'm sorry." I scanned the short rejection. "Well, you'll just have to apply for next year." He nodded.

"That's what I figured too. Another year working at Graduate."

We sat still, holding hands, allowing ourselves time to deal with the bite of disappointment. After a bit, I nudged him and smiled. We had each other. He smiled back.

A few weeks later, Michael phoned. "I have a surprise for you, but you have to come to Penndel to see it."

"You're taking me to your softball game!" I said. Michael and Joe played in a league, and I cheered with the fans. We left on a Friday evening and chatted through the rush hour traffic—his usual, calm manner surrounded by a curious, happy anticipation. I tried to wheedle some information out of him.

"I won't answer any questions about the surprise," he said. "You just have to wait."

He took unusual care opening the door to his second-floor apartment. Before I could comment, a blue-gray, half-grown kitten with green eyes greeted us. I dropped to the floor and gathered up the handsome, little cat.

"It's a boy," Michael said, beaming. "I was crossing Route 1 two days ago, and he was a step ahead of me. He would've been squashed like a bug if I hadn't grabbed him."

"He's gorgeous," I exclaimed, petting the purring cat. "Have you named him?"

"Nope. I wanted you to meet him first."

"He looks like a Russian Blue, but with a pointier, pretty face." It only took a few minutes before I said, "Let's shorten 'Nikita' to 'Nika'."

"Nika, you are a handsome cat," Michael said, trying the name on for size. "It fits him."

And so, Nika became part of the household in Penndel. Without warning, Nika yanked a piece of roast beef from my hand and ran with his prize. "You little bug!" I scolded. I knew he had been starving. I didn't know he would never forget those hunger pangs. Affectionate and wild in a healthy kitten sort of way, he played, purred, and charmed us with his sweet personality. The vet pronounced him disease free, in good shape, and about six months old. Now, he belonged to us.

Later that year, Michael and I were together at the Penndel apartment. Sitting on the couch with Nika in my lap, Michael changed from conversational to quiet and serious. He came toward me, an earnest look on his face. "You know, we're together almost all the time. We should get married."

"Well, no one's asked me," I said.

His serious face disappeared with a grin, as he came down to eye level and asked, "Will you marry me?"

"Yes, I will, if Fell gives his permission."

"I can do that," he said.

Albert Fell—the gentle man who loved my mom and showed me what a father should be like, who showed me how a man should treat a woman—became the man who gave Michael permission for my hand in marriage. In general, Fell laughed and responded with humor as much as Dad frowned and responded with criticism. Mom had accepted Fell's marriage proposal with a Valentine's Day wedding planned. I called him "Daddy" and my father "Dad"; Love and affection poured out for two very different men. My sisters did the same.

God reigned—clear, consistent, even making use of a medium. All powerful, bringing good out of evil, a road forward out of difficulty—*the God of love and mercy at work.*

Michael's letter of acceptance to the Certificate Program in Physical Therapy, University of Pennsylvania, for the graduating class of 1975, arrived in April of 1974. Our joy overflowed with a celebration at DaVinci's Restaurant, a short walk from my apartment. On the way to DaVinci's, we passed a jeweler, where I sometimes perused the sparkling contents in glass cases. Too early for dinner, we stopped and scanned the gold, silver, and gems. I studied the displays for an engagement ring that I would want to see, every day, for the rest of my life. Michael and I both liked the simple settings with a single stone. Nothing caught our eyes that night.

At dinner, our waiter set a massive, wood bowl on a stand near our table. In went a raw egg, olive oil, fresh romaine, and grated cheeses. Well-tossed, crispy, garlic-coated croutons finished the dish: the best Caesar salad in Philadelphia.

"You want a taste?" I teased. Michael's dire allergy to eggs would lead to hives and a trip to the ER without immediate administration of Benadryl. He laughed.

Crab cakes, broccoli, and French fries paired with a glass of *liebfraumilch* (a sweet German wine) followed my salad. Michael's filet mignon came out medium, sizzling, with baked potato, sour cream, garden salad, and an olive-ridden, dry martini. Glass held high, I said, "May you become a fine, fellow physical therapist at Penn!" Our glasses clinked, and we settled down to celebrate.

I found myself in the jewelry store once a week in front of the ring case. I don't recall when I discovered *my ring* in the store; but the fact that a sapphire instead of a diamond glowed from the ring's center surprised me. In yellow gold, the unusual, square-shaped ring cradled a single, intense, blue stone in a bezel setting. Size seven and a half, it slid on my left fourth finger, a perfect fit.

"Michael, I fell in love with a sapphire ring instead of a diamond."

"Really?" He sounded distracted. "At the jewelry store we visited?"

"Yup. If you hate it, get me something else; that is, if you still want to marry me." That rated a chuckle.

On my December birthday, 1974, Michael and I sat at a secluded table at DaVinci's. He had already given me a funny card. Our wine waited, while a small but lavish box on my dinner plate received my undivided attention. Glossy, Persian blue paper and an elegant, blue-and-white bow suggested professional care in wrapping the little gift. *Is it my sapphire, or did he pick a diamond?* Underneath the wrapping, I read "Jonathan Stember Jewelers" on the white box. Inside, a blue, velvet box invited me to open it. "Is it my ring?"

Michael shrugged, looking pleased with himself. "Open it," he said.

Light struck the stone as the box opened, and midnight blue sparkled in a gold, bezel setting. I inhaled so sharply I made a noise. Michael moved to my side of the table, sealing my joy with a kiss. Taking the ring from its velvet nest, he slid it on my left, ring finger and kissed me again.

Engaged, I gazed into the face of my fiancée, my best friend, and my *gift from God.* Elation rose as Michael held me, pulling me to him until we couldn't get any closer in public. Misty, I stared at my hand, at the rich blue gemstone set in gold—*created by God, just for this moment in time.*

23

WEDDING PLANS AND REMINISCENCE

"If it is possible, as much as depends on you, live peaceably with all men."
— Romans 12:18

Fell and Mom, 1975

"I do," Mom said to the minister as she looked into Albert Fell's adoring eyes. On Valentine's Day, 1974, Mom wed Fell—a day my sisters and I still remember, with great affection.

Fell helped Mom with the divorce lawyer and a cash settlement for Dad. Although hurt, my father ended up with money and tried to move on with his life.

My introduction to Carrie Anne, Dad's steady flame, occurred in his new apartment on Locust Street. My two sisters and I were invited to meet

168

"the new girl in town," and I hoped I'd love her as much as I loved Fell.

I greeted her cordially. Petite and shapely, Dad looked at her with longing eyes. She lit up a cigarette and took the first puff, a shock since Dad hated cigarette smoke.

"Oh, I'm so sorry, Carrie Anne," I said. "I'm really allergic to cigarette smoke."

"So, go to another room," she said in frigid tones.

My first meeting with Carrie Anne dumbfounded me. I worked with all kinds of people daily. Her reaction puzzled and offended me. That meeting would characterize our entire relationship, until death did us part.

I have regrets. Dad invited Michael and me to dinner one Saturday evening. I'm sure Carrie Anne cleaned and started preparations for a lovely meal. Tired after a week of work, neither Michael nor I had the energy to walk on thin ice with Dad. He could be touchy on a good day; with Carrie Anne added to the mix, the atmosphere could become volatile. We cancelled. I don't think she ever forgave me. I tried to make it up to her, but she rejected all attempts. She never accepted any relationship, although I offered, up to the end of her life.

Mom had twenty-five years with my father and twenty-five years with Fell. But the difference between the first twenty-five years and the second compares storm to sunlight. In his second marriage, Dad received from Carrie Anne the treatment he had given Mom in his first marriage of poor choices and control. He persevered with her and still stayed in contact with me, even though I became persona non grata to Carrie Anne. Dad's wife got along with Lynne better than with me. But for some reason we've never understood, she tried to cut Gay off altogether.

Dad and Gay worked around Carrie Anne's vitriol. We all did.

My job at Magee came with a family atmosphere. If one therapist needed help, someone always had the expertise required. We became a close-knit group at work, congregating at our favorite watering hole, Watson's Pub, on Friday nights. Michael met me there, and we enjoyed icy beer on tap before going back to my place. Our pub hangout became the fertile ground where a ski trip to Sugarloaf Mountain in Maine took shape. Two inveterate skiers in our group played prime mover roles and made reservations for all of us.

Once there, Michael and I started on the bunny slope but graduated to intermediate trails by the end of the day. We skied the intermediate slope three times, before I hugged a rock and kissed a tree on the last run of the day. I twisted my knee when a binding failed to release, but I skied to the bottom of the mountain. Walking to the lodge, Michael slipped on black ice in the parking lot and crashed on the blacktop, richer by a few bruises.

We took the next day off the slopes—lounging in our room, talking, reading, and watching TV. My engagement ring flashed blue on my hand. We hadn't talked about a date. "Honey, when do you want to get married?"

"I want to have a job first."

"You're graduating in the summer. You should have a job by the fall, right?"

He nodded. "How about October? The weather in the beginning of the month is still really nice."

I looked at a calendar. "The first Saturday in October?"

"Sounds good," he said.

I wrote our vows that day and set the date in my journal: "October 4, 1975, Wedding Day."

"How does this sound?" I asked Michael, his nose in an *American History* magazine. "And they shall be equal partners, united in marriage, signified by the lighting of this candle." I continued, looking at him. "Then both of us will light the candle at the same time." I waited a second for his response.

"That's nice," he said and returned to his magazine. I'd heard weddings were for the bride; Michael seemed to be living proof. He left the details to me. I took charge, a blissful obsession. Michael cleared each detail of the plans with no changes, other than a few words in the vows. Within two weeks after the ski trip, I had booked the entire wedding, including the church, reception, minister, and flowers. I had simple instructions for my four bride's maids: floor-length dresses, autumn colors, and something they loved enough to wear again. One of the most important purchases of all remained: my wedding gown.

I called Dad to invite him and a guest. I had great news for him: from ballpark figures, this wedding would be considerably less expensive than the average nuptial affair. He expressed enthusiasm when he heard the approximate price for the reception and my ongoing search for a reasonably priced, unique, wedding gown. Things didn't get sticky until he asked, "Is your *mother* going to be there?"

"Sure, and Fell too."

"I don't know if I can come."

"Aww, that's too bad, Dad. You'll be missed," I said. After a silent thirty seconds that stretched on, I added, "You know, I can seat you and Mom at opposite ends of the room for the reception; and you can sit wherever you want on the bride's side, near the front of the church."

"Could you do that, honey?"

"Sure, Dad."

For a minute, his acceptance disappointed me. I wanted Fell to walk me down the aisle; but I knew it would hurt Dad beyond repair. I told Mom and Fell, who appreciated the thought. They both agreed Dad should accompany me down the aisle. We all knew it was the right thing to do.

Good reports from friends trickled in about a restaurant and reception venue. The appointment with Mr. Rainer at Collegeville Inn surpassed my expectations. Magnificent assortments of cut flowers in bouquets; table arrangements; small, standing candelabra with live flowers and ivy twined from base to candlesticks; all looked ideal. Several ring- binders filled with glossy photographs included pictures and lists of sumptuous buffets with charming choices for our wedding cake. After a wedding food tasting, and Michael's approval, I signed the contract—with an added flourish to my signature.

My wedding gown posed a problem. I visited The Bride's Shop filled with wedding dresses, ranging from six hundred to thousands of dollars. Worse yet, none of them fit my style or personality—too frou-frou. A country girl at heart, The Peasant Garb carried dresses for all occasions in my petite size and style. I wanted something quaint and light, not white. I focused on the petite rack of long dresses and chose by color. I picked up an off-white, long- sleeve made of lacey, crocheted cotton. I pushed the other dresses back. The homespun, ivory gown of muslin material had lace-like crochet-work at the collar and a laced bodice. I whisked the dress off the rack and into the fitting room. My mirror image looked back at me with a peasant-style wedding dress that fit my height and each curve of my body. The hem fell just below my ankles. I admired the creamy color, no virginal white pretense. I stood staring at my reflected wedding dress, recalling the dialogue with Mom.

I couldn't be anything but honest with her when Mark moved in with me during college.

"Mom, I will never marry a man without living with him first, after what you went through with Dad." I didn't expect an answer.

But she said, "Violet, I'm sorry all of you kids had to go through that time. There's no way I can change history. But I have three beautiful daughters, who I wouldn't trade for the world!"

I brought my attention back to the present. Ecstatic at such a find, I grinned and fished out $35.00 for my perfect wedding gown. I thought of Mom as I walked home with the gown over my arm. Opposite in style from her elegance, she wouldn't be surprised. She never expressed surprise when Michael moved to Walnut Street with me during his physical therapy certificate program at Penn, especially since our engagement. She approved that he insisted on having his degree before we married, a decision I also respected and admired.

I admire him! I thought with a smile that faded as I thought of Dad.

My father couldn't be defined as a husband to be admired; although he often said to Mom, "What do you want? I don't smoke, drink, or run around."

Mom didn't realize she could have said, "Neither do I!"

But as I looked back on my life, I recognized that by second grade, God had taken the place of the Father I didn't have: kind, gentle, fair, honest, worthy. *Water over the dam...but so much water!*

I walked home from work still thinking of Mom, her philosophy, and how it affected me. After the divorce, she had told me, "God would not have wanted me to suffer any longer than I did with your father." *Unfaithfulness* did not appear in Dad's list of sins. I didn't find *mental cruelty* and *miserly actions* addressed in the Word as worthy of divorce.

The Bible being "the Word of God" never entered conversations in my family. "It's a book written about men, by men, and for men," Mom exclaimed, when we discussed abortion, divorce, or anything that would change life from a worldview to one grounded in the Bible. The Good Book brooked no credence with Mom, not until many years later.

But in the meantime, for me, both cross and crucifix portrayed symbols of a torturous death—rather than *recognition of death's defeat through resurrection and sacrifice for all mankind.* An understanding of these concepts that would transcend beyond the superficial came many years later.

Until then, even a cursory assessment of my life exposed mistakes, begotten by my ill-conceived notions. The seeds of understanding Jesus as a personal Savior had been planted and sprouted in my teens—but not yet grown to mature faith and practice.

Time rolled on as our wedding approached. *How would it go?* We were about to find out.

The Lord had already helped me with my family. I trusted He would take care of the wedding too.

24

THE WEDDING

*"Marriage is honorable among all, and the bed undefiled; but
fornicators and adulterers God will judge."*
— *Hebrews* 13:4

COMBINING two households becomes a worthy first challenge for a
couple on the brink of matrimony. How do you introduce a half-
grown kitten into an already-bonded trio of two cats and a dog?
That's what we had to figure out.

When Michael moved in with me, Nika had to be introduced to
Mink and Saki. Shani and Nika had already met in Penndel. With
cats, this sort of family blending can be dicey, since they're territorial
with other felines. When we surveyed the physical layout, we discovered the perfect "no-man's-land"—two flights of stairs with a landing
outside the apartment entrance.

I held Nika, while Michael went up and let the rest of the family
out. He held Shani back, so the cats could meet each other without
the excited Airedale. Saki and Nika sniffed noses first, with me in
watchful attendance. Mink followed. With no hissing, raised hackles,

or paws, Mink and Saki turned and started back up the stairs with Nika at their heels. We had "three Musketeers" and a dog. Shani and Nika became acquainted in the Philly apartment, with Nika up on the couch at Shani's eye-level. Mildly wary for a couple of minutes, they nosed each other in acceptance and never looked back—one happy family.

Michael and I continued to enjoy one another's company. His humor could be raucous, quiet, ornery, sensitive, salty or sweet. He made me laugh, his touch everything I needed or wanted.

I teased him that I was *a serious individual of German stock with salt-of-the-earth sized hands.*

He was *my laughter and my love.*

Then, he said he *sent in twenty-five cereal box tops, and I came in the mail.*

We laughed, worked, loved, and explored the streets of Philadelphia together, as time passed.

The days counted down to October 4, 1975. We had everything in place for our wedding. A honeymoon week on Cape Cod, Chatham, Massachusetts, awaited us. The advertisement read: "cozy, New England style-house, fifty yards uphill from the bay, fireplace and bicycles, rent for a week or season."

Taking no chances, I inspected everything the day of the wedding —a sun-filled, Indian summer, short-shorts kind of a day. I arrived at the church just as the delivery man came. Standing candelabra for every pew in the one-room Norriton Presbyterian Church, circa 1698—and elegant, glass-covered candlesticks for each deep-set window were expected. All flowers had been sent to Mom's home.

The same minister who married Mom and Fell the year before agreed to marry us after an informal meeting with Michael and me. Reverend W. Osborne Rowland, a kind man who smiled often, believed God gave us more latitude than conservative pastors of the day, then or now.

I unlocked the church for the delivery man and began opening boxes. Puzzled by the large-sized boxes holding the candelabra, no mystery remained when I saw the oversized, finished product standing by the first pew: large, almost crude, brass candelabrum with a string of plastic ivy and fake flowers wound haphazardly around the pole. They dwarfed the simple, rich, dark wood and white painted pew—and looked nothing like the candelabra from the sample photographs. The glass covered candlesticks, though oversized, looked elegant and sat well-proportioned on the deep-set sill of each tall window. I sucked in a breath through clenched teeth and gathered my wits before speaking to the man, busy unpacking boxes.

"I'm so sorry. You're going to have to take these back," I pointed to the candelabra and glass protectors. "They're not what I ordered. But we will keep the candlesticks and globes for the windowsills."

"I can't do that. I'm just following orders on where to deliver this stuff," he said as he continued to unpack more of the offending items. I moved closer to him and impeded his unpacking. "Let me be a little clearer," I raised my voice a notch and enunciated, unconsciously mimicking my theatrical mother's attention-getting voice. "I am refusing this portion of the delivery. Pack it back up, and take it back to Collegeville Inn. Please."

The bewildered delivery man looked at me, as his mouth soundlessly opened and closed. I continued, "You are not responsible. I am the customer, and this portion of the delivery has been refused."

"I have to leave these here!" he exclaimed in desperation.

"If you leave these here, I am not responsible for loss or damage. I need this church ready for a wedding at six o'clock this evening. These boxes will go back with you *now*."

He eyed me with increasing displeasure.

"I will go right now and discuss this with Mr. Rainer at Collegeville Inn. I promise, if you load this up now, you will have done your job." He peered at me, and I saw some light of understanding in his eyes. "If you load up right now, I'll follow you out of the driveway to Collegeville; Mr. Rainer and I have a lot to discuss."

He reversed his process and began packing. In ten minutes, he finished. Dressed in ice blue short shorts, sandals, and a T-shirt, I met Mom as she arrived with the pine boughs to decorate the candlesticks under glass for each windowsill. After my hasty explanation, she discussed how many single candles and glass-covered candlesticks to leave with the resigned delivery man.

I left for Collegeville Inn, three dimensions of angry. The drive took fifteen minutes.

"I'm sorry; Mr. Rainer can't see you now, miss."

"I'm getting married at six p.m. tonight. I'm refusing a delivery of oversized, plastic-garnished candelabra. If you want to take responsibility for the refusal and non-payment, I'll need that in writing," I said.

She caved, reaching for the phone. Five minutes later, I sat in Mr. Rainer's office.

Please, Lord, help me not to lose my temper in an unproductive or nasty way. Guide me and let me be clear with this man who had sample pictures of candelabra twined with fresh flower-and-ivy garlands but delivered plastic. Help me have my wedding tonight. Amen.

The office door closed, and Mr. Rainer appeared like a storm cloud before the rain. "What's this I hear about you not liking the candlesticks and flowers?"

"Not as advertised, and not what you promised. *Plastic* ivy and flowers?"

"Princess Anne would love the way they look," he exclaimed, his color rising.

"Then Princess Anne has bad taste," I countered, firm. "I will not pay for that delivery of candelabra. I will pay for the single candlesticks and glass globes that will be used in the church windows tonight."

"What do you mean you *won't pay*? I have a signed contract!"

"Yes, for fresh ivy and flowers twined about diminutive candelabra, like the sample pictures you showed me. You can say you have a contract. But as far as I'm concerned, there's false advertising involved here. Your book of pictures that helped me pick my wedding package did not show any arrangements with plastic ivy and fake flowers."

He blustered some more, repeated himself, and expected me to fold.

"Mr. Rainer, I hoped you would be fair with me. Now, I'll promise you something. If I don't get my money back for those big brass candelabra, plastic ivy, and flowers, I will be your worst nightmare. I will personally picket your establishment and write daily letters to the editors in the local papers. You will wish you never met me! I'm supposed to be home right now for my wedding pictures. You know, your son-in-law is doing the photography package. Look at me, in shorts and a sweated T-shirt. Look at the time! My husband-to-be is already waiting. I'm a half hour from home, and you're making me late for my own wedding. So, make up your mind."

He glared at me but opened a ledger with checks. He used his calculator, filled out a refund check, and handed it to me.

"Thank you." I grabbed my purse and left at a run.

Back at home, Lynne tore apart and recreated the patch of flowers that was supposed to be crown shaped. We took all the pictures I wanted to see in my album, and Mr. Rainer's son-in-law apologized as he observed the frantic preparations. Even though I shaved my legs over the sink, while my maid of honor ran interference for me, I arrived an hour late for my own wedding.

All that time, Michael sat with Reverend Rowland and had no idea of circumstances.

Two weeks before the wedding, my childhood and teen memories caught up with me. I talked to Michael about breaking off the engagement. A prince, he ever so gently peeled me off the ceiling and grounded me in the present. He agreed I would handle all the money and bills, the home books; his mother did the books in his family home. This would help assuage my fears of losing control of my own finances to a spouse, as my mother had done. I dried my tears and smiled—satisfied, at peace.

But now, two weeks later, Michael sat by the altar on our wedding day, waiting for his bride, an hour late.

By the time I appeared in the church doorway, an ashen gray color tinged his face. Not one unoccupied seat remained in the tiny, sweltering church. My dad walked me down the aisle to the music Michael and I chose. Michael, Reverend Rowland, and I got through the ceremony pleasantly, though still somewhat shellshocked. And then, almost suddenly, we stood together, husband and wife.

In the limo to the reception, with twenty minutes alone to talk, Michael finally smiled.

Pictures - Violet and Shani, while Michael waited at the alter...

The rest of the evening continued in an *interesting* vein. The band showed up half an hour late. I had three glasses of champagne on an empty stomach and, unwittingly, insulted a friend's husband. When the emcee introduced Michael and I for the first time in public, he mispronounced our name. I stopped them from bringing out the wrong cake—the one with white plastic columns and swans. They found and delivered the right cake—the one with candles spiraling around and around from top to bottom, laced with fresh-cut flowers complementing the icing roses.

Our guests had a wonderful time. No one knew of anything amiss, except Michael, me, and Mom.

We danced the required dances and visited each table. My stomach rejected the idea of food, and I had nothing but ginger ale from the bar, after my champagne-tainted rudeness. We decided to

"Honey, I'm so sorry I was late, but wait till you hear what happened!"

go back to Mom's and Fell's to unwrap our gifts before going to the honeymoon suite at Valley Forge Towers.

When we reached the house, I ate a late dinner of scrambled eggs. Opening our wedding gifts, the thoughtful, creative presents, and touching cards provided the bright spot we needed. Michael and I headed for the Towers by midnight.

At the registration desk, I gave our name and explained we had reservations for the bridal suite, while Michael brought in our overnight bags.

"I'm sorry, Ma'am. What did you say your name was?" the receptionist asked.

"Batejan, *B* as in boy, *a-t-e-j-a-n* as in Nancy."

"Oh, my," she said with a frown. "That room is taken. It was scheduled in the name you gave for Saturday. It's after midnight, so it's Sunday now."

"All right," Michael said, after we exchanged looks. "Get us in another room, and we'll have that complementary bottle of champagne on ice."

Champagne and Smiles—"So that's what happened!"

"Oh, dear," the receptionist frowned again. "Since it's after midnight, officially, it's Sunday; that means we can't give you champagne. Pennsylvania blue laws, you know."

When they found us a room, I headed straight for the shower to wash the day off of my body and gather the screaming fragments of my mind into a calmer state. Then, Michael and I curled up together and went to sleep.

But the weather had been beautiful...

Sun-sparkling Sunday, we picked up our furry friends and prepared to leave for our honeymoon in Cape Cod. Mink and Shani were coming with us. We planned to board Saki and Nika at the vet's. When I made the boarding reservations for October 5, the receptionist told me, "Bring them when you're ready, and good luck with your wedding." I phoned, expecting to leave an "on our way" message. Instead, I listened to a recording. The veterinary practice had closed early. It was Sunday...

The six of us had a fairly uneventful trip to Chatham, if you overlooked the flat tire.

After I unpacked, I wrote an apology to my friend's husband. We explored and mailed the letter. Later, I thought of each wedding gift as I wrote thank-you notes—a pleasant, evening chore, beside my husband and a glowing fire.

Indian summer continued throughout our honeymoon as if in apology for the wild wedding ride. On the bay, with a week to *just be* with my love, I let go of all the wedding day craziness. We biked in shorts and light shirts; found the last, red rose of summer; waded in the chilly back bay near our front door; and rested by a glowing, evening fire. I found little shops where I purchased earrings and an antique shop where Michael and I bought Mom Batejan a pale-blue, hand-blown, glass bowl. I bought my mom a tall, porcelain, seal-point Siamese cat sitting on its haunches. We took in the sites like Plymouth rock, ate lobster, and basked in the warmth of the waning sun.

We did something we continued throughout our lives. We played and cuddled with the furry critters and each other, during a flawless honeymoon.

There's no doubt God has a sense of humor. He answered my prayer; we had our wedding. And after the devil's foiled attempts at mayhem, the Lord ended our wedding week with the quintessential honeymoon, to launch our married lives.

25

OUT OF THE CITY

*"The earth is the Lord's, and all its fulness, The world and
those who dwell therein. For He has founded it upon the seas,
And established it upon the waters."*
— *Psalm 24:1–2*

AFTER OUR HONEYMOON house on a Cape Cod bay and the last
rose of summer, Walnut Street in Philadelphia assaulted us. Conges-
tion, horns, crowds, block after block of multi-story buildings with
one tiny Rittenhouse Square of green—the city collided head-on with
our back-bay minds and rested bodies. Within a week, the hamster
wheel turned again. Quiet country with tranquil, green openness and
earthy scents infused my dreams. "Are you dreaming about the
country and the ocean?" Michael asked.

"Yes," my shoulders shrugged, then dropped. I missed the sound
of birds calling, the smell of dew in early morning, trees dancing with
wind and bare feet in grass.

"Me too," he said. *Country calling us home.*

The real estate section rustled as I folded the paper in half. My finger followed each boxed ad down the page. Our goal: *get back to the country*. One ad stood out.

"Look!" I pushed the newspaper toward Michael. "It's a house with a small yard for rent in Narberth near the train station. And it gets better! 'Non-smoker preferred.'"

"Give them a call," he said as he scanned the paper. "Wouldn't that be nice?"

I had lived with city noise and the crush of people since my college years at Temple University. Back then, five days a week, my commute on the subway portrayed city people as less friendly, a bit harder edged, and less likely to go out of their way for a stranger. My sophomore, abnormal psychology course agreed—bad, good, and in-between people coexisted. But the text cited multiple studies of attacks on public transportation with no onlookers offering the victims any help. Not surprising—until junior year, when my own, potentially volatile experience didn't support the research.

The "non-smoker preferred" advertisement brought the unforget-table incident to mind. All four years at Temple University, subways —non-smoking areas, dirty, graffiti-laden, dark, and dangerous—took me to class daily. A man had died of a gunshot wound at my Broad and Columbia stop during freshman year. One nippy, fall day, a trim, black man in a three-piece, tan, corduroy suit and tie boarded the subway train. "No smoking" signs glared in red print everywhere. He sat behind me. Within minutes, cigarette smoke permeated the surrounding air. I turned, glanced at the cigarette, and smiled at him. "I'm so sorry. I'm allergic to cigarette smoke." He stared at me. "Could you please put it out?" I asked, my voice soft.

His expression remained neutral. He said nothing; but the hand with the cigarette crept closer to me on the seat rail and settled imme-diately behind my head. Smoke curled upward, wafting into my face. My eyes widened in surprise. His expression never changed; his actions spoke for him. Eyes watering, breathing through my already stuffed nose, my index finger and thumb reflexively flicked the cigarette into his lap. He leapt into the aisle, swearing, and moved to the door in front of my seat, his previously handsome face unrecognizable, contorted with rage.

"I'll spit on you," he yelled and swore again. He tried. The best he could do was drool down the left side of his chin.

Seated, unafraid, I laughed at him. He stumbled as the train lurched to a stop. Still seething, he retrieved his briefcase and shouldered his way to the door of the train, at *my* stop. I waited until he left the car before I grabbed my purse and books to go. Before I got to the door, a small, dark hand gripped my arm. I looked down into clear, brown eyes and a coffee tinted face, filled with quiet humor.

"Honey, you're not getting off this train at that stop," she said in a low, pleasant voice.

It took me only an instant before I replied, "You're right. Two more blocks are not too far to walk."

She nodded, a slight smile lighting her eyes. We stood together like traveling companions, until the doors opened again. With my quick hug returned, I stepped off the train and walked two extra blocks that day. The kindness and wisdom of a petite, black woman, who listened to that still, small voice and got involved, will be remembered. *There are good people in both city and country; but perhaps I met an angel that day on the subway.*

Nearly eight years of city life passed before my spirit finally rebelled. Both Michael and I craved a quieter, open living space with trees and grass. Train fare wiggled its way into our proposed household budget as we devoured "house for rent" ads.

"Hon', we have an appointment scheduled with the owner of the Narberth property. Her name is Eleanor Wray."

A nicely-rounded, middle-aged woman met us in the driveway of a welcoming, two-story house. Her ready smile matched lively blue eyes. I liked her on sight.

After brief introductions, she said, "I live in the addition in back; the front half is the original house. Narberth is such a nice, small town." She gestured up and down Dudley Avenue. "You're two and a half blocks from the train station, have your own driveway, front and side entrances, and a nice little front yard. There's even a picket fence." She pointed to the postage stamp, front yard with a classic, white picket fence facing the front porch and door. I saw a bow window on the left side of the house by the driveway. Tingling with anticipation, I moved closer to Michael.

"This seems like a fairly quiet street," he said. "And curbside parking as well as the driveway."

Mrs. Wray nodded. "Parking's never a problem. Shall we go in?" We followed her up steps, across the generous covered porch, to the front door. The living room, an expansive, airy space, opened to the dining room through a large arch with just enough wall on either side for some separation. The dining room had space next to the bay window for a table and chairs. Shuttered with louvered folding doors, the long kitchen had hook-ups for a washer and dryer. The kitchen side door accessed the driveway.

At this point, Michael and I shared a look and hand squeeze of excitement at the sight of our new home. Two large bedrooms were more than we needed. At the top of the stairs, the dated, black and white, ceramic-tiled bathroom had an oversized tub and shower. Within a week, we signed the lease. In a month, after moving help from friends, we became commuters on the Bryn Mawr Local train line.

It took a couple of days to settle into the well-proportioned house where our furniture fit as if it belonged. I had just hung the last picture, when someone knocked on the door. Shani barked the alarm as she ran to meet and greet whoever stood on the other side: Mrs. Wray.

"Oh, look at this!" she exclaimed in surprise.

"Shani, sit!" The little Airedale sat, ears perked, eyes on me.

"I see she's very well behaved," said Mrs. Wray. "Why didn't you tell me you had a dog?"

"There was no mention of pets when we spoke—just the non-smoking."

With some guilt, I admitted the obvious. "We were afraid you wouldn't give us the lease with the pets until you got to know us a little better." I gave her a sheepish look.

Mrs. Wray reached toward Shani. "Okay," I said to the dog. She sprang to her feet, tail wagging and yipping with joy at her freedom. Shani licked the outstretched hand, and Mrs. Wray's face broke into a happy smile.

"I've been missing a dog," she said, as the three cats trooped in one at a time. "Oh, more surprises!"

"Please, come in," I said.

As soon as the door shut, Mrs. Wray knelt on the floor. Saki and Shani positioned themselves side by side, their front paws in her lap.

"Look how well they get along!" She petted each one. "My problem of missing pets is solved." She glanced around the two rooms. "The front yard is yours to plant any flowers you like. I can see by the bay window there are orchids and African violets in with your plants. You have a green thumb."

226 Dudley Avenue, Narberth, Pennsylvania. Impatiens blossomed as a border garden to the front porch, and potted tomatoes sunned themselves on the side-door stoop; they kept us stocked all summer. Mrs. Wray enjoyed the crop too.

We watched our N-scale model trains go over bridges and through miniature country sides. Our spare bedroom turned into the train room for relaxing and creating. Mrs. Wray invited us to swim and sunbathe. The inground pool took up most of her backyard. We sat and chatted, friends rather than renters and landlady.

When exuberance overflowed, Michael and I chased each other up and down the stairs, shrieking with laughter, followed by the dog who joined in the noisemaking and fun. We ran into Mrs. Wray at the mailbox the day after one such playful frolic.

"Did you invite some wild banshees over yesterday?" she asked with a mischievous smile.

"Oh, none that don't already live here," I said laughing. "We love this house! Sorry for the noise level. We got a little rowdy playing around."

She laughed. "Oh, I don't mind. I remember those days with my husband too. I'm so glad you are the ones who found the ad and rented my house!"

We probably would have stayed in Narberth longer had it not been for the Pennsylvania marriage tax. The first year we filed a joint tax return with the IRS produced a terrible shock. Uncle Sam demanded a large sum of money that made me grit my teeth. Our accountant who broke the bad news also gave us some advice: buy a house, and take out a mortgage.

Michael had changed jobs by this time. He wanted more freedom to use up-to-date treatment techniques and a broader range of experience. His last affiliation at Jefferson University Hospital had been just such an opportunity. When he applied for a job there, they hired him on the spot. Therapists at Jefferson rotated through all the different specialties within physical therapy, with top-notch educators.

Grateful for jobs we enjoyed, we thanked God for our many blessings in prayer before meals. But our free and relaxing weekends did not include Sunday Church. We hadn't completely grasped the need to be with other believers in worship—the need for Bible study and the company of others who loved the Lord. At this point, Sunday was just another day to play.

After the tax bite, we discussed home location, finances, and work. Such big decisions required thought and planning, which took time. We considered buying land versus a house on acreage. We needed a house within our price range and commuting distance to work. We let God decide where the house would be. Of all the geographic locations possible, ads in newspapers consistently took us to Chester County, Pennsylvania.

Driving around the countryside, a favorite Saturday pastime, we looked for houses or land for sale. "3.6 acres in Pughtown, $17,900, negotiable," read a *Sunday Bulletin* ad. The realtor gave us directions. The hill, more like a small mountain, on Cooks Glen Road proved too steep for our plans.

Michael turned on Saw Mill Road. Every style of house seemed represented in this wooded, hillside community. The narrow, dirt road gave way to a fine, gravel track. Every once in a while, we'd stop and look.

"What do you think of this one?" one of us would ask.

"Really nice, but not in our price range."

Nearly at the top of the hill, on the right, a little hovel surrounded by rhododendron and woods came into view. It looked like a hobbit house. We got out of the car where the blue and white sign read, "For Sale by Owner." White plaster walls with a tar paper roof kept the weather outside. The home looked hand built, by someone unfamiliar with the building trade.

The last vestiges of winter stalled a fairy garden's spring awakening. The remains of ostrich fern and tiny eruptions of lily of the valley surrounded by moss flanked a clear, quick running stream through the backyard. Any kind of running water made me think of the river where I was raised.

Big slates of varying size approached the front door. The owners, Mr. and Mrs. Miller, invited us in. A brief look gave us the first impression of a tiny place, heated toasty warm by wood burning stoves on a chilly March day. Curtains instead of doors cordoned off two bedrooms. The lot measured 150' x 82,' all for $11,000. We thanked the Millers and took their phone number.

"The house is not well built. We'd have to install a shingle roof," Michael said as we discussed the property. "I'll bet it's on a floodplain too."

"You're probably right," I said. "It was dark and cramped inside, but I love the location."

"Me too." After thinking for a minute, he said, "Let's talk to Fred."

The next day, we went back to the hobbit house with Fred, a fellow alumnus of Michael's Neshaminy High School days. He had a degree in engineering.

"This is a large undertaking for a first home," Fred said. "If you wanted a hillside get-away, second house, it would be perfect. Otherwise, the lot's too small," he said.

His assessment of the house and lot rang true. We crossed the hobbit house off our list, knowing that God had the perfect place already in mind. *It would be in His timing.*

26

GOD'S TIMING

"If the Lord delights in us, then He will bring us into this land, and give it to us, a land which flows with milk and honey."
— *Numbers* 14:8

ON A BREEZY, April day in 1977, the Bryn Mawr Local rattled its way toward Philadelphia. Michael had the newspaper turned to the "Homes for Sale" ads. As I watched the passing scenery, I felt him sit straighter in his seat, as we swayed with the train's motion.

"Look at this," he said, moving closer so I could see the paper. "Home for sale, 2 bdr, 2 acres, porch and pool, Chstr Spgs."

"Chester Springs with two acres," I read, my attention focused. "Wow, there's a dream, huh?" I looked at Michael.

"We have to look at this. That's close to your mom and Fell, right?" he asked.

"It's next door to Kimberton where I went to high school. It's a great area; actually, it's perfect!"

"We'll need money for a good down payment. We don't have enough for that and the settlement," he said.

"Dad said when we first started house hunting that we could

borrow $5,000 from him. Let's look at it before we take on second jobs!" Michael smiled in agreement and handed over the intriguing ad. As soon as I got to work, I made an appointment for Saturday with the realtor.

I called Dad at lunch. He listened to my excited description of the property. Without small talk or conversation, he said, "Violet, I decided to marry Carrie Anne. I just bought her a $5,000 engagement ring and a $750 wedding band, so I can't help you right now."

He said it without apology, remorse, or even mild regret.

Blindsided, I managed, "Right, Dad. Thanks." I hung up, too angry not to vent. I dialed Mom, still in the home where I was raised and grew roots near the Schuylkill River, the template of perfect real estate for Michael and me. Because we were renting, Mom and Fell's place, and Michael's parents' place still claimed the name "home" for both of us.

Fell answered the phone. I told him what happened. "We have an appointment to see it Saturday; but there's no use going. I could just spit, I'm so mad!"

"Of course you should go see the place. We'll help you out," he said as if there was never any question.

"Oh, Daddy, thanks! That's amazing! I've got to get back to work right now, but I'll let you know what we find."

I had called to talk to Mom, never expecting help from her. Everyone could see how much she and Fell loved each other, both making up for lost time. But Fell's offer— done without thinking, without pause—spoke of a father who really cherished his kids. Fell had just treated me like his own daughter, and it melted my heart.

I wrote down the address the realtor gave us, so we could look at the land and the home's exterior. Saturday turned out to be a warm, crystal clear, sunny day—ideal for a drive in the country.

"These directions are wrong," I said, hunched over the hand-written page. "It's not a left on Yellow Springs, it's a right."

After a quick U-turn, we crossed Route 113 and found the sale sign. The inclined driveway with woods on both sides gave no sign of a house, until we approached the steepest part of the hill. A field opened on the right with a tiny house set deep into the hillside, with a backdrop of forest on the north and east sides. A dirty, in ground pool out front had no cover.

Rutted, dirt, and gravel, the driveway turned right off a common lane. Straight ahead led to a house on the hilltop with a hand-carved sign in a garden below: *"AERIE." An eagle's nest. What a great name for a house perched up high*, I thought. The empty driveway ended near "our" house. We clocked an eighth of a mile from the main road, all uphill.

I rolled my window down and listened. An occasional whirring of insects, birds singing, and wind in the trees refreshed me. The cooing of a turtle dove and wind in pine trees brought my childhood home to mind. It had been an ideal environment to be a child—bare-foot in the grass, climbing trees, and riding bikes at break-neck speed through the woods. I always assumed I would have kids; and I wanted a baby. But I married Michael knowing he didn't want children. It would be a mutual decision—or nothing.

We wandered over the property, across the lane, down a deer trail, and back to the pool—full of leaves, algae, toads, frogs, and tadpoles—a stagnant pond in cement. Chairs in the grass by the cement pool deck each had a standing ashtray on a stem stuck in the ground, like a bizarre flower gone wrong. It looked like they had been there all winter. Beer cans had been tossed in the now-dead weeds below the pool. *How strange*, I thought, *to have a piece of Eden and neglect it like this.*

The tiny house sprung up from the hillside against a backdrop of tall trees—two-stories, white, asbestos shingles, a box with black shutters and lattice-work windows—like a Swiss chalet. A wrap-around deck hugged the west and south sides with a west-facing front door. We peered in windows and saw hardwood floors in the living room, three cots, and a few chairs—like a summer camp dorm room.

Looking at the grounds from the deck two stories up felt like a treehouse view. Two acres, bordered by woods and a semi-isolated location fit our long-term vision. The house would work, short-term, until we could afford an addition.

"We've got to get Daddy up here, now! This will be sold in a heartbeat."

"Let's go," said Michael.

Chattering like a pair of guinea hens with excitement, we arrived at Mom's and Fell's door in a blink. Daddy looked down from a ladder, paintbrush in hand. I nearly pulled him off balance in my excitement.

"You've got to come and see this house *now*! We have to put an offer in fast, before someone else buys it!"

"It's priced to sell," Michael added. "It's a real find."

Mom and Fell followed us. They stopped just after coming up the hill in sight of the house. When they pulled into the driveway, I ran to Fell as he unraveled his six-foot frame from the station wagon. He turned in a circle, hand shielding his eyes from the sunlight—360 degrees of green without another house in sight. Fell whistled in appreciation. Then we inspected the house: cheaply built, the washer and dryer stuck in the cellar with no stairs in sight, a true handy man's special. The pool looked to be in good shape other than neglect. Two acres of prime land in this area made sweat equity worthwhile.

Mom told me later that Fell and she decided after they came up over the rise and the house came into view. She said that Fell stopped the car for a minute, turned to her, and said, "We can't let the kids miss out on this place!"

We saw the house with Mr. Mayor, the realtor, and offered $2,000 under the asking price. Entrance to the laundry in the basement required a walk outside down a hilly, dirt path. The basement door hid under the deck facing south down the hill. The deck needed to be replaced.

Only one other party scheduled to see the house. Now the waiting game began for acceptance or rejection of our bid. I could still see the green expanse of unbroken, woodland backdrop and the tiny jewel of a house set in the hillside. If we got this house, by some act of God, we would never need to move again.

On May 4, we received a phone call from the realtor. "The home-owner's bargaining. She wants $2,500 more than your bid." We kept our offer the same.

Five days later, I called Mr. Mayer. "The owner wants $1,000 more than you offered; but she'll throw in the beer fridge in the base-ment and the riding mower," he said.

"We'll call you right back," I said, Michael at my elbow, holding his breath.

I called Fell, who said, "Go for it!"

We phoned Mr. Mayer again and changed our lives with three words: "We'll take it." Michael grinned beside me.

"It's yours, once I receive the check," he said with a smile in his voice. I hung up. Michael grabbed me, and we danced around the living room, whooping and shouting with joy.

On Wednesday, May 11, Daddy gave us a check, and the realtor came for the final signing of the revised Agreement of Sale. "Just a couple of signatures left," Mr. Mayer said. "The owner already signed."

"I'm surprised there was only one other person seriously looking at the property," I commented.

Mr. Mayer looked up from the paperwork. "I didn't mention it? There *was* another buyer: a builder, who wanted to put 40 percent down, cash."

"What happened to him?" Michael asked.

"Within a week, he got a call from the company he worked for. He took a job transfer to California for a big raise. End of deal." Mr. Mayer chuckled. "You two have some angels watching over you."

We needed those angels again. Neither Michael nor I had estab-lished a good credit history. Other than purchasing a new Subaru station wagon, we had no major purchases to earn a solid credit rating as first-time home buyers. All the major banks in our area refused us a mortgage.

"Let me see what I can do," said Mr. Mayer. He also gave us the estimate for closing costs, more expensive than we expected.

The time for moonlighting had come. The Hospital of the University of Pennsylvania hired us for chest physical therapy, with a start date two days later. We worked Monday and Wednesday nights and every other weekend. In between, Michael, Shani, and I drove to Chester Springs, sat on the grass, and looked longingly at "our house" from the far corner of the property.

In two months, Mr. Mayer found a mortgage for us. Settlement, scheduled on September 15, 1977, gave us time to earn our closing costs. My lawyer friend, Amy, helped me once again, this time with the legal end of our settlement. "I'll have to do a crash review of real estate law. I'm more familiar with drug busts," she said with a cackle.

We kept the grueling work schedule and squirreled away money. On September 14, 1977, Amy spent the night with us. Settlement felt like we signed our lives away, as Amy read through the legalese, and we placed our signatures on multiple pages. By 10:00 a.m., September 15, we became homeowners—and Amy came to see our new house.

As tiny as we remembered it, we paid for the grounds and woods —and it felt like my family home. Lower Pine Creek paralleled Yellow Springs Road at the bottom of the common lane. No dusty, river road wandered by; but the same wildlife roamed on our hill that had lived in the silt basins. A "Garden of Eden" feeling, surrounded by nature, made us stand still. And then came familiar sounds: wind in evergreen trees and doves cooing, with a wood thrush trilling in the background.

We owned a piece of God's creation to live on, as long as He allowed, with His help—all in His perfect timing.

27

EDEN HILL

"Through wisdom a house is built,
And by understanding it is established;
By knowledge the rooms are filled
With all precious and pleasant riches..."
— Proverbs 24:3–4

EXHAUSTION DID NOT ADEQUATELY DESCRIBE the way I felt. Michael's look mirrored my own. Fell and Mom left us in our repainted home just after I finished scrubbing layers of grease off the kitchen cabinets. The first overnight stay—in our own, fully-mortgaged, dollhouse-sized home—came at the price of comfort. Sleeping bags rolled out on the floor looked inviting. Bed frame assembly proved too much for our fatigued bodies.

Michael waved a legal-sized page at me. "Here's the mortgage," he said, trying to sound lighthearted.

We sat on the floor together under a lamp on a bedside table, looking at the price of the house and amount paid at the end of a thirty-year mortgage. I reread the figures and realized I read them correctly the first time. At 9 percent, the end amount paid totaled multiples of the house's price. Shaken, I went to the bathroom and brushed my teeth. Michael folded the mortgage papers.

"That's a bit of a shock," he said.

"To put it mildly. Did you expect it to be that expensive?"

"No." He put a hand on my shoulder and moved me sideways, as he reached for his toothbrush. We couldn't both fit in the bitty bathroom. With a quick kiss goodnight, I gave Michael room to brush his teeth. Even though a job interview coming up cried for my attention, our newly inhabited house held my thoughts captive.

We crawled into our sleeping bags, too tired to do anything requiring consciousness. As I mentally revisited the condition, size of the house, and overwhelming total payment, I wondered, *Did we make a terrible mistake?* But our inked signatures on the mortgage proved, mistake or not, *obligation and ownership.* I cried myself to sleep.

Five days before my interview for chief physical therapist at Southern Chester County Medical Center (SCCMC), Dr. Derry asked to see me. The respected chief of staff at Magee showed me to a chair and came to the point.

"I understand you're applying for a position at Southern Chester County Medical Center under Cameron O'Brian, the physiatrist there."

"Yes, at the end of this week."

"I know you're a fine therapist. This is a wonderful opportunity. But I also know Cameron O'Brian very well. When you go for the interview, make sure you have a solid list of questions about your benefits and hours. Above all, get *everything* in writing."

The intense look in Dr. Derry's eyes as he spoke flagged the importance of our discussion. His advice sounded a trumpet of concern and caring. Dr. Derry's warning heralded serious consequences if ignored.

"I'm so glad you told me. I will have a very complete list of questions for him. Do you know the hospital at all?"

"Not really, other than it's quite small, and Barry Cade is CEO. He's young and talented, from what I hear. It sounds like a good fit for you. Just get all your Is dotted and your Ts crossed. After your interview, would you let me know how you made out?" Dr. Derry asked like a grandfather.

"Of course! And thanks so much for the heads up!"

My odometer clocked thirty-two miles away from our house to SCCMC, one way. But, after Route 30 Bypass and a bit of Coatesville, God's rural countryside encompassed me.

I found Dr. O'Brian's office on the second floor of the medical office building.

"Well, so nice to meet you at last," he said. "How about a quick tour before our meeting, and then I'll treat you to lunch at the hospital cafeteria."

The hospital glowed—spotless, impressive in cleanliness. Dr. O'Brian made a cursory introduction to Barry Cade—wavy brown hair, snapping brown eyes, only a few years older than me. The physical therapy department—one large room with three whirlpools and three curtained booths—boasted the same thorough housekeeping seen in the hospital corridors. The usual electrical equipment appeared in good shape. A nice-sized desk faced the far wall. Parallel bars on a wooden base stood between the desk and whirlpools. Finally, three high treatment tables, called plinths, furnished each curtained booth. My new department needed nothing else to function well. Only one drawback: in the cheerful, single-room department with candy-striped curtains, no windows looked out or allowed natural light in. Fluorescent light replaced the sun with no options. *Oh, well...*

"Could I see the policies and procedures manual?"

"Ah, that will be part of your job. There isn't one," Dr. O'Brian said in a breezy manner and changed the subject.

"How much vacation and sick time is included?"

"Oh, you just tell me when you need some time off, and it will all work out. And sick time, you're young and healthy! You're not going to get sick!"

"I never heard of a policy like that. I'll need specifics and everything in writing regarding my job description and benefits. If you are to be my boss, I'll need the agreement, signed by you."

"I knew you were the one for the job the minute I laid eyes on you," he said. "You're thorough; but this would be an informal arrangement."

Dr. Derry had been an angel to prepare me for this snake oil salesman. I thanked Dr. O'Brian and politely declined his offer of a hospital cafeteria lunch. I told him I couldn't take the job under those circumstances. He blew more hot air at me for the next five minutes, until he realized I wouldn't be swayed. We agreed he would phone me when he had a proposal ready in writing.

A whisper spoke deep inside me: *talk to the CEO before you leave.* In the past, when I ignored that still, small voice, I invariably found regret. To my relief, Barry Cade seemed anxious to talk to me. In his office, I explained my problem.

"SCCMC and the beautiful country setting are calling my name; but I can't take the job with Dr. O'Brian."

"Ah, I see," said Cade after I explained the circumstances. "I think we can come to an agreement with you as a hospital employee. You will report directly to me as a department head and director of physical therapy." He thought for a moment. "There's only one problem. You have no executive experience."

"Well, that's a problem we can work around," I said smiling. "If you don't like the job I'm doing in three months, I'll resign." He laughed out loud and nodded approval.

Barry Cade and I discussed my upcoming employment and the hospital's needs like old, compatible, work acquaintances. Considering the lack of PT policies and procedures, he added to the salary and benefits associated with the job. Then, he included a raise in salary at the end of three months. I stood—feeling young for this honor, controlling my rejoicing and excitement with a tight rein—and shook his hand. I walked out of SCCMC as the future department head of physical therapy, drove out of the parking lot onto the quiet country road, and whooped at the top of my lungs.

I thanked Dr. Derry the minute I returned to work at Magee.

"Barry Cade is a good egg," he said with obvious relief.

Garnet Schiller gave a cool but appropriate response when I tendered my three weeks' notice. Giddy with excitement, I bought a new work wardrobe complete with a white lab coat. This job demanded some changes.

"Surprise!" the gang shrieked. I gasped, shocked for a minute at the familiar Magee faces, all gathered to say goodbye to me. Cake, punch, and good-natured teasing about me being a *department head* set a happy tone. I left Magee with fond memories and a lasting friendship with Margo, the assistant chief PT. Magee Memorial Hospital had branded me, forever, with the true, profound identity and knowledge of physical therapy I would use for the rest of my career.

Although Michael loved his work at Jefferson, daily drives on the Schuylkill Expressway forced him to look for another job. He resigned after signing on as a staff PT with Coatesville Hospital. We carpooled together—no trains in Chester Springs—and made the shoe-box-sized house our haven.

The house purchase transported us home to country life: digging in the moist, dark-chocolate earth that smelled of beginnings and endings; planting asparagus, tomatoes, potatoes, Chinese pea pods, onions—and bordering the garden with marigolds as a rabbit repellant. On the hill together after work—in our own personal Garden of Eden, a retreat from the world—I named the place God gave us, "Eden Hill." We learned to live in and love the thirteen-hundred square feet of space.

As winter blew in that snowy year of 1977, we found some obvious flaws in our mortgaged treasure. By late November, our front-wheel-drive car's wheels spun with no grip on the road, over layers of wet leaves or more than one inch of snow. On those days, parked at the bottom, we hoofed the eighth of a mile to the house. With a record snowfall that first year on "Eden Hill," we trudged our way to a level of fitness unknown since high school sports.

Our electric lines hung on poles through woods from Yellow Springs Road to our yard, before they dove underground to the house. Any strong wind brought branches down with the lines. We left work early one snowy December day and found a cold, dark house. The power stayed out for three days. Candles provided our only source of heat and light, besides bundling in ski clothes with all the animals huddled in bed; my orchids and African violets also survived in the bedroom with us. Snowed in, we had no choice but to wait until the storm sighed and moved on. Through the winter, our savings account for a four-wheel-drive vehicle grew in a small but consistent way.

"We've got to do something about the power going out," Michael said. "We can get by with candles for light, but we can't deal with this cold." He snapped his fingers. "A wood stove would fix everything." I started researching the next day.

By spring, with Dad Batejan's expertise, we installed an airtight wood stove that could heat the whole house. A brick hearth and fire-proofed walls with floor-to-ceiling brick in the living room corner housed the stove, shaped like a rounded pyramid with three legs. A fireplace screen allowed us to watch the brilliant, leaping flames. Clever design made the stove door open and retract, or close in airtight mode for maximum heating.

After cutting logs with the chainsaw, Michael's sledgehammer, wedge, and axe rang out and split logs into burnable pieces. Heat radiating from the wood stove warmed me with a glow like the summer sun in July. As oil became more expensive, and our pleasure grew in the wood stove's satisfying heat, we chose wood heat most of the time. It took us another year to purchase a four-wheel-drive Subaru that would make it up the hill in most conditions. Our new hearth warmed us with or without electricity. Oil always heated our hot water—and occasionally, the house.

Cosseted in God's gifts, both house and jobs, we wanted for nothing. We began searching for a Christian church, having recognized our need to worship within the community where our roots would grow deep and wide. The time for corporate meditation on God and His Word had arrived. For now, we worshipped together each Sunday with our Bibles and devotional. Our faith in Jesus Christ brought Michael's Romanian Orthodox upbringing and my Lutheran background together. *God drew us closer, and His perfect timing continued to reign.*

28

WITH CHILD

"As you do not know what is the way of the wind, or how the bones grow in the womb of her who is with child, So you do not know the works of God who makes everything."
—*Ecclesiastes* 11:5

FOR THE PRESENT, Michael's Coatesville Hospital job contented him professionally and financially. At SCCMC, as the patient population grew, I needed an aide to free me for physical therapy treatment and assist me with patients who required the help of two people.

Barry Cade set patient visit goals that sped to achievement. Faye Harris, LPN, came aboard as my physical therapy aide. Of three applicants for the job, Faye won the position with ease. Older, wiser, with more life experience under her belt, Faye's LPN degree had earned her a place on the nursing staff at Southern Chester County Medical Center, where I had first met her. She made a smooth and welcome transition to my department. As a woman of color, she embodied my belief that intellect and goodness had no external markers. Her common sense and compassion led the way, while her knowledge of the nursing department helped me appreciate problems faced by the staff.

"Come on, Vi," Faye said. "You have one patient at a time, and the nurses and aides up there have a bunch. Don't melt down on them because they lost track of your schedule."

"Well, how am I going to keep a schedule in PT?" I asked.

"Why don't I call fifteen minutes before we're ready so the patient's waiting, and I can bring them down. Transport can take them back to the floor."

I looked at her in admiration. "Woman, what would I do without you?"

"Probably put your foot in it." We laughed together.

Faye's plan smoothed out all of our scheduling difficulties. Every once in a while, she played my "Dutch Aunt" when impatience or arrogance arrested my spirit.

"Vi, you jumped all over Harriet because that patient wasn't ready. Did you know her mother died three days ago? She nearly cried when you walked out the door. She won't be real forgiving, if you don't apologize."

Faye's tirade stopped me, openmouthed. I closed my jaw, thought for a minute, nodded, and returned to the nursing floor. Harriet accepted my heartfelt apology and sympathy. She smiled when I told her I felt like an idiot for making such a fuss.

The nickname "Vi" had never felt right to me. Normally, I corrected people. Yet, it sounded fine coming from Faye, the only person in the world who got away with it. We worked as a team throughout my employment at the country hospital, and I thoroughly enjoyed her company.

Treating inpatients, outpatients, and bedside patients as well as eating in the cafeteria allowed me to meet all the hospital staff and many people in the community. Department head meetings, held once a month, gave me a platform to watch each department cell function as an integral part of the larger hospital organism. We belonged to the SCCMC family, creating a feeling typically unknown in larger hospitals. *I felt at home.*

Though everyone knew me as a PT, the cafeteria's salad bar snagged my claim to fame at SCCMC. Yellow, over-cooked broccoli raised its limp head in my world, once again. I wanted a fresh salad with my lunch. The idea of a petition seemed like a good one. I collected signatures from all the departments and made an appointment with Barry Cade.

At first, he appeared upset. "A petition! You're going behind my back with a petition?" An uncharacteristic hint of anger sounded.

"Oh, no!" I said, regrouping. "It's a *show of interest.* How else could I know if other people wanted a salad bar too? I wouldn't waste your time without a true show of interest!"

That stopped him. He took his time and looked at the long list of names.

"Hmmm. Actually..." Barry picked up a pen and added his name to the list. "I'd like a salad bar myself."

In three weeks, a gleaming, stainless steel and glass salad bar stood in the dining room. I happily put together a chef's salad from the ample array of choices and sat down. As soon as I sat, everyone at my table looked at me, pointed to something over my head, and roared with laughter. I turned to Faye in confusion.

"You didn't see it, did you, Vi?" She pointed to a paper banner taped to the salad bar's overhead cover behind me. It read: "The Violet Batejan Memorial Salad Bar." The whole dining room broke into laughter; I had missed the sign with eight-inch-high letters.

"Wow," I said grinning as I scanned familiar, faces. "And I'm not even dead yet!"

SCCMC lay thirty-two miles south of our home. Once past Coatesville, back roads took me the rest of the forty-five-minute drive. Homes, pastures, horses, riding rings, and fields of corn, wheat, and soybeans checkered the landscape. In the spring, brood mares and foals gamboled about their pastures and paddocks. Amazed at the life

I lived, contemplation and prayer became my habit on Fern Hill Road, my favorite shortcut toward Rt 796. Populated with large horse farms and forest groves, peace reigned—and life, rooted in prayer, flourished. When I passed wooded areas and fields, I often prayed, "Lord, guard the little animals. Please keep them safe and clear of my car!" From mice to deer crossed my path—by His grace, never in danger, only enjoyed.

One afternoon on my way home, I spotted a small flash of color on the side of the road in my rearview mirror. I stopped and watched a kestrel with a late lunch in his talons. Preoccupied, he didn't fly, as I backed up for a better view. The multicolored feathers of the male falcon shone in the sun. Slate blue-gray capped his head and extended down with some white stripes for added decoration. Wings tapered into black, flight feathers. Bright, rusty brown filled in between his wings; tail and back stippled in black, his breast displayed black dots and a softer rust color. I sat enthralled with the small falcon, who ignored me and feasted. I left before he flew. The glow of God's unique and unmatched palette of colors worn by the kestrel with easy grace stayed with me, imprinted in my memory for easy access whenever I need reminders of magnificence.

During the three blessed years at SCCMC, Michael and I talked occasionally about having children. I wanted a baby with this man I adored and called husband. He knew I wanted to hold his child in my arms. There were times I cried, hidden from view and out of Michael's hearing.

But he knew. One cold, March night, he whispered as he held me close, "Let's have a baby." I needed no convincing.

Three months later, the girls in the lab brought the results of my pregnancy test to PT in person. They couldn't hide their excitement. I raised my eyebrows in a silent question, and they both nodded *yes* together. We did an abbreviated dance of joy and hugged before we went back to work. I called Michael and told him, "God answered our prayers." He came home with a delicate bud vase painted with blue flowers that looked so real I wanted to smell their fragrance. *What more could I want?*

Michael and I had long conversations about my leaving SCCMC and being a full-time mother until the baby reached two. We discussed our present jobs. It would be tight financially on one salary. Within a week of our good news, I made an appointment with Barry Cade. His secretary waved me into Barry's office. I sat in the familiar chair that faced his organized, uncluttered desk.

"I have some good news," I said.

"Good news is always welcome."

"Michael and I are having a baby," I said with a big grin.

He congratulated me, but before he could say any more, I continued, "But I have some good news for you too!"

Now, he looked curious. "Really?"

"I'm planning on becoming a full-time mom for at least two years; so, I will be resigning as of a week before my due date, which I don't have yet."

"That's my good news?"

"Nope. The good news is, I found my replacement." I paused for a long second. "Michael is interested in the job."

"Now, that *is* good news!" he said smiling. "We will still have to advertise the job, but I've met Michael several times. He's not an unknown quantity." He looked down, then back at me. "You, by the way, are his best reference."

Other than normal hormone changes, I felt wonderful during my pregnancy. I had one unusual side effect. For breakfast, I always made two soft-boiled eggs on crumbled, buttered toast. As the spoon cut into the soft egg, yellow yolk oozed out over the toast. Without warning, I gagged. Eyes closed, I waited until the storm in my stomach calmed. I sat still for several minutes. Then, without looking at my carefully prepared breakfast, I picked up the bowl and placed it on the floor in front of Shani. The perky Airedale snarfed down my favorite breakfast in less than a minute. Avoiding eggs became a minor inconvenience.

Violet & Mike Batejan, L.P.T.

Southern Chester County Medical Center--New Beginnings.

Nothing stopped me from working normally or preparing for our new arrival. The baby's room, done in textured paint, shone with a pale yellow. Mom gave us a walnut stained cradle, cut from plywood, sturdy, and well made with a heart cut into the head and footboard. All the wood furniture had a dark stain that complemented the yellow walls. The nursery lit my face in a smile, a kingdom all its own.

My drive continued as a time of decompression between work, with pressures that affected even the best of jobs, and home, our respite from the world. Summer green turned to fall colors, which fell as time moved the seasons and us forward in time. Saturated with anticipation and happy preparation, we revolved, contented, in our own fairy tale world. A new deck hung on the west side of the house. The pool—winterized, with a cover to keep the water clean three of the four seasons—would not be open yet when our child arrived in March. The baby's room progressed toward completion, until only the curtains were missing.

As snow season came and went, Michael and I bandied names about, sure of "Michael" for a boy. So far, no girl's names surfaced without one of us making a sour face. The baby turned, somersaulted, punched, and kicked. *Probably a linebacker,* I thought as I watched my abdomen roll from side to side. My little one added twenty-five pounds to my petite frame, as pregnancy approached full-term. I set a resignation date, and suddenly, it was time to leave.

My fellow staff members at SCCMC gave me a great send-off and baby shower. Thoughtful gifts, some handmade and intricately crafted, left no doubt of the love and best wishes each represented. I left my fulfilling job two weeks before our baby's St. Patrick's Day due date. Michael took over as department head in *"my"* physical therapy department. Our hearts brimmed, ready to blossom with new life in our *home sweet home.*

The Lord moved the seasons toward spring. Purple and white crocuses poked toward the earth's sun-warmed surface early in March. *All gifts came from God, our generous Good Shepherd; Michael and I waited with unsurpassed excitement.*

29

NEW LIFE COMING

"By humility and fear of the Lord Are riches and honor and life."
— *Proverbs 22:4*

I HELD the curtains in my hand with the sales slip from Strawbridge's. The baby's room shone bright with afternoon sun, although a coating of snow covered the ground outside the window. Feeling satisfied, I tore the plastic open and felt the poly-cotton fabric, while admiring the eyelet embroidery. Orange, rust, yellow, and red embroidered flowers bordered a chocolate ruffle, with the body of the café curtains done in off-white. They were the only curtains in a large selection that I could picture hanging in the sun-lit baby's room.

As I admired the freshly dressed windows, a sudden realization dawned. With ruffles and eyelet embroidery, these curtains reflected *a little girl's room*. I thought, throughout most of my pregnancy, that I carried a lively boy. I had been calling "him" my little "linebacker." But it appeared, if my choice of curtains was a harbinger of the future, that a little girl—who still had no name—fooled us.

That evening, I showed Michael the completed room with the crisp, new curtains. A wind-up, primary-colored mobile hung over the walnut-brown crib. Pictures of cunning, little animals dressed in clothes decorated the walls—my favorite, a mother mouse, babies tucked in a row, as she hung out the wash. The rich mahogany frame set off the cheerful, colored, metallic foil which formed the figures and background.

"So, my love, what is the first thing you notice?" I asked Michael.

He surveyed the room with a pleased look and said, "It's perfect for the baby."

I nodded. "Yes, but which baby?"

He wrinkled his brow.

"A boy or a girl?" I asked.

He looked at the well-appointed room once again and, gradually, his face registered surprise.

"Ohhhh, we better pick a name for a girl!"

After I explained the Lord's hand in my trip to Strawbridge's, we went through the whole list of girl's names during dinner. Only one name suited both of us: *Jessica.*

Six days after I left SCCMC, I awakened filled with energy and anticipation. Chores flew to completion. Folded cloth diapers next to newborn disposables filled the shelf under the changing table. Four letters, stamped and sealed, finished my correspondence. Hungry after writing, I prepared a chicken sandwich paired nicely with chicken gumbo soup. The Campbell's Soup I had grown up eating tasted of okra and tomatoes, rich and hot. Dishes cleared; sun streamed through the window. Nearing mid-March, a walk would feel good.

I immersed myself in the clean, damp, earthy scent of impending spring and meandered along Yellow Springs Road. The Standard-bred stallion perked his ears and left the early, spring grass. He nuzzled my jacket, asking for carrots and apples. I didn't disappoint him.

By the time I trudged up our long lane, I had walked a mile, round trip. Pleasantly tired, I stretched out on the living room couch, covered with a small quilt, and napped.

An odd dampness awakened me an hour and a half later. *Five o'clock.* Michael would be home in an hour. I sat up, and water gushed. I stopped the flow with my hand. In the bathroom, I captured some of the fluid to describe it to the ob-gyn. It looked clear with some lacey membranes floating about. The answering service took my number. Dr. Connors was on call.

Of all the four doctors I saw, Connors ranked last on my list. I stressed to each of the MDs that I wanted perineal massage to avoid an episiotomy. Dr. Connors appeared bored and said, "I'll make a note of that."

Birthing classes prepared Michael and me for labor and delivery, *hypothetically.* My well-being hinged on Michael's presence. I didn't care if Dr. Connors made it or not. I expected my athletic, flexible body to sail through these uncharted waters.

The phone rang. "Hello, Dr. Connors here," a cheery voice said. "I hear we're having a baby tonight."

"I don't have any contractions yet. The amniotic fluid is clear, but is it supposed to have bits of tissue floating in it?"

"That's perfectly normal. Any pain?"

"No. I don't have any symptoms at all."

"Still perfectly normal. If you don't begin contractions in twelve hours, call me, and we'll induce you. If contractions start, come in when they're five minutes apart. Now, relax and I'll see you tonight; we'll have some fun!" He disconnected.

Michael sounded like his usual, unflappable self when I called. "Okay, hon', I'm on my way. How are you doing?"

"I'm fine; no need to hurry."

My pre-packed baby bag waited on the living room couch. I scanned our peaceful, well-loved house—so small, every room could be seen from the hall outside the bathroom. I memorized the way it felt, the silence, the two-person home growing to a family home of three. I prayed and assumed the pretty, ruffled curtains foreshadowed a little girl's arrival.

Dear Lord,
Bless this child of love, that she may thrive and prosper,
That she may walk in Your ways, all the days of her life,
And dwell in Your house forever.
Bless Michael and me with Your wisdom, love, and patience
As our world changes through Your precious gift of life.
Keep me focused on Your light, Michael's love, and bring her into the
world safely.
Bless the three of us as a family, my Lord.
In Jesus Name, Amen.

The first contraction stopped me in mid stride. Movement paused, as my body took over—squeezing, clamping down, contracting—then gone. When my breathing and ability to walk returned to normal, I checked my watch. In five minutes, the sequence repeated. Michael came home, loaded my bag in the car, and we met the OB nurse in the office.

"We're going to have a baby tonight," she said. "You're doing great with the contractions. Stay here until you dilate a little more. Then I'll send you across the street to the hospital; you're at 4 centimeters now. I called Dr. Conners. First babies take a little longer, so he'll get here in time." I nodded, breathing through another contraction.

Why don't the contractions hurt? I thought. *Thank you, Lord!* They were intensely focused on pushing the baby toward the waiting world. *It's like being paralyzed with my mind clear and body on autopilot.* In another hour, at 6 centimeters, we started out for the hospital.

In the parking lot, Michael joked, "You know, we're so close; it's just across the street. You wanna walk?" Knees bent, breathing through a strong, prolonged contraction, I eyeballed him with a stabbing stare. My look rocked him back a step; he regrouped with grace. Arm around me like a brace, he held me close and waited. When movement returned to my legs, he helped me to the car.

The hospital staff shuttled Michael to another room to change into scrubs. A hospital room masked in everyday furniture, the birthing room was furnished with comfortable chairs, a couch, a recliner, and a hospital bed which I crawled into with gratitude. *Good to lie down,* I thought, relieved.

Inability to move increased for longer periods of time. Focus centered on breath, contractions, and communion with Jessica. *You are loved, little one. I'll be holding you soon.* Between each intense, downward press, speech occurred in brief phrases that died down to monosyllables. "Put your right hand into the sleeve...that's it. Let's get this gown straightened out...good." I shivered in the chilly birthing room. A warm blanket descended over my chest, abdomen, and arms. "There, dear. That's better, isn't it?" In slow motion, I searched for the nurse's face, saw her smile, and nodded. Contractions intensified, Michael still absent.

"I want to push," I grunted to the nurse. "HUSBAND!"

She did a quick examination, and a shocked look widened her eyes. Wheeling, she hollered, on the run, "Page Dr. Connors. Get her husband in here STAT!"

Back at my side, she spoke quietly to me. "You can't push yet; I know it's hard not to, but we have to wait a little bit. You're going through transition. You can't push until you're more dilated."

"HUSBAND," I said with a hard look. I didn't care about the doctor. I needed Michael.

Michael walked through the door, still pulling on his scrub shirt. Speaking softly, he took my hand. My world corrected. I grabbed his hand and focused on his eyes. Transition felt like exponential hyper-sensitivity, my mind unsettled, helpless—my body uncomfortable but programed and doing its job without any volitional assistance. *How strange!* I thought, disjointed, unreality edging in. Michael's face held me in the present—real, loved, supported. I wanted to tell him, *Stop breathing on my face; it's driving me crazy!* But my tongue didn't work, speech no longer an option. My eyes and face communicated. Michael breathed with me, coaching. But each time he exhaled, his breath brushed my hypersensitive face. I exhaled on his face and shook my head. Within two breaths, he had it, gave a tiny smile, and turned his face slightly away from mine without breaking eye contact. Short-lived relief transitioned to, "No, dear, you can't push yet. Just breathe. The doctor's here, getting into his scrubs." She patted my forehead with a cool, damp washcloth. *Lord, I feel you. I still don't have any real pain! How can this be, after all the terrible stories I heard about labor and delivery?*

The door opened. Dr. Conners came in. "Okay." He clapped his hands and rubbed his palms together. "Let's see where we are." He lifted the sheet. Calf supports and stirrups cradled my legs. "You have some pushing to do before this baby sees the light of day," he said.

As quickly as I progressed through labor, pushing went on, and on. The monitor showed contractions, cueing Michael and the nurse to help me sit halfway up, so I could push with gravity and muscles assisting the baby's slow exit. In between bearing down with all of my might, I slept. "All right, we're crowning. One episiotomy coming up, and we'll have a baby before you know it!"

I wanted to scream at him. *What happened to "massage to ease the baby out" like I had requested of you when I could talk?* But things happened too quickly now. With a few more pushes, "It's a girl!"

Welcome to the world, Jessica.

"Come on, Dad. You can cut the umbilical cord." The doctor handed Michael the scissors.

I saw Jessica for a minute, before the nurse took her to be cleaned up, weighed, and assessed in general. A ruddy little thing, she had a good healthy cry, ten fingers, ten toes, and a thick shock of brown hair. Michael and I held hands and smiled at each other, as we gazed at our daughter.

Birthing the placenta surprised me with more pain than bearing the baby. I felt the episiotomy stitches; but by then, I held Jessica, the most beautiful, wanted, baby girl ever born. Michael petted my hair and stared at his daughter. Born at 9:28 p.m. she weighed five pounds, thirteen ounces, and measured nineteen inches long. The nurse reported the information and wrapped Jessica in a blanket. The staff transferred me to a room to rest, and Jessica came with me in her clear plastic bassinette on wheels.

With a kiss and hug, my exhausted husband went home. Jessica rooted, making sucking motions with her baby mouth. She latched on and nursed, melting any anxiety I felt about problems breastfeeding. Transferring the sleepy baby from my arms to her bassinet, the night nurse said, "Get some sleep, Mom. Rest up here while you can." She rolled the bassinet to the nursery. Eyes closed, comfortable lying down without the weight of a baby, my body felt like leaping for joy. *We had a daughter.* Labor and delivery took three and a half hours without anesthesia, so I would recover quickly.

A thousand thoughts went through my adrenaline-laced brain. The nurse gave me good advice; but my wired mind couldn't sleep. Two hours later, still wide awake, I heard Jess crying.

"My baby's crying," I explained to the nurse. "I'm too excited to sleep anyway. Could you please bring her to me?"

"There are several babies here tonight," she said.

"Yes, but my daughter is crying." Dutiful but skeptical, she went to the nursery and returned with my daughter in full cry.

"You were right," she laughed.

The next morning, Michael came to pick us up. A movement drew me to the window. Cedar waxwings flitted back and forth, eating juniper berries. I had never seen them in our area. Shaped like cardinals, their color combination of rust, tan, yellow, and gray with black masks over their eyes and tiny, orangey-red wing

markings made them look like elegant, flying bandits. I watched the animated flock as they feasted until the berries were gone. Amid snow flurries, with Jess in her new car seat, we traveled back to our own hillside kingdom.

Joy mixed with a multitude of emotions, as I turned and looked back to the Lord's precious gift. Outside, snow flurries floated down like confetti, a fitting celebration. *Thank You, Lord! Thank You!*

30

UPSIDE DOWN

"But Jesus said, 'Let the little children come to Me, and do not forbid them; for of such is the kingdom of heaven.'"
— Matthew 19:14

MOST PARENTS COMPLAIN of the first three months of a baby's life as a difficult transition. Jessica slept through the night at six weeks and spent the days nursing and sleeping. I held her by the hour and stared at her miniature face, drinking in her tiny humanness. I held my husband's child, an honor and privilege I thought unlikely a year ago. As I contemplated the wonder of our baby daughter, my thoughts yielded to grateful prayer.

Three months slipped by quickly. Although I had ample milk, I thought a supplemental formula may give me some freedom to use a bottle in public. After research, I found an expensive, "hypoallergenic" formula and tried it. She liked it and gulped it down. Within fifteen minutes, Jessica's shrill scream brought me running. Her body curled with tense muscles. She cried so hard that she made a crowing sound.

My family doctor heard her, when I called in desperation.

"Did you put that baby down crying like that?" she asked.

"There's nothing I can do to comfort her," I said in tears. "I put her down to call you!"

"Bring her to the office right now," Dr. Suguira said.

She prescribed paregoric. Jess calmed down within ten minutes of receiving a dose given by the doctor.

"The formula gave her severe colic. The one you chose is usually quite good. It seems she is sensitive to some of the ingredients." Dr. Siguira looked up at me from her four-feet, eleven-inch height, a petite Japanese woman loved by our family for her skill and kind, no-nonsense style.

"I don't think you should try formula. Start her on baby vegetables at six months. She could start having cereal in the next week or so. Nurse her as much as she wants. Call me if there are any problems."

That night, Jessica did not sleep through the night. She had me up six times, crying unless I held her in the rocking chair, bounced her, or walked. Her discomfort did not stop. Fussiness at night went on for almost a year. Days were not much better. The doctors found nothing wrong. Jess became "a colicky baby."

One night, I awakened to the usual wailing. I had nursed her an hour ago. I dragged myself out of bed and gazed down at the crying child. Exhaustion, helplessness, loss of control, and anger at 4:00 a.m. converged. I felt an urge to throw the red-faced, screaming infant—this *most wanted baby in the world*—against the wall to shut her up. At that moment, I understood child abuse by an exhausted parent. I picked her up with a caress, rocked her, walked her, and jostled her until she settled. I managed two hours of sleep and thanked God for that.

Taking a shower became an impossible dream. If I put Jessica down, she cried. I discovered the sound of my hair dryer soothed her. With her stroller in the bathroom and the blowing hair dryer stuck between the towel rack and wall, she stopped crying, and I got my shower.

Sleep deprivation robs vitality. I went from being a successful professional bringing in a good salary to being a failure at motherhood, in my estimation, with no salary. Michael came home to an emotionally and physically bankrupt wife, who might still be in her pajamas without a shower.

My past job haunted me. At work, I knew when I would eat lunch; patients were scheduled; I talked to adults in intelligent conversations; I was respected for my expertise. Recently, I could not even string a sentence together with another adult on the phone. My mirror revealed a haggard, desperate-looking woman I did not recognize. *Who was I?* My world had been turned upside down by an infant, a gift from God, the most wanted of children.

My dream turned into a nightmare. Michael no longer enjoyed coming home from work.

Gradually, Jessica started eating soft baby foods. When we introduced fruits, I bought the cheap pears in heavy syrup and mashed them. Within fifteen minutes, I had to use the paregoric to stop raging colic so severe that Jess curled into a ball and turned purple screaming. Once I got her calmed down, I called the pharmacy and asked them to read the ingredient label on the formula that launched our problems. The common ingredients in the formula and the pears were corn syrup and corn solids.

Other than colic, Jessica seemed a normal, healthy baby who reached all her milestones on time. She looked fine, but I didn't. Sometimes the pediatrician looked at me as if I had a screw loose when I described the problems with Jess. I had to be careful in my choice of foods, which went through breast milk. If I ate corn, we had severe colic. The complexity made it difficult to nail down exactly which foods caused the colic. We proved corn beyond a doubt. Michael and I called the two hours between 4:00 p.m. and 6:00 p.m. *arsenic hours*; the poor biddy thing screamed non-stop. She seemed to gain some relief if we bounced her up and down. Her Jolly Jumper, suspended from our kitchen doorframe, became a best friend.

In the midst of this, Dr. Sugiura retired. After discussing the allergy issues with my new family doctor, I asked if I should wean Jessica. She suggested I do this gradually, so I could eat more normally and wean myself of nursing her as well. I talked it over with Michael. We agreed to have her weaned by the time she turned a year old. Torn between my need to have some semblance of normalcy and the best option for the baby, I prayed and spent time reading anything to shed light on my dilemma. Nursing her intertwined our love bond.

This year floated with tears of exhaustion, frustration, and anxiety. At the same time, amazement at this growing, adorable, wriggling bundle trumped all the bad stuff. Her physical symptoms eased when she ate solid food as well as nursing.

Our one-of-a-kind, lovely child grew out of colic. When Jess turned eight months old, I had returned to work one day a week, while Michael watched her. He had no problem. I relished doing my PT at SCCMC on Saturdays. Sitting down at a regular time for an uninterrupted lunch and a chat with other staff members created a rare treat, medicine for my spirit.

Our nighttime ritual culminated with nursing before bedtime, so with weaning, bedtime nursing had to end. I gained strength in my conviction by comparing our weaning to a mare weaning her foal. In mid-March, after Jessica's first birthday, I rocked her without nursing her for the first time. She did not fall asleep in my arms, as I hummed songs that drifted into my mind. After ten minutes, I put her in bed, said, "Night, Night," and walked out with her door left open a few inches.

A TV performance of *The Red Shoes* played, an insufficient distraction. I went back into the nursery, patted and talked to the inconsolable baby, before returning to the living room.

Michael held my hand, as Jess and I cried for the next hour. Whinnying mares and screaming foals, longing for each other after being separated, came to mind. They needed to learn to be apart. Our daughter needed to learn this new bedtime ritual. And she would in time.

As Jess slept longer during the night, the old schedule still awakened me. On tiptoe, I crept into her room. Her chest rose and fell—asleep, not dead. Gradually, I slept through the night along with her, and my world became brighter. Laughter returned to our lives. We started feeling like a family, instead of a war zone. Our kingdom had survived. I thanked God that we had a healthy, beautiful child with the first year of battle behind us.

Verbally gifted and mentally quick on her feet, Jessica challenged me at every turn. Plato's well-used adage, "Necessity is the mother of invention," held true, and I learned to think just as quickly in response to my daughter.

Time without Jessica, time for just Michael and me—for talking, touching, keeping our *best friend* status alive—became a vital challenge. One night, with Jess at the difficult fourteen-month-old stage, Mom and Fell volunteered to babysit so Michael and I could see a movie. On the way back to Mom's, Michael sailed past my family home and drove toward the river road, a different intention on his mind.

"You know, we just passed Mom's," I giggled, sliding my hand up and down his thigh.

We parked in moonlight on that warm, early June night, danced in the dark, necked like teenagers, and needed more. Loving each other with uninterrupted pleasure didn't take long. The river road scene created a more private setting compared to a time, years before: a rushed midnight possession of one another in a deserted train station parking lot. Tonight, our station wagon and blanket provided a comfortable resting place. But the hilarity and newlywed exuberance of hot sex in the front seat of a stick shift sedan came to mind as an unmatched past experience that still made us laugh and want more. Recalling, sharing past passion and deep connection, affirmed our love, strengthened our bond. Those nights enriched our union and became part of an intimate history that still makes us smile and feel the fire.

I credit a book by Dr. James Dobson called *The Strong-Willed Child* with saving my sanity in the next stage of never-ending, child-rearing changes. It helped me become a mother who taught her child healthy boundaries. Michael showed more talent in this stage, but I learned.

Punishment became an interesting conundrum. Imaginative and creative, Jess had fun while standing in the "naughty-corner." Experimenting, I sent her three steps down into our stairwell for time-out. She hated it. I became creative as she. My guardian angels worked overtime. But day-time drama beat night-time colic. We thanked God for a healthy, imaginative, verbally-gifted child.

When Jessica turned two, we enrolled her at Charlestown Play House, where she attended "The Twos." After "playschool" let out, Jess went to a sitter close to home. Mary Jo had a gift caring for children and babysat six kids from toddler to school age. I worked during Playschool hours at Northern Chester County Community Nursing Service, a home care agency. Home care physical therapy gave me one-on-one time with patients doing the job I loved.

Ruth, another physical therapist, worked with me. Everyone loved Ruth, who became my best friend. The Nursing Service required one afternoon a week for meetings, to touch base with our supervisors and communicate face-to-face with staff. Jess played under my desk while I worked. My job had built-in flexibility, a dream for moms with young kids.

During the summer, Jess stayed with Mary Jo while I worked. I came to pick her up fifteen minutes early one day, as Mary Jo supervised the children cleaning up at day's end. She turned to me and said, "You're going to have your hands full!" She pointed to Jess watching the children put toys away. "Jessica, you have to help too," Mary Jo said.

Jess responded, "Jake, there's one over there. Tara, there's one under the couch..."

"No, Jessica. You have to put toys away too," Mary Jo said and handed her a doll destined for the toy box. With a big sigh, she complied, a slightly pained look on her face. I hid my laughter.

Jessica continued at Charlestown Play House until public school kindergarten. My first kindergarten, parent-teacher's meeting started out well. After telling me I had a bright and verbally-gifted child, Jessica's teacher quizzed me. "What do you do if Jessica wants something from another room?" she asked.

"I tell her to go get it," I answered.

"What if she wants something she can safely reach in the refrigerator?"

"I tell her to go get it," I said, light dawning.

"Does she put her own toys away?"

I laughed. "You expected a mother who pampers her child, waits on her hand and foot; am I right?"

"She does seem to expect things to be done for her," she said.

"I know what it looks like. But we don't spoil her at home. She is expected to clean up her toys. I know she seems to have a 'to the manor born' attitude, but neither my husband nor I wait on her." After this conversation, we had a fruitful meeting with some problem-solving in dealing with this amazing, bright, and strong little girl.

Now that I had a second income, Michael and I looked at our tiny house with new eyes. More space, with an addition, became an exciting possibility. When Jess turned four, workmen began appearing on the hill at 8:00 a.m., as we added another half house to our tiny domain. Pouring over books to design the kitchen fed my creative side. Michael and I worked on the exterior design and windows. It took fourteen months to complete, but we had our dream home—the home I said we would never want to leave. My world became calmer as Jess grew. Michael and I had a downstairs bedroom suite with more privacy. My world righted itself, no longer upside down.

God granted me my fondest wishes and prayers: a loving husband, a house in the country, our child, and a solid profession. But it was still early in my life. *He had lessons for me to learn beyond my home and work. He had a plan for my life I couldn't foresee.*

Eden Hill looking like a Christmas Card.

31

VALLEY OF THE SHADOW

*"Yea, though I walk through the valley of the shadow of death,
I will fear no evil for You are with me..."*
— *Psalm* 23:4

IT SHOULD HAVE BEEN an ordinary February night as I made dinner for Jess and Michael, but I felt jumpy and strangely distracted. *What is wrong with me?* A telephone ring seemed like a fire alarm, the noise adding to my already jangled state. I tried to shake off the feeling as I reached for the receiver.

"Hello?" I paused. "Hello?" Silence greeted me on the other end. I closed my eyes and tried to calm my rapid-fire heartbeat. *Something's wrong.* When my mind cleared, one thought came through like a jagged bolt of lightning. I had to call Ruth, *now!* I dialed the phone number from memory and visualized her lovely face. Her wavy, auburn hair, green eyes, and kindness radiated beauty, inside and out, that could not be completely devastated by a three-year battle with breast cancer. At thirty-six years old, she had clawed and scratched to survive with her indomitable will to live. God must have agreed; she was still here.

Ruth was my best friend. We could talk about anything. Well, almost anything. Death became our one forbidden subject. When I tried to discuss the obvious, she claimed that only "positive thinking" and a strict physical regimen would return her to health. She tried everything: chemotherapy, shamans, special copper wiring in her house, special food, coffee enemas—and, I'm sure, things she never told me. Death was a "negative thought" and a taboo subject.

On my last visit, her ninety-pound, emaciated body shocked me. Masking my feelings, I massaged her neck and shoulders, only to find a multitude of cancerous lumps under my fingers. Her speech, punctuated by fits of uncontrollable coughing, confirmed her X-ray findings: the cancer had spread to her lungs. But her eyes remained alive and angry.

As the memory of those invasive lumps, her skeletal body, and angry eyes faded, tears blurred my vision. I wanted my best friend back. I wanted her to laugh and run with her four- year-old daughter. I wanted to see her embrace her husband with love in her eyes. I wanted to call her on the phone and talk without her becoming angry and frustrated. She had told me to stop calling, because she was too short of breath to talk on the phone anymore. But when I called that night, she begged for help, her wheezing voice barely recognizable.

"I'm having panic attacks," she said, fear shadowing each word. "I haven't slept for three nights."

"Okay, Ruth. I'm on my way," I told her in a calm voice, belying my inner turmoil. I knew I needed to sound steady, soothing, the way I spoke to a frightened patient in physical therapy during my workdays in home care. I must have succeeded, because she hung up without another word.

Michael would put Jess to bed. She was five now, a year older than Ruth's daughter, Amanda.

I prayed as I drove. *Please Lord, heal her*, I thought of Lazarus, *or take her home. Give me the strength to accept Your will. Help me help her tonight. What can I say to her? Give me the words that will help her, Lord.* I understood Ruth's need.

It is so easy to say, "Trust in God and let go of the fear." But how do you actually do it? How do you trust God and let go enough to leave a husband and a four-year-old daughter? Ruth certainly did not come to this place without a fight.

Her mother had tried to talk to her about Jesus and was met with stony rejection. Jesus, Savior, forgiver of sins, Lover of our souls. I heard it all as well. *How could I talk to her, with my own faith riddled full of questions?* I cringed at the thought of wearing cross jewelry—something that celebrated the device of a brutal death. Yet, of all the world religions I studied in college and tried over my college years and beyond, I kept coming back to Christianity. Even so, the idea of *only one way to heaven* made me wince at all the people going to hell. Jesus said He was *the way, the truth, and the life;* that *no one saw the Father except through Him.* I still wrestled with those words written in red, since He wanted *none to perish.* The car hurtled through the cold, damp night.

"What can I say to her, Lord?" I started at the sound of my own voice; I had spoken out loud.

Driving the last mile, I continued to pray out loud. "Help me, Lord. Give me words to comfort her." I breathed slowly, deeply, to center myself in the Lord's presence. A peaceful warmth flowed through and around me—a cloak of serenity.

As I drove through the night, I realized I had to deal with Jesus. I believed in miracles; I believed in God. But my spiritual questioning left the "Savior" issue unresolved. *Only one way for everyone? All* paths did not lead to God in the Bible.

The house, lit up like a beacon in the dark, looked like there was nothing amiss. But Ruth leaned—elbows straight, hands on the dining room table—as she swayed from side to side. Her husband, Tim, held her, supporting her from behind, humming a folk song. Her eyes were dilated pools of panic.

"I can't stop moving," she said, as I took her in my arms and began the macabre rocking. Tim stood by, drooping with exhaustion.

I spoke to her gently, softly, whispering at times, swaying back and forth until she gave me an opening to broach the root of her fear: death.

"Do we have to talk about that?" she wheezed, annoyed.

"If you face it, you won't be so frightened."

The rocking stopped. "Tell me *you're* not afraid of dying!" she bristled.

"I'm not ready to go yet, but I'm not afraid. All of my earthly burdens will fall away, and God will take care of me." *I sounded so sure!*

"Maybe I'm not trying hard enough to get well." Defeat, fatigue, and guilt lined her face.

"No one could have tried harder," I said. Tim nodded, as we made eye contact, and he left us alone. I took over Ruth's care for the evening—to be with her and give her tired family a break. The evening unfolded as if it had been planned. It felt so right, so natural. There were no thoughts about what needed to be said, no questions about what needed to be done. This evening, this moment in time, seemed to be a culmination of all my experience, from the time I was in first grade and "doctored the wounded soldiers" on the playground, through my present daily work as a physical therapist.

It also seemed to encompass all the experiences I had with God through churches and my sense of the Spirit of God. Raised in a Lutheran church, I spent a year in an Independent Baptist Church, sporadically attended Quaker Meeting in college, married in a Presbyterian Church, and at present claimed membership at a Quaker Meeting. I still hadn't found what I sought in a church.

Strange, this situation. I never expected to help my dearest friend, as she approached the portal of death.

Ruth and I had met as home care physical therapists. Bright, compassionate, and strong, she seemed to have life under control. I patterned my record keeping after her patient notes. She was my example in parenting. Now, it was my time to support her.

She sat next to me at dinner. "Have you tried venison?" she asked hoarsely.

"No, I haven't. Do you like it?"

"Here, try some." She offered me a piece on her fork. Her eyes had a hardness to them, as if to say, *"Let's see if she eats it off my fork, a fork that was in the mouth of a cancer victim..."*

As I smiled, my eyes sent her a message in return, *"I'm not afraid, and I love you..."* I ate the meat from her fork. The hardness vanished, as her eyes softened and her face relaxed.

Four-year-old Amanda talked to her father, miming a character in a funny, high voice. Her grandparents laughed and joined in the make-believe character conversation. I nudged Ruth and said, "Look at your strong little girl!" Our eyes met, as my gaze urged her to see Amanda, safe with Tim and her parents. *She would be all right.* Ruth nodded that she understood with a reluctant smile.

Dinner done, dishes cleared, Ruth and I lingered over tea.

"I need a bath," she said.

I held her hand, as she walked to the bathroom, amazed that she needed so little support with her skeletal legs and so little flesh left on her frame. We talked comfortably as I sponged her back. By the time we finished, she dragged with fatigue. The bath cost dearly in precious energy. With a father's loving embrace, Robert lifted Ruth into bed, then went out with Tim. Her mother, Wanda, and I made her as comfortable as possible. As we propped pillows, tugged and smoothed sheets and blankets, fear crept back with its incessant motion. Ruth moved her head and arms in agitation.

"God will help you," I said, with words beyond my own thoughts.

She looked at Wanda, then at me, long and sorrowfully.

"I don't believe in Him enough. I've done terrible things." Eyes closed, she rested and gathered enough oxygen before she continued. "God doesn't want me in heaven."

Wanda and I looked at each other, stunned. *What was she*

saying? I had seen fear do strange things to people, but this caught me completely by surprise. Ruth was quiet, her face lined with hopelessness, her breath ragged with emotion.

After some thought, I said, "Ruth, let's do a little visualization, the kind we use in physical therapy when patients don't believe they can do something difficult."

Ruth opened her eyes and focused on my face. "I want you to take everything bad you ever did and put it in a big pile. Can you do that in your mind?"

She nodded, her breath quieting, and closed her eyes.

"Now, throw some gas on the heap and torch it. Can you see it burning?"

She nodded again and was still for a minute or so. Then she said, "There's more. I haven't burned it all."

"So, gather a second pile."

She did. Then she gathered and burned a third pile as well before resting again.

"Ruth," I said cautiously, "nothing can keep you out of heaven, if you ask God to forgive you when you let Him into your heart."

She looked at me, a look filled with such self-loathing, I almost flinched. She paused, then said, "But I had an abortion..." her voice trailed to a whisper. Her green eyes examined mine. I returned her look. When she found no condemnation there, she turned to her mother.

"Do you think I'm horrible?" she asked, her breath wheezing.

"Of course not," Wanda said, as she softly brushed Ruth's hair back from her face, fingers lingering in a caress.

"What's wrong with me? I'm pro-choice. Why am I feeling this way? I've kept it a secret all these years. It happened before I married Tim." She squeezed her eyes shut as if that helped block the thought. "It was *inconvenient*." Her voice cut short, as she tried to catch her breath. "I had an abortion, because a baby was inconvenient!" Tears left a trail from the corner of her eye to her jawline.

We were quiet for a long minute, each of us holding Ruth's hands as she vented the pent-up grief and guilt.

"Everyone makes decisions that they don't realize will affect them for the rest of their lives," I said. "That was a terrible situation and decision for you; but you're forgiven, if you ask the Lord from your heart."

Her tear-filled eyes pleaded for help, as she struggled to breathe.

"Slow your breaths down, Ruth. You know how. You used to teach this too!" A wan smile touched her face, and soon, she had it under control. Her face smoothed with relief as the minutes moved on, grains of sand in an hourglass. Eyes closed, she was quiet long enough to be asleep. Just as I was about to tiptoe out to the kitchen for another cup of tea with Wanda, Ruth stirred. Her next words caught me off guard and, by Wanda's expression, I was not alone.

"Someone came in the front door."

We knew no one came in, but I felt compelled to follow Ruth's vision. Wanda nodded to me in apparent agreement.

"Who is it?" I asked.

"A man came in. He's telling me I have to pay him for all the things I've done."

"Tell him your debts are paid. Jesus paid them, and you believe. Tell him to get out!"

Ruth's brow wrinkled with concentration. After a shuddering exhale, her face eased again.

"Boy, was he mad! He slammed the door and patched out of the driveway!" she flashed a real smile, like sun breaking through darkness.

"Now, invite God in," I heard my voice say.

"I'm not good enough," she said, wilting.

"Do you remember the story of Jesus's crucifixion?" I asked. She nodded. "He asked God to forgive His tormentors, because they didn't know what they were doing. Even a thief hanging next to him on a cross was promised paradise with Him, when he showed faith in the last hours of his life! Your debts have been paid," my voice insisted. "With Jesus, you are forgiven!"

Ruth seemed to drift off again. It took a few minutes for her to speak. Again, I wondered if she had fallen asleep. My mind reeled with the effortless words that came from my mouth, words that felt so uncertain in my heart. *How could I reconcile my lack of faith and the Gospel message I had just spoken out loud?* Wanda smiled at me; too puzzled to respond, I nodded my head.

"There's a big tent," Ruth said in a low voice.

"Tell me what you're seeing, so I can see it with you."

As Ruth spoke, I could picture a good-sized, cream-colored tent— crowded with people.

"I can't see what's going on," she complained.

As if observing her in the crowd, I saw her craning her neck around the throng of humanity, looking toward the front. There were benches in rows.

"So, stand on a bench in the back. What do you see now?"

"A kind, loving man being dressed in rich, purple robes."

"What does he look like?" I asked.

"Like all the pictures I've seen of Jesus," Ruth said in a dreamy voice.

"Oh, Ruth, go up front!" *Could it be Jesus in her vision? Yes,* I thought, answering my own question, *it could!*

"I'm all the way in the back. I can't butt in," she said, shaking her head.

"The Bible says the first shall be last, and the last shall be first."

Ruth thought for a moment. Then she nodded and made her way to the foot of the stage.

"Now, touch His robe."

Her hand moved, reaching up from the hospital bed—reaching... Suddenly, she pulled it back, as if startled. "He wants me to come up on stage with Him!" She frowned.

"Ruth, you're not seriously going to refuse Jesus, are you? This is a gift. Please, go to Him!" There was certainty in my voice. *Maybe this vision was for both of us. I had been sent here.* My whole being felt an awe I had never experienced.

Ruth described being supported by pillows, as Jesus ministered to her. I saw hand-woven pillows—like soft jewels, with gold, sapphire, and emerald-green, metallic, cloth covers.

"Oh, He has beautiful green eyes!" she said, her voice filled with wonder.

Green? Well, who knows? I thought with an internal laugh.

"All this around Him, and He doesn't mind. He loves us anyway!" She fell silent for a bit. Slowly, awe changed to sorrow. "Oh, no! He's weak like me. We're back-to-back, leaning on each other. We're holding each other up!"

"Jesus was human *and* God. There was no need for Jesus without us and our sins. We lean on Jesus—and Jesus took on the weak, human form for us. You're not the only one responsible for your body. God is ultimately *the* responsible One."

Ruth smiled and closed her eyes again—resting, calmer than she had been the whole evening. Her mother and I sighed together, as if breathing for the first time in a while. My body sent fatigue messages to my brain—heavy, undeniable, urgent.

"Ruth, you don't need me to stay any longer tonight. Between you and God, you'll be fine, whether you live or die."

Her green eyes were luminous with newfound peace.

"Tomorrow night is Friday," I added. "I can stay the whole night with you then, if you want me to."

She nodded. Her eyes smiled, but her muscles were too tired to move her lips.

I hugged her like tomorrow might not come. We were not promised our next breath, let alone tomorrow. Her mother and I held each other tightly, bonded for life by this night's sharing.

I sang on the way home and thanked God for His work. I would never have done it the way He guided me this night. The words were not mine. They were not words I would have chosen. But they were right.

3 2

GOING HOME

"O Death, where is your sting?"
— Hosea 13:14

AT WORK THE NEXT DAY, I was on an adrenaline high. *Ruth touched Christ's robe. He laid hands on her.* I prayed I would witness an incredible, healing miracle. My body tingled with anticipation at the thought of seeing God's work, as my car found its way back to Ruth's and Tim's house on Friday night.

As I entered the silent home, I knew my miracle had not occurred. Ruth lay on the bed, no longer able to move her arms and legs. Wanda, Robert, and Tim hovered near, concern and sadness masking their faces.

"Need some water," she said, acknowledging my presence only with her eyes. As I held the glass with the straw to her mouth, she tried to move, but her ravaged body remained still, beyond her control.

"Would you like to be on your side, instead of your back?" I asked.

"I can't hear you," she rasped, her breathing ragged and irregular.

I nodded, smiled, and mouthed, "It's okay."

The family greeted me, one by one, with a touch, hug, or simple eye contact. Bound by love, we wanted to be there. We wanted to wait with her. There were times she drifted off—eyes still open, but vacant. For a ten-minute period, she was "not there," her breath uneven. Then she returned, needing her head held, so she could lean forward to breathe in shallow, labored gasps.

I helped silently. Her family ministered to her, moving her as she wished, even if she had been lifted the same way only five minutes before. By 11:30 p.m., she seemed more settled.

"Would you like a cup of tea?" Wanda asked me, as we carried a few dirty dishes, napkins, and utensils to the kitchen.

"No, thanks, Wanda." I stopped and put one arm around her shoulders, as I glanced at both Robert and Tim. "I think you are all exhausted. Why don't you let me sit with Ruth, and you can get some sleep? I'll just put the kettle on and take the tea in with me."

We hugged, knowing that nothing would ever be the same.

The family drifted off to bed after each one said goodnight to Ruth. I stayed in the kitchen, so their time could be private. Then, armed with chamomile tea, prayer softly came through me and circled heavenward: "*Father, hold us in Your hands, as I watch with Ruth. Take her gently, Lord. Help us; we love her. Amen.*"

Midnight, alone at her bedside, felt like I was in the Garden of Gethsemane, as Jesus had been, pleading that God consider saving His life—yet submitting to the will of the Father. *Please, God, keep me awake.* Ruth turned her head toward me, her eyes fully open for the first time in the last hour.

"I'm so cold," she said, shivering.

Blankets already were heaped on the bed covering her. Like caring for someone freezing, I climbed into the bed and cradled her head on my chest, her body nestled close to mine. The shivering waned, as warmth soaked through us. I stroked her auburn hair and held her to comfort my soul for a few precious minutes. And then, she needed to move again.

"SSS okay," she said, weakly pushing me away, back to my bedside chair, empty teacup and dim lamplight.

My chair touched the bed. I held Ruth's hand under the covers. She slipped into that strange, vacant state for another half hour. When she returned, she couldn't get comfortable in any position, until I sat her up with her head forward, resting on my shoulder, her chest rattling with fluid.

Marshaling all her strength, she lifted her head, eyebrows raised, emerald eyes smiling. "This is more than you bargained for..." Her voice quavered, but her own special brand of humor reigned in full measure. I laughed and hugged her carefully. She was too weak to respond.

Gradually, she was able to lie down, propped with pillows, her hand in mine. She tried to speak again. There were words, and she spoke them out loud; but they were not in a language I could understand.

"Ruth, you're not speaking English anymore," I said.

Her eyes drew me in—deeply, urgently trying to tell me something.

Slowly, I understood. "You're seeing where you're going, aren't you?"

Calm acceptance surrounded Ruth as she agreed with a satisfied look. She closed her eyes again, withdrawing her hand from mine.

"It's okay," I said, taking her hand again.

Once more, she pulled away. It took some time before I realized I had become the problem. Without thinking, I was holding her there. She had to leave, and I had to let her go. Placing her hand under the covers I listened to her breathe—three or four shallow breaths, then nothing; three breaths, then nothing. It had been that way on and off all night. But now, it quieted...then became still. I touched her cheek and felt the chill of death.

"I love you," I said, as I held her cool, vacant face next to mine. "Go with God, my dear friend."

A poem I wrote long ago came to mind:

Carve my name upon the stone
Though the body that bore it is gone
My spirit roves free through the green of the wood
'til the angels lift me to my dawn.

I was not required to know all the answers—the Lord was there with me, with all of us. Ruth had been healed; I *had* witnessed a miracle. God simply did not do it my way.

A year passed. And I was still crying. The last year since Ruth died, I cried at the same traffic light, five days a week, as I headed for work. Although it didn't make sense, I didn't cry on the way home. But whether the light turned red or green, the intersection of Route 30 and Route 10 became some kind of trigger on the way to work. Immeasurable loss, heartache, and memory bubbled up, surfaced into my eyes, rolled down my cheeks, and wrecked my eyeliner. Her smile, auburn hair, and green eyes rose along with the pain of her absence. *My best friend, gone.*

This crying jag was not a scene I shared with anyone. It stayed between me and God. I functioned normally at work and at home—well, almost. I couldn't talk on the phone with Ruth anymore. I guess, as far as mourning goes, I shouldn't complain about ten minutes each workday and a little make-up repair. But her loss hurt from the roots of my hair to my toenails. The underground, missing piece to my world remained palpable, still present within me. The pain at knowing I couldn't see her, commune with her in the flesh proved more pervasive than my outward ten minutes of crying.

Cymbidium orchids bloom in the winter. Mine were full of blossoms that February. I will never forget the pair of fragrant, white-petaled, lavender-throated blossoms behind Ruth's right ear the day of her viewing. The same plant still blooms in my home, January and February each year. I had plenty of flowers on the orchid from which

239

to choose. She wasn't there to admire the flowers, or to speak to people who passed her bed for a final farewell in her home. And that silence felt right. Cancer that robs the body of breath, that metastasizes beyond compatibility with life, must end; the suffering must cease. And it was finished for Ruth.

Cymbidium Orchid

But not for those left behind. We breathed normally and did our jobs. There were individual differences. Ruth's parents, husband, and daughter would, naturally, be most affected. Then there were Ruth's many friends. She had been everyone's best friend. I wasn't the only one still weeping.

So a year later, when the grieving continued, I didn't feel concerned. On the anniversary of Ruth's death, I finished work early. Late February light still glimmered with evening sun as I approached the little, stone bridge, a quarter mile from home. A sudden motion caught my eye on the far-right windshield—a flash of blue. The bluebird came into focus slowly, as the world around me seemed to freeze in place. It flew directly across my path, inches from my windshield, and paused as it neared the driver's side. Its small head turned toward me, glinting black eyes directed at mine, with a form of intelligence in its gaze. A rosy breast faded to gray at its tail, detailed down to the outline of each feather; the wing feathers outstretched in flight, yet suspended like a video in slow motion.

The finely-etched bluebird looked at me, as I heard a voice in my head—not me thinking of a voice. This voice talked to me, and it sounded like Ruth's.

"Stop crying," the stern, feminine voice said.

I had a good, last look at the magnificent, bright bird before three words, without a voice, came to me: *bluebird of happiness*.

The bird disappeared, with no continued line of flight—there one minute in brilliant color, and gone the next. A sense of peace lingered, surrounding me. My shoulders felt lighter, my back straighter, as if a load that pulled me down suddenly let go. A long, deep breath made me realize I hadn't breathed for a while. Outside the car, my world seemed brighter, more vibrant. The weight of sadness and grayness of grief had gone.

God gave me a bluebird that looked me in the eye. He healed my spirit and lifted the sadness, grief, and loss. I haven't cried for Ruth since that day. I will see her in God's good time.

OH BABY!

"Behold, children are a heritage from the Lord, The fruit of the womb is a reward. Like the arrows in the hand of a warrior, So are the children of one's youth."
— Psalm 127:3–4

"I AM NOT DOING this stupid homework!" Jess exclaimed as she threw her backpack on the floor.

"Why? Let's see it," I said as I retrieved the backpack and handed it to my scowling eight-year-old daughter. She pulled the mimeographed sheet out and laid it on the table.

"It's about wrapping a gift. Who would wrap the box before you put the gift in it?"

I looked at the offending homework assignment and saw an elementary exercise in sequencing. She had to number the steps in order.

"So, tell me the answers on your 'stupid homework' sheet." Jess numbered the steps and turned her brown-and-green, hazel eyes to me. I handed her a pencil. "Now, write it on the page, and you're done in fifteen more seconds."

"But it's stupid!"

"It's easy for you. It might not be easy for everyone in your class. It's homework, whether you think it's stupid or not. You're wasting play time. Do it, and put it in your backpack." She rolled her eyes at me, as she wrote the correct answers on the paper.

A beautiful child—athletic, well-spoken and quick—her eyes were brown, shot with green, like her father's. Her birth answered a fervent prayer. I continued praying, because I didn't know how to parent her. Quicker than me, Jess seemed quite similar to Michael in personality. That demanded *binding arbitration* when they argued—with me as judge.

At age 10 her fourth grade teacher, Mrs. Mack, had Jess tested for the gifted program at my request. I scheduled the follow up conference with bated breath. Jess seemed bored with school. Gifted in writing and English in general, she didn't show the same type of gifting in math. Mrs. Mack agreed with my testing request and its reason. I settled into a fourth-grade sized chair as she retrieved the folder.

"Well, you were right about Jess being gifted in verbal and written skills," Mrs. Mack said, showing me the high score. "But you can see she's average in math."

"Will gifted classes be available in her high scoring areas?" I asked.

"Unfortunately, no. The children must be gifted in both areas to qualify. I wish I could help her, but she won't take kindly to extra work not given to the other students."

I agreed with Mrs. Mack's honest answer. Jess would have a fit with any extra work. We had to think of a way to present a worthy challenge under her radar.

"Michael, we have to do something about Jess," I said when he came home from work that night. "She needs a special challenge, something active to burn energy and make her want to climb a step higher at the same time." I told him about the conference with Mrs.

Mack. "If we don't find something she enjoys with physical and mental challenges, we'll be in real trouble when she's a teenager."

"Yeah, I know. But what?" His question hung in the air.

I thought for a minute before the answer came to me. "What about horseback riding? We have lots of stables near us. I've always loved horses."

"Sounds like one possible solution," Michael said.

Jess took to riding. "Mom, I want a pony of my own," became a mantra as she walked, trotted, and cantered with good form. Ever one to plan ahead, I discussed working off partial room and board for a pony with the owner of the barn. Her answer came with a caveat: only if I supervised Jess and helped too. I began riding in adult group lessons with delight long submerged for lack of time and money. A problem with sciatica after a car accident in 1980 resolved, as my core strength and physical endurance shot upward.

On a warm Sunday while Jess stayed with a friend, Michael and I left church for a drive toward Lancaster. "Look," I said, pointing to the "Horses and Ponies for Sale" sign. "Let's stop." A cute, flea-bitten, gray pony grazed in a ring on the property. In the office, the farm owner pointed through the window to the little gray. "That mare is $250. She's six years old and gentle. We think she's mostly Welsh Mountain Pony. Try her if you're interested," she said, eying my apricot dress, nylons, and heels.

She must be kidding, I thought, looking down at my just-above-the-knee Sunday dress. *But at that price, this pony won't be here long.* "Do you have tack for her?" I asked.

"Just a bridle."

I hadn't ridden bareback since I was fourteen. Michael looked dubious but gave me a leg up. The little mare stood thirteen-and-a-half hands high, big enough for me, small enough for Jess—a potential, productive solution involving both energy and intellect. My dress rode above mid-thigh as I straddled the warm, furry back. Michael held my shoes, after agreeing the pony might be a good idea. "Don't fall off," he said. I rolled my eyes and laughed.

The small mare walked and trotted without enthusiasm. Cantering required pummeling her with my heels and voice. Even so, the pony showed promise, with good gaits and temperament. She allowed me to touch her all over and lift each foot off the ground.

"What do you think?" I looked at Michael.

He petted the little gray's forehead. "She's nice. The price is good. Get a vet to check her out if you think this is the right move."

Fifty dollars down, we bought the pony pending a good vet check. "Lady Take a Chance," became a joint venture for Jess and me. She proved a willful rascal in the beginning, rearing and scaring Jess. At her side, I calmed my daughter.

"Hop down and let me get on her," I said, taking the riding crop from Jessica's hand. The pony stood still until I nudged her with my heels. I felt her gather to rear and took the reins in one hand. Horizon tilting, Lady went up, rearing high in the air. My hand rose and fell hard, as I walloped her between the ears with the crop's butt. The pony came down as quickly as she reared, quivering and wild-eyed at the sudden contact with her head. "We won't have any of that," I said in a soothing voice, rubbing the side of her neck. She stood, quiet, for a few minutes as I talked and petted her neck and flank.

At my signal, she obediently walked, trotted, and cantered around the ring in both directions. We pulled up in front of Jess. "It's your turn now." I hopped off, picked up a lunge line, and snapped it to the pony's D-ring snaffle bit. "You'll be fine," I said, pushing the pony out to circle on the lunge. And she was.

Jess and Lady Take a Chance, Grand Champion, Short Stirrup,
Ludwig's Corner Horse Show.

Lady and Jess traveled the local show circuit in "short stirrup division." As Jess approached twelve years old, her growth told us this would be the last year riding Lady. Blue, red, yellow, green, and pink ribbons plastered the walls of her room—her final addition, the multi-colored rosette of Short Stirrup Grand Champion in walk, trot, canter, and jumping. As sad as we felt parting with Lady, Jess needed to graduate to a horse. Lady would continue carrying children to victory in short stirrup classes.

A bay gelding stood in the crossties, restive, eying his new surroundings. Bought at the New Holland sale for a trial by our riding coach, the dog food dealers missed out on this racetrack has-been. His substantial winnings came after he had been gelded; so once his track career ended with no stud fees possible, the New Holland auction gave the owners an easy way out. The horse needed a couple of weeks to purge drugs given at the track from his system.

During that time, the handsome bay rolled his eyes and danced—nervous, unsure at the end of the lead rope. As always, I tried him first, after he acclimated to his surroundings.

But Jess remained spooked by his early skittishness. While Jess rejected the new horse, I fell in love with him. He became "Perfect Timing," nicknamed "Mikey," the first horse Michael ever groomed.

Our coach returned to the New Holland sale and brought a magnificent, dappled-gray mare home. She had a lost, hopeless look in her eyes that proved prophetic when a painful limp, diagnosed as navicular deterioration, sent her back to the auction.

Bay and beautiful, the next horse nuzzled Jess and captivated her in that one single action. Officially a teenager, she named him "Spitting Image" and called him "Josh." Sweet and intelligent the horses took up three weeknights and weekends. Michael learned to ride but never developed a love of the sport.

"I smell like a barn," he complained before choosing to watch Jess and me in selected competitions rather than ride.

Mikey reached over the vet's shoulder and pulled a pen out of her pocket. He twiddled it in his mouth, eyes glinting with pleasure at our laughter. His mischievous, benign-but-cute stunts endeared him to all who encountered him. I had the horse I longed for all my life; *the prayer of yesteryear answered, not in my time, but in God's.*

34

BROKEN

"He who dwells in the secret place of the Most High
Shall abide under the shadow of the Almighty.
I will say of the Lord, 'He is my refuge and my fortress;
My God, in Him I will trust.'
Surely He shall deliver you from the snare of the fowler
And from the perilous pestilence.
He shall cover you with His feathers,
And under His wings you shall take refuge."
— *Psalm 91:1-4*

THE HEADACHE WAS NOT A MIGRAINE. My head felt pressurized, a
volcano about to explode. Medication didn't touch the pain. Fatigue
replaced my usual, boundless energy. I tacked up Mikey for a lesson,
a day after the headache. My muscles felt heavy, incapable of holding
me up, let alone ride.

The next week, spaghetti at lunch made me so sleepy I could
barely function. I found any kind of pasta, bread, sugar, fruit, or
starchy vegetables made me either short-tempered or deadly fatigued,
among other symptoms. Months of trial and error eventually yielded

a list of foods that fell on the "okay to eat" or the "do not eat" list. It reminded me of severe, food-related colic Jessica had as an infant. For me, most fruit, wine, potatoes, rice, wheat, peas, corn, and milk interfered with my ability to organize paperwork, keep my pleasant temperament, or drive a car without getting lost in familiar places. Reading or working on my novel, *Sara's Way,* turned into energy vampires. I couldn't afford to do either if I wanted to work, drive, or do anything but stare at a wall.

On an internet search, I thought my symptoms boiled down to one diagnosis: hypoglycemia, also called low blood sugar. I read a book about carbohydrates and their impact on blood sugar levels. The thin volume's author explained my cognitive, visual, endurance, and energy problems from personal experience. All my favorite carbs suffered instant amputation from my diet. Eating became a labor-intensive activity, potentially dangerous when severe symptoms arose from mistakes.

Learning how to deal with food as medicine progressed with baby steps. I became unable to drive that year. When I made a food mistake, I could get lost in places I knew well, either the same or next day. Irritability brought out murderous-eyed Hyde, requiring medication to cope with work and family. Early on, I looked at a patient with such raw anger, both he and my aide responded with open mouths, as my neurological filter malfunctioned.

Problems escalated. My memory went on vacation. I couldn't recall a phone number without writing it down and covering each number as I dialed. My ability to write physical therapy patient notes quickly, or organize a cluttered desk, vanished. On my way to the grocery store, I drove the wrong way into a one-way exit; everything looked unfamiliar in a place I'd been a thousand times. I came home from work and fell into a dead sleep on the couch. Yet, my ability to create treatment plans with sound physical therapy skills didn't suffer; I never missed a day of work, with my aide, Karla's, help.

The short fuse coupled with no energy for details changed my personality. As I went from doctor to doctor, no one had answers. My family doctor gave me Xanax for the irritability and anxiety, which probably saved my marriage.

"I would understand if you divorced me," I sobbed to Michael. "I'm not the same person you married. I'm broken!"

"Honey," he said, "we'll get through this together."

My world fell apart, and no one knew why. I felt like my body betrayed me. Michael took over the lion's share of thirteen-year-old Jessica's care, as well as meals and laundry. I worked, came home, and crashed.

Three weeks after the volcanic headache, I visited my horse, who had been ridden by other people for lessons at the stable. Normally affectionate, the Thoroughbred had his head over the stall door, but he backed up when I came near.

"Oh, Mikey! I missed you so much," I told him as I offered a carrot. His gentle, luminous eyes didn't betray his feelings, but his body language did. He turned his back on me. My sweet horse stood with his head in the stall's back corner, until I left in tears.

"Sell him," I told my coach, John. "I'm not getting better; I'm getting worse. I can't ride him, and he's miserable."

John, riding coach and owner of our latest barn, called within a week. "I have a buyer who wants a horse for her daughter. She's going to try him tomorrow afternoon."

The next afternoon at the barn, I watched a twelve-year-old girl groom, tack up, and ride my beloved horse. A good, little rider, she warmed Mikey up slowly before asking for a faster gait. The graceful bay dutifully swung into a comfortable canter at her command.

"Mom," she yelled with glee, "did you see that?!" She pulled up with care and walked Mikey across the ring to the fence where her mother stood.

"Yes, Tammy, I did see it. He has nice gaits and goes into a very nice canter; but he's a little short coupled."

"Mom, he's the one," Tammy said, definite. "You know how many horses we've looked at. He's perfect!"

I walked over to Tammy's mother. "I'm his owner," I paused and smiled at Tammy. "I can't ride anymore. The only reason I'm selling him is that he needs a single owner. He's miserable being used as a lesson horse. Tammy can crawl under his belly without him batting an eye. He's really a kind, sweet boy."

She paused, studied me for a minute, glanced at her daughter's glowing face, and made a decision. "We'll take him, as long as the vet says he's sound," she said with a smile, as her daughter gave a triumphant yell.

God's gift: a perfect girl for Mikey. "You won't regret it," I said misty-eyed.

The Lord gives, and the Lord takes away. Blessed be the name of the Lord.

35

LEARNING CURVE

"He who dwells in the secret place of the
Most High shall abide under the shadow of
the Almighty. I will say of the Lord, He is
my refuge and my fortress; My God, in Him
I will trust."
— Psalm 91: 1-2

I FELT safe in only one place: our home. My job at Highland Medical Center remained possible because of my aide, Karla. She sheltered me, protected me. I did the physical therapy problem-solving needed for each patient; Karla carried out the treatment with my guidance. Patient notes, problematic before because of my organizational and sequencing issues, turned into Mount Everest. I sat, stared at the progress note forms, pen hovering. Disorganized thoughts milled about my brain, squeezed out onto paper at a snail's pace. Unable to safely drive, Michael dropped me off at work and picked me up. Never done with my paperwork, any lateness on Michael's part became a blessing.

Karla developed into a dear friend who made it possible for me to keep my job. Until the job changed.

Michael came to pick me up one evening, looking serious. Actually, worried would be more accurate.

"I had a meeting with Barry Cade this morning," he said. "They want you to go on site to teach body mechanics and correct equipment setup for businesses in the area, which would add to the money Highland brings in. Our present Highland treatment statistics showing productivity aren't meeting expectations. We don't have the patient numbers to keep you working without adding in another money-making activity."

I felt my stomach drop. "I can't do that. I can fake it here on days when I can't complete a full sentence, because Karla covers for me. I can't do off-site work. I never know what state I'll be in when I wake up, and I'm not safe driving in unfamiliar places."

"I understand," he said. "I don't know how we're going to handle this one. Let's go home and sleep on it."

That evening, the light blinked on our message machine. I listened and wanted Michael to hear the message too.

"This is Jake Turley with a business opportunity. My partner and I are looking for a motivated individual to run a private practice in West Chester." The message continued with a contact number.

"You're not going to call, are you?" Michael asked.

"I have a feeling this is important. I can't do the job anymore at Highland. It can't hurt to talk to him." Michael shrugged one shoulder. He didn't like the idea. But I felt God nudge me. We couldn't make it on one salary. Michael agreed.

Jake Turley set up a meeting with me, even after I explained about recovering from an illness—although "recovering" didn't accurately portray this point in my illness. When the day of the appointment came, I drove without a problem, thanking God all the way. The interview went well. Jake Turley understood I needed a break in the afternoon, and I expected to schedule my own patients. The physical space and setup looked Spartan but adequate. On the whole, the job seemed good from a physical and financial standpoint—a good salary with benefits. I talked to Michael about the opportunity, and he agreed I couldn't stay at Highland. With the job in West Chester, I would drive the same route every day and be able to stay in one place until I came home. It looked like my best option.

So far, I had been on a year-and-a-half learning curve with my undiagnosed medical condition before I left Highland. In that time, I learned I could partially control my symptoms by eating minimal carbohydrates and maximal protein. The other symptom stabilizer: nightly medication for sleep and, as needed, for 'anxiety.' Many times, especially in the first two years, symptoms controlled me. Stress, excitement, a disagreement with Michael, food, physically overdoing it— one, or a combination of these, would crash me. The medications made an undeniable difference with no side effects.

Before I left SCCMC, Michael, as my department head and boss at Highland, told me I had to attend an end-of-the-week meeting at the hospital about Highland's future. The minute my eyes opened that morning, brain fog engulfed me. I had tried brown rice with my meal the evening before, a bad move. Michael left early. I had two choices: try to make it on my own, or stay home and miss the meeting. Medication gave me enough function to drive.

I knew the way, but suddenly, nothing looked familiar. I knew my location, but not how to get to the meeting.

"Michael," I said, in tears, "I'm lost. I'm in Exton and can't figure out how to get there."

"Okay, Violet. It's all right. Can you get to Highland in time for your first patient?"

"Tell me how I should go."

"You have to get on 30 Bypass to Route 10."

"Wait, let me get some paper and write down directions. I can't figure out how to get to the bypass from here." Michael, ever patient, gave me directions from my location. *Lost in my backyard—God help me!*

During this period, for the first time in my life, depression attacked me; but it came in an unusual way, without reason—a sudden onset, as if a black cloud darkened the sun, filling me with hopelessness and isolation.

Thank God, this rare event only laid me low at home. The couch in the living room held me, curled in a fetal position, as I cried quietly. These episodes took two hours to run their course. Michael always came and sat by me.

"Honey, is there anything I can do?" he asked, rubbing my curved back.

"No," I sniffed. "I'll be okay in a bit. Just let me be." I patted him with love and dismissal at the same time; I had been here before. I knew what to do. But the first time I experienced this black hole, I felt cut adrift, without help. Eyes locked shut, only darkness engulfed me. *Lord, where are you in this place of desolation? You must be here somewhere!*

Light and focus came gradually. On the screen of my mind, a majestic image of our blue-green earth, rotating on its axis, came into view—like a magnificent moving picture. In this dark place, God, like the sun at night, hovered on the other side of the earth. I had to wait for the world to turn to see the sun shine again. God remained—omnipotent, omnipresent, omniscient. He could love me from the other side of the planet. I was never alone. This darkness would pass. *Focus on the Son, and all will be well.*

And it was. I knew how to wait out the episodes, after the Lord's explanation on the movie screen of my mind.

Approximately two hours later, as if a switch had been flipped, the darkness lifted, the hopelessness vanished, and I returned to *the living* again. I popped up to a sitting position, smiled at Michael, and said, "I'm back," like I had just arrived home from the grocery store.

Before I became ill, Michael and I had made plans to visit the Chesapeake Bay Eastern Shore. One of Fell's friends owned a small house on the bay in Rock Hall, Maryland. In April 1993, he offered us a week's stay at the end of June, since he would be away. Only one month after my strange affliction struck, the time came for our vacation on the Chesapeake. I had not ventured out except to work and grocery shop—necessities. The idea of packing food and clothing overwhelmed me; leaving for a strange place terrified me. The morning of our planned departure, fear paralyzed me in bed.

Michael saw I hadn't moved. "You have to get up if we're going to have any time left today after traveling."

"Honey, I don't know if I can do this," I said in a small, quavering voice. "I'm afraid to leave the house feeling like this."

He came and stood by my bed, concerned. "We don't have to go. If you think it's better, we'll stay home."

Torn, I realized staying home would ruin a free vacation for Michael, Jess, and her best friend, Jenn. We always took a friend for Jess on vacation. "Just let me stay here for another few minutes." He nodded and went into the bathroom.

Oh, Lord, please help me, please help me. Jesus, help me, I prayed.

Without warning, a loud voice in my head shouted "GO!"

Michael turned back just in time to see me leap out of bed with an awestruck look on my face.

"We're going," I said and went to get my suitcase.

I stayed at the cottage while Michael took the kids to the Naval Academy in Annapolis. Without fear of having enough energy for my job, I did things that were impossible to do at home: A book came to life as I read. Journal pages filled with writing. Artwork flowed onto paper. My body and mind let go of worried care for the first time in a month. God presided, answered my prayer, told me to go, and I did. His gift didn't go to waste: vacations became possible.

I had scored against the dragon within. *You're going to make it.* My affliction, disease, disability remained a mystery. But I had just begun to fight the monster.

If I couldn't win, I would go down fighting to the end. God stayed by my side, strengthened me, and led me into the fray.

3 6

FIGHTING THE DRAGON

"Is anyone among you suffering? Let him pray."
— James 5:13

ON THE CUSP of a new job, my dart prayers kept flying heavenward. I decided to pursue one more physician for a diagnosis before giving up and "living with it," whatever "it" was. Dr. Hawthorne's degree in neurology and reputation persuaded me to make the appointment. Although I had joint and muscle pain, the majority of my most debilitating symptoms appeared to be neurological, brain related.

The doctor sat ensconced behind a large, neat desk as he leafed through my complete medical history and blood work. My blood pressure and temperature read low-normal with my pulse slightly elevated, nothing unusual. He finished his short, physical exam, asked me a few questions, and stared at me intently.

"I can't find anything wrong with you," he stated. "As a matter of fact, all of your tests are excellent."

"Then what is wrong with me?" I asked in desperation. "I'm not imagining this. I had to sell my horse. I can't walk a quarter of a mile without sleeping for two or three hours to recover. My life is in shambles!"

He tapped his finger on my medical records. "Many people believe they are ill. I'm sorry. I can't help you."

With that, the appointment ended. I left, dazed by his finality and the implication that the issue lived in my head. I received the same look from my family doctor; the shades behind his eyes lowered. "Nothing wrong with the tests." End of story. Apparently, I would have to "live with it."

I turned to my work, as I tried to move on with my life. The new job started out on an interesting note. There was only one patient on the schedule. Jake Turley explained a physical therapist before me "ran the business into the ground." As a salaried employee, my finances wouldn't suffer. It meant starting on the ground floor with the practice's marketing and referral base. *No problem*, I thought.

Carol, the office manager, seemed friendly. As we became acquainted, she explained West Chester Physical Therapy and Fitness Center's past. A terrible car accident had sidelined the original, very successful owner. She hired a PT to run the business, but he made no attempt to attract new patients. Finally, as a last resort, she sold the business to Jim Shindler. His sidekick, Jake Turley, didn't own any stock in the company; he did the advertising and general management for Jim.

My interview with Turley and Shindler went well. I knew I had the job. Turley—five feet, ten inches, and balding had a joke for every occasion. Shindler—dapper, six feet tall, curly brown hair, and dark eyes—had a dead-serious persona compared to Turley's light, friendly humor. Where Jake Turley had watery blue eyes and talked easily on almost any subject, Jim Shindler had shrewd brown eyes and spoke only about business. Impressed with the friendly affect that Turley portrayed and his apparent good communication skills, I jumped in the ring when Jake offered me the job. My new position would start three weeks later.

Amid tears, I said goodbye to my friend and protector, Karla. We would keep in touch.

The next meeting a month later turned interesting, when the two explained I should purchase West Chester Physical Therapy and Fitness Center in six months, after I made it a great success. They said this as if my success were bound to happen, making this sudden leap sound plausible and reasonable. Caught off-guard, I told them several months would have to pass before I could even consider such an offer.

Michael, like I, expressed amazement at Shindler and Turley making such an offer. It seemed so far-fetched that we shrugged and went on, as if it had never been mentioned.

But Michael's professional life took an unexpected turn. Barry Cade, the CEO of SCCMC and Michael's boss, called him in for an appointment. Michael would no longer be department head of the PT department. "Nothing personal, you understand, Michael," the CEO said. "I'll announce the changes and explain more at the next department head meeting. I wanted you to know your salary won't change." Stung with a move that had been whispered as mere speculation the month before, the business decision came to light as planned at the next department head meeting—and "effective immediately." A well-known rehabilitation center took over management of Michael's department. Within a year, Michael slouched home, more disgruntled than usual.

"I need to look for another job," he said in disgust. "I've been at SCCMC for fifteen years in middle management. I want a total change within PT. Maybe I need this push to move on."

I mentioned to Jake that Michael may be looking for a job. "Tell Michael not to take any job yet. I think there's a physical therapy job opening in one of our Intermediate Unit [IU] contracts."

Michael surprised me. He was interested in the IU job. "Honey," I said, "You've never worked with pediatrics. What makes you interested in this job?"

"I wanted something completely different. This job could be

made-to-order. I bought a book on pediatric physical therapy, so I can discuss the needs of the IU. I want to be familiar with the testing used for kids."

The job, at the Delaware County Intermediate Unit, boasted an excellent salary and summers off as a part of the school system. Michael came home pleased with the interview. "Honey, they offered me the job at the IU, and I like the job description. The salary is great, and I'll have summers off. What do you think?"

"It sounds wonderful. You're okay with the drive?"

"It's a little more traffic, but no big deal. The biggest thing this job has going for it is I'm working on my own. It's totally different from hospital work, and I'm not middle management."

"Well, it sounds like the DCIU job checks all the boxes on your wish list." I watched Michael's face as he thought about this opportunity. His jaw didn't look tight, and his brow had no furrows in it. He looked more relaxed than I'd seen him in months. I told him so.

He smiled at me, a good smile without tension. "You know, I think you're right. I think I'll like working with the kids."

"So you're going to take it?" I asked to make sure I read him right.

"Yeah, I think I will."

A future tea party showing Michael's imaginative "kid capabilities."

His DCIU responsibilities revolved around elementary schools in two school districts: Chester Upland and Penn Delco, including Rose Tree Media, a private school. Although Chester Upland, located in a rough neighborhood, could have been a problem, Michael never had any trouble. The neighborhood men knew his car. He helped their kids, and they knew it. He worked school hours and came home with funny stories about the kids. His enthusiasm buoyed my heart. I felt relieved and began to relax.

Michael now worked for AMC, a company that staffed home care and IU contracts. Jim Shindler, who also owed West Chester Physical Therapy and Fitness Center [WCPT&FC] owned AMC. Michael did home care during summer vacation. While working on improving our client base at WCPT, I filled in my afternoon schedule with nearby home care patients.

One sunny afternoon, I treated a new home care patient that changed my life. As I took Pat's history and began hearing about her symptoms, my ears perked up, and I listened more closely. Then, a light bulb went off. I recognized most of my own symptoms were being described by Pat. I told her some of the problems I experienced with my mystery disease.

"Violet, you have Lyme Disease," Pat exclaimed. "Go see Dr. Toren in Roxborough. He's the only one who helped me."

"Lyme Disease has never been mentioned by any of my many doctors. It was never on the radar. I guess God had a larger purpose in our meeting," I said. "You're helping me!"

I began researching Lyme Disease and found a published list of symptoms; I had thirty-two of the thirty-four. Michael drove me to see Dr. Toren, an internist, who listened intently to my description of life before this "illness," and life after. He looked at my symptom list and sifted my records. At the end of the visit, he gave me a lab slip for tests, one called a "Western Blot," a test for Lyme Disease.

Next visit, Dr. Toren reviewed my test results. "Your Western Blot Test indicates two bands that relate to the Lyme spirochete. According to the Center for Disease Control, Lyme is not treated unless there are five bands on the test. But I'm going to start you on Doxycycline," he said. "You have had severe symptoms for two years, so let's see how you do, and we'll go from there."

The Doxycycline cleared up my joint pain, but not my brain fog, memory, or cognitive issues. On my next visit, he changed the antibiotic to Ceftin, large caplets the color of a robin's egg. After the first dose, my symptoms became worse.

"Don't worry," Dr. Toren said. "It sounds like a Herxheimer

Reaction. When the spirochetes begin to die off, there can be a temporary increase in symptoms for the next several days."

The next time I visited him, I drove myself, braving the Schuylkill Expressway to Roxborough. But my cognitive symptoms and memory had not returned to their original abilities. After six months, Dr. Toren decided to change my prescription. "I want to start IV antibiotics, since we've had good partial results with oral doses. I'll have a home care nurse come to your house to place the IV. We'll use a drug called Claforan."

A PICC line, placed in the crook of my elbow, threaded up a vein in my arm where it ended near my heart. But my physical job displaced the IV catheter within three days. Dr. Toren sent me to a surgeon to insert the catheter into my chest. During the surgery, I surfaced and heard the surgeon complain that I had tiny blood vessels. I surfaced again a littler later and said, "Did you get that little sucker in there yet?"

"Harry...!" the surgeon warned the anesthesiologist. After that, I awakened in recovery.

A specialized IV nurse taught me "sterile technique" in changing my dressing to protect the catheter. I learned the sterile sequence to hook up IV tubing to the "Groshong Catheter" in my chest. The first dose, I broke for lunch, snagged the bag of antibiotics from the refrigerator, and hooked it up to my catheter. I ate and did paperwork, until I noticed an arctic chill coming from the inside out. Shivering, I realized too late that the bag of fluid dripping into my chest was 40 degrees Fahrenheit. Next time, I tucked the bag in my waistband and carried it around with me for an hour or so before hooking it up. Body temperature IV fluid worked just fine.

I settled into the treatment regime and turned my eyes toward the future, hoping to increase my activity level at home—including the care of our sixteen-year-old daughter. The disease dragon had a name, and slaying it became my goal.

God at work is an awesome power. I knew my life would get better. If the Lord closed a door, He opened a window.

37

DECEPTION

"...He [Jesus] said, 'Assuredly, I say to you, one of you will betray me.'"
— *Matthew* 26:21

IN THE MIDDLE of my quest for health, Jim Shindler moved our office and started a gym called "Fit for Your Life." Patients arrived at our PT office, located in back of the gym, after walking through state-of-the-art gym equipment. Two weeks before the equipment arrived, Jake came into my office with a handful of forms.

"Violet, I need you to sign a bunch of Medicare forms. Clear your desk for a minute." He had organized all the forms, layered under the top one, with only the signature lines showing.

"Thanks, Jake. You didn't have to go through all this trouble."

"No problem, Jake said." I signed the forms in three minutes, and he whisked them away.

I had started IV antibiotics. The brain fog and fatigue got worse before they got better; I had enough experience to understand the reaction as normal. By now, with a good patient population, Michael and I realized we could make the business successful. He worked with me after his school day ended at the IU and all summer. The more Michael and I discussed buying the practice, the better it sounded. I asked a lawyer at church if we needed counsel.

"Do you trust them?" he asked.

"Yes, I think so," I said.

"Then you should be okay."

We bought the practice in July, 1995, on my youngest sister's birthday. Michael and I met on the same day in 1972, twenty-three years before we signed the purchase agreement for West Chester Physical Therapy and Fitness Center.

It turned out that our new business needed a few old wrinkles ironed out of the works—big wrinkles we hadn't seen before the purchase. One afternoon, I received a phone call.

"Violet, I hope you don't mind the first name basis. I didn't want to butcher your last name."

The man on the phone introduced himself as Jim Shindler's attorney.

"You need a lawyer. Jim is not paying the rent on the commercial property, and he's not paying the equipment bill you co-signed."

"What do you mean the equipment bill I co-signed? That's not my equipment!"

"I have a copy of the agreement of sale for fitness machines with your signature on it, along with Jake Turley's. Do you sign things for your practice's billing?"

"Yes, of course," I exclaimed. "When we bought the practice, we kept Jake Turley as our billing manager. He's always giving me things to sign."

"Well, I'm afraid you signed some things under false pretenses. Shindler and Turley, your business managers, are not living up to their contract. They have not paid Carol, your billing secretary, for the last month. You need to get a lawyer who I can discuss this with. I'm supposed to be representing Shindler; but I've been down this road before with him, and I don't want to see you get burned."

"Which lawyer would you recommend? You've been kind enough to alert me to this fiasco. Who would you like to work with?"

"Alan Abrams." He proceeded to give me Alan's phone number. "He's in practice with his brother who's a divorce attorney. He's sharp, fair, and communicates well; this is his specialty. You'll like him."

I cornered Turley when he came in that afternoon. "Who do we rent from, Jake?" I asked, all innocence. Jake's expression betrayed suspicion and concern.

"Why?" he asked.

"I'm paying you for the square footage we use for WCPT. I want to know who the check goes to." He shrugged and pulled a card out of his wallet: *Lambert and Reamer Realty*, the card read. *Harold J. Thornton*. The phone number and address were there as well—everything I needed to check out the lawyer's story before Michael came.

I called Harold J. Thornton and made an appointment to see him. Before I disconnected, I asked him a single question. He answered succinctly.

"Yes, the rent due is one month in arears."

"I will see you at 1:00 p.m. tomorrow to discuss this situation. Thank you for your time."

As if on cue, Carol came into the office. "Violet, I have to talk to you," she said.

"You haven't been paid."

"My paycheck bounced," she said scowling. "I talked to my husband, and he said I should resign."

"Can you give me at least couple of weeks? All this is breaking today. They're not paying the rent either. I know you have been patient."

"Sure," she said. "You know, I thought it was strange. Jim Shindler was really angry that the health insurance reimbursements were not in by the time you two bought the practice. There were thousands of dollars outstanding, and the money is just starting to trickle in now."

"I paid several bills that were overdue. It looks like Shindler wanted to run with the profits and stick us with the bills," I said, reflecting on the timeline of events.

"I'll stay as long as you need me. You'll need to hire someone I can train in the billing," Carol said. "I'm going to stay home and take care of the house and my husband for a while after this job!"

Michael, and I dissected the situation together; we began scheming. "Shindler has our company checkbook," he said. They're supposed to be managing the business portion of our practice. Give me that lawyer's phone number. Let's get an appointment now, and get our company checkbook back from Shindler!"

The next day, I sat in a pleasantly furnished office at Lambert and Reamer Realty. "Mr. Thornton, I'm sorry you were not paid last month. We paid Jim Shindler a third of the rent, since that's the square footage our physical therapy practice covers. I will pay you personally from now on."

"I can't accept a partial payment," he said. "I'm so sorry."

"You should take the partial payment. I don't know if you will get anything out of Shindler. My husband and I have an appointment with an attorney this week to sever ties with Shindler and Turley.

Mr. Thornton looked out the window for a few seconds before turning back to face me. "All right," he said. "You make a good point about something being better than nothing."

We closed the meeting in agreement. I asked, as an afterthought, "We will need a property close by. Will you look into commercial properties for our business?" I gave him a West Chester Physical Therapy & Fitness Center, P.C. card.

Mr. Thornton—probably twenty years my senior—gave me a fatherly smile, took the card. and said, "Of course. It is a pleasure doing business with you."

I badgered Jake Turley to bring us the company checkbook from Shindler's office for a week. Finally, Michael said to me, "Tell Turley I'm picking up the checkbook tomorrow at Shindler's office. It better be there, ready to hand over to me."

Since Jake hadn't picked up the checkbook from Shindler, I told Jake that Michael would the next day.

"But you can't do that," Jake exclaimed, horror-stricken.

"Jake, you knew I was ill when you hired me. You and Shindler stiffed Carol on her last paycheck. You haven't paid the rent for this place. We own that checkbook. Michael will be at AMC to pick it up tomorrow. I wouldn't cross him. He *will* make a scene if it's not there waiting for him, I guarantee!"

Jake's face turned a pasty color, tinged with gray. I walked away from the cheat and liar who I had trusted and considered a friend. Michael picked up the company checkbook the next day without incident. He and I hugged and sighed with relief.

Next, we had to move the practice.

God worked with us and for us. He shined light into all the dark places, so we could make things right with His help. The best would come with time—God's time.

38

BEAUTY FOR ASHES

"...He has sent Me to heal the brokenhearted...
To comfort all who mourn,
To console those who mourn in Zion,
To give them beauty for ashes,
The oil of joy for mourning,
The garment of praise for the spirit of heaviness; That they
may be called trees of righteousness,
The planting of the Lord, that He may be glorified."
— Isaiah 61:1–3

ALAN ABRAM'S MODEST OFFICE, located on a back street in West Chester, looked like an unassuming brownstone with a brass plaque outside the door: *Abrams & Abrams, Attorneys at Law.* Slightly stocky but not muscular, Mr. Abrams looked soft and a bit over-weight. Shorter than Michael's five feet eight inches, his balding, sandy hair gave him a non-descript look. He wouldn't stand out in a crowd, yet a presence about him made me comfortable.

Alan dove into the matter at hand. "I talked to Dave, Jim

Shindler's lawyer. He called me, actually. Very helpful! You have quite a situation here."

We laid out the contract with AMC, our articles of incorporation for West Chester Physical Therapy & Fitness Center, and our PT licenses. Alan already had a copy of the AMC contract. He also had the co-signed equipment contract. I saw my signature clearly displayed.

"I've known about this mess exactly five days," I said. "I'm stunned that this is happening. I have no knowledge of how my signature got on that equipment contract other than trickery!" My voice hardened as I pointed to my familiar handwriting.

Alan nodded. Michael picked up the document and looked at the damning signature. He caught my eye, affirming my distress. "That's your signature, all right," he said.

I nodded. "Now what do we do?" Michael and I both looked at Alan.

"Do you have any idea how you signed this contract?" Alan asked.

I sat—quiet and rational amidst the internal, raging storm. When I could trust my voice, I said, "I think they thought I was sick enough that they would get away with this. It's a form of fraud and robbery all wrapped up and whitewashed. I was ill and trusting enough to sign all the Medicare billing without reading it. My bet is he slipped it in with all the billing that needed my signature to process."

Alan nodded. "I can't tell you how many times I've seen this. It's a prime example of why I have a job. Tell me the sequence of events from the beginning."

I remembered getting bills totaling over $1,800 for equipment and stationery that were three months old with "*Third Notice*" in glaring red. I phoned the companies and explained we were new owners, and the bills would be paid as soon as possible. They all seemed very understanding, and each one expressed relief, that I phoned after months of silence and no payments. I gave Alan a verbal picture, and we listed all the business incongruencies we could remember.

"Just a few more questions," he said. We spent the next hour discussing details. Alan crafted a battle plan.

On our way back to West Chester PT, Michael and I took a drive in the neighborhood of our present practice site. Attractive office parks and commercial space for rent looked plentiful. We dropped the rent check off to Mr. Thornton, who waved us over. I introduced Michael to him as handshakes were exchanged.

Mr. Thornton said. "I know you're looking for an office space. There's a very nice group of professional buildings just diagonally across from your present location with a space for rent. Here's the card for the realtor." He handed me a card and nodded to both of us.

"Well, good luck to both of you! Let me know how you make out with the real estate."

We thanked him and drove to look at the office park on Boot Road and Paoli Pike. The handsome, dark brick edifice—one of four buildings centered in the parking lot—stood facing a busy road. Each business had a unique sign on the left side of the door. Chocolate brown trim outlined each building, an artistic and professional touch. A prime location, with easy access to a main road, the site seemed perfect for our practice. We made an appointment for the next day.

The building housed three offices, 100B and 100C at ground level with an elevator or stairs to 100A, "Shannon Architectural Design and Construction." Jack Shannon's name was on the card in my hand. We knocked and walked into a busy, open environment with windows facing a grassy courtyard. A dry, faux creek bed of fist sized, pink granite, river stones, ran through the center of the yard, spanned by a whimsical bridge from one side to the other. Complemented with a weeping cherry, gracefully cascading in full, mauve bloom, the scene had a charming and soothing effect. Each building's back windows viewed this sunny, green courtyard and opened for fresh air.

"Oh, you have come at the right time," Jack Shannon said with an outstretched hand. Of medium build, he had a florid complexion with a shock of silver hair. "The bunch in 100C moved out in the middle of the night leaving furniture behind—*big* furniture." He turned to his desk drawer and pulled out some keys. "It's just downstairs." He started for the door. "If you're interested, you can have any of the furniture they left. It'll save me from putting more junk in storage." He chose the stairs instead of the elevator, a testament to his trim frame.

Cheap, multi-hued, tan carpet covered the floor. But other than paint, carpet, and partitions, the space seemed perfect. Bright with natural light, a large room for our office faced the tranquil, courtyard scene. The large outer room had space for three curtained treatment cubicles, a large mat table, a partition for a waiting room, and a separate reception/business office. I could picture the layout.

"We're just starting to look for office space, but this is the right size," I said. Michael gave me a look, *Don't give away too much information.* With an imperceptible nod to him, I said, "We have a few other places to look at before we make a decision."

"We are interested. We'll see if the timing works," Michael added.

"And the desks and chairs could stay if we decide to sign a lease," I said.

Shannon gave us the details on rent, utilities, and water as well as condominium fees. Not inexpensive, but in our financial ballpark. Once in the car, Michael and I talked with excitement. We called Alan to let him know we found a new location.

Armed with indisputable facts, Alan extricated us from our former management contract. Both attorneys worked together, allowing us time for lease signing and renovations. Jack Shannon, our new landlord, recommended an architect who designed and drew up plans for the out-build. He created the blueprint format and suggested a reputable builder who could complete the project in our timeframe. Dovetailed, smooth cooperation among so many people meant God's signature was on the plans.

In six weeks, as construction neared completion, we chose off-white walls with a slate-blue tint and wall-to-wall, blue-and-green, loop Berber carpet. The office glass rose from waist height to the ceiling with a pass-through window for patient registration. Chart file cabinets and one of Shannon's left-behind desk and chair sets furnished our business manager's office. A patient waiting area—partitioned from the treatment room by a three-quarter height wall—had three upholstered chairs, with a small pie-crust table and Victorian lamp. The tiny waiting area, although eclectic in design, looked welcoming like the rest of the office. A variegated philodendron in a classy container sat on top of the three-quarter wall adding a touch of living green. We were ready.

During the six weeks of construction, treatment continued at the Fit for Your Life location, while our out-build bloomed. In a seamless move, all of our patients would be re-routed to the new building one block away after construction finished. Secrecy prevented either of the former managers from denying us access to our equipment and patient records. As a bonus, a small room would be rented to a massage therapist who worked at "Fit for Your Life." Bill Manfredi—an honest, high-energy man in his twenties—had a degree in athletic training and massage therapy, a good fit and income source for our practice.

Michael and I positioned our large, free desks so they faced each other. The comfortable, expensive office chairs had also been left behind, gifts from God through Jack Shannon.

I received a call from our former realtor, Harry Thornton. His company was contemplating a lawsuit including me, WCPT, Fit for Your Life Corporation, and Jim Shindler for breach of contract. He wanted me to know ahead of time about the suit.

"Harry, do what you have to do. You know I've paid our square footage and tried to be honest with you."

"I know, Violet. I'll see what I can arrange," Harry replied.

Our lawyer called me in a week. "Harry Thornton sent me a copy of the suit against Fit for Your Life. Neither West Chester Physical Therapy nor you, Violet, are named. The suit holds your company and you personally 'harmless' in the action."

"That's incredible," I exclaimed.

"Yes, it is," he said. "And quite, quite unusual."

God was at it again. Michael and I prayed thanksgiving, gratitude, and praise. I wrote a thank-you card to Harry.

Our office moved out of Fit for Your Life on a Friday afternoon after the manager left for the day. A moving company took care of the big items with their truck, while Bill Manfredi, Michael, and I packed boxes to go. Carol had our new office manager trained in the preceding weeks. She would start Monday when we opened for business, free and clear of Turley and Shindler, our former management team. In the rapid move, we left our sound system—radio, CD player, and speakers—in the Fit for Your Life gym.

While Bill Manfredi worked at Fit for Your Life another week, he set up his own massage therapy practice in our office and prepared for his new job as a stretching coach with the Philadelphia Eagles. I phoned Saturday afternoon and told him we had forgotten to move the stereo from the old place. "So just come over and get it. Turley left already. He turned purple when he saw all your stuff was gone!"

I laughed. "I can picture that. I'll be over in fifteen minutes."

In the middle of the Fit for Your Life gym, with people on the workout equipment, I turned off the CD player. Bill helped me dismantle the components and load them in the back of my station wagon. Five minutes later, we had everything unloaded at our new address.

"You better get back before they miss you," I said to Bill after thanking him several times.

"I'm going to put this thing back together, so you can have music when you open on Monday. I'm not in a hurry; someone's watching the shop."

With Bill's help, we had music on Monday morning. Our patients loved the new office. The practice thrived, and so did we.

273

Nearly a year later, I drove past Fit for Your Life, now an empty building. I called Carol to see what happened to her. She said Jake Turley and Jim Shindler took the fitness machines and gave them away to family and friends instead of returning them to the company they'd bought them from. Shindler never paid for them. Jake Turley moved to Hilton Head, South Carolina.

Carol quit before Fit for Your Life folded. Turley and Shindler never paid her final paycheck. "No surprise," I said when I learned of this.

"My husband wanted me to quit anyway," Carol said. "The aggravation wasn't worth the money. Creditors called non-stop, and they wanted me to lie. So, now I'm happy taking care of Charlie and our home!"

"Come visit us sometime, now that you're footloose and fancy-free," I said. Carol chuckled and agreed.

Soon after I talked to Carol, I received a phone call from the equipment company that furnished all the fitness machines to Fit for Your Life. The gentleman noted my signature was on the contract.

"Yes, but I didn't know I signed it. Jake Turley must have put it in with all the Medicare bills that I had to sign. I was very ill at the time. I'm sorry."

"Oh, I see; here is a note. We heard from your lawyer, Alan Abrams. Our company has decided not to pursue you or your company. But, please, Ma'am, could you tell me where Jake Turley lives? He's the one responsible for the equipment."

"I'm sorry. I don't have an address, but the last I heard, he moved to Hilton Head, South Carolina."

"Thank you very much," he said.

A week after the equipment company called me, I received another phone call, this time from Jake Turley himself. After minimal opening conversation, he gave the real reason for his call. "Why did you tell them where I lived?"

"Did you pay them?" I asked.

"What business is that of yours?" His surly tone lit my fuse.

"You know, you have a real nerve saying that to me. You tricked me into co-signing for that equipment, defaulted on the rent, stiffed Carol, and stuck us with bills while pillaging our PT profits. Of course I gave them your general location. You lied to me. And you owe them the money!"

After a tiny pause, I heard a click and a dial tone. He hung up, and became part of an "interesting" history.

We spent three, happy years building our practice at the 100C location. Late one afternoon, Michael came in with thought-provoking news. "I ran into our neighbor at the mailbox. He said that Unit 200C next door is going up for sale. Our tax deductions would be a lot better with a mortgage than rent, and the rate will be fixed. Our rent's going up again. Do you want to look at it?"

"Definitely," I said.

We moved into our own, spacious, double condo—one building down from 100C—after the usual process of outfitting a new location. What a joy for my creative side, as I designed the new space, choosing carpet and wall colors with Michael.

My youngest sister, Gay, needed a job just when we needed a new office manager. Our daughter, Jessica, also worked with us one summer. We were able to pitch in and help with her expensive, out-of-state college tuition, so her loans would be less.

Michael's and my desks still faced each other; he treated his patients on one side of the condo, while I treated mine on the other. We had the best of all worlds when a second opinion or a medical question needed addressing. Patients' personalities and diagnoses matched with our preferences. Each of us had favorite specialty areas within physical therapy. And, I could still kiss him in the back room, the best of the precious perks, working together with someone I loved and respected.

The practice became the joyful peak of my career with the love of my life, Michael—all created by His design: beauty for ashes. Wrought by God through turmoil, strife, kindness, and love, all hammered by hand into a practical, precious vessel for which I will be forever grateful.

"Mom, how can you leave here? You've spent a lifetime in this house that your father built." I looked behind her, scanning the magnificent home and grounds.

She smiled with a tinge of sadness and patted my cheek. "Honey, it took me a long time to learn, thanks to Fell, that this house is just another *thing*. Life is not about a house. I want Fell to enjoy life, not be tied down to four acres of mowing every week of the summer. I want to enjoy life with him too."

Caring for the family home and four-and-a-half acres had become a burden for Mom and Fell. Even though Michael and I were blessed to live only seven miles away from them, Daddy wouldn't ask for help with the yard work. Mom and Fell made plans to sell our family home near the Schuylkill River and move to a condo in Chesterbrook. At least it wasn't much farther away. Camera in hand, I walked from room to room, snapping pictures of the artful décor that we kids took for granted until we had to say goodbye.

The yard in full bloom and Mom's unique, elegant decorating style lived on, preserved through my camera. My goodbye to "Earl's Haven" turned into a photo album. Mom smiled.

My sisters and I lived in only one home until we grew up and left. Earl's Haven slipped away from me only in a physical sense, because the same kind of beauty and wildlife surrounded Michael and me at Eden Hill, our own home. The family home of my childhood still lived in my mind, whooping with joy, jumping down the hall stairs, streaking through the house and out the back door on bare feet. I had lived my early life surrounded by woods, meadows, and river, dappled sunlight and breezes, bird songs and whirring cicadas, glowing dawns, dusks, and star-fire. The imprint on my childhood and teenage years held lavish, immortal color, substance of God's creation, held close in my memories.

Eden Hill held the same natural wonders at a different stage of my life. No loss, just a trade, the gift of one place for another, childhood to adulthood as is time's responsibility.

Chesterbrook also proved a trade at the right time—God's blessing and timing, of course.

3 9

OUT OF THE NEST

...when I became a man (woman,) I put away childish things
— *1 Corinthians 13:11*

JESSICA's senior year of high school ushered in unexpected changes
—what a surprise. She chose to switch from horses to swimming and
we sold Josh to a good home. He turned into a fine, competitive
jumper. When it came time for college, Florida Tech called to Jessica.
I worried. *So far away from home!* There would be no homemade
chicken soup delivered when she had a cold. Jess decided on a school
at the south end of the East Coast, with further discussion futile. If
we vetoed her choice, any failure at another school would be seen as
our fault. So, I went and sat by the pool on a cloudless, sunny day—
and prayed.

A red-tailed hawk circled overhead, keening. It circled lower and
lower, repeating its wailing call. I could clearly see its markings and
red tail. Flying still lower, it keened more urgently. My heart opened
as I felt this mother hawk tell me: *If she could push her babies out of
the nest, I could too. All would be well with the Lord, who made her
soar and gave me the message.*

When we drove Jessica to college and moved her into the dorm, I had a wonderful sense of accomplishment. I cried, leaving the campus for home.

"She'll be all right, Violet," Michael said with a sympathetic look.

"Oh, honey, I'm not crying because I'm worried about her. I'm crying because we got her here alive! I kept you two from killing each other. You're so much alike."

"Ah," he said with a little upturn of his mouth.

I laughed and wiped my eyes. "All kinds of memories bubble up in my mind. Remember when she turned fourteen months old, and Mom and Fell babysat her?"

Michael smiled at me and patted my knee, "I'll never forget it. What movie did we see that night?"

"I don't remember the movie. But, on our way home, I remember we went right past Mom's and parked down the river road to continue our 'date.'"

This time, Michael grinned at me and said, "It's lucky that neighbor didn't call the police any earlier!"

Laughing, I said, "Yeah. I had just buckled Jess's car seat in the back, when they came at us with spotlights."

Michael said, still grinning, "You stuck out your hand and pointed to your wedding band."

"And I said, 'We're married. My Mom is babysitting our fourteen-month-old just up the road.'"

Michael nodded. "They got a good laugh out of that."

"And we did too. They disappeared so quickly." We chuckled for a few minutes about that particular memory. "We could reminisce all the way home with Jess stories. Remember when she took karate?" I asked.

"That was one of the best things we did, the karate lessons. She needed an outlet. Her instructor really did a good job teaching her the meaning of respect," Michael said.

"And Master Goh made sure the kids knew karate was only for self-defense. I remember in fourth grade, she came home and said,

279

'Mom, I might get a detention.' When I asked her why, she told me she used karate on the playground. She helped some of the girls being bullied by a boy. It sounded like this kid bullied them on a regular basis," I said.

"I remember. Jess swept his feet out from under him, and the playground monitor ducked behind the school building, laughing. She knew this kid as a bully who got what he deserved." Michael shook his head. "Jess is a piece of work!"

"No two ways about it," I said. "I told Jess we would back her in this situation, but she would have to serve detention if they decided to punish her. And she was okay with that."

"But the teacher never reported her, did she?" Michael asked.

"There was never any detention. I asked Jess about the boy that she swept. Apparently, he stopped bothering the girls after that."

We were quiet for a few minutes before I asked Michael, "What's your favorite Jessica story?"

"It's a toss-up. The time she asked to 'borrow' my car keys at our church spaghetti dinner to get something out of the car and went for a joyride. She didn't know how to use a stick shift, and her cousin was with her in the car."

I rolled my eyes. "She was fifteen. That's the first time we grounded her for a month. Scared me to death! My sister almost bit my head off after that little stunt. She could have gotten little Lynney and herself killed. That kid's guardian angels worked overtime that night. What's the other story?"

"The time she changed the grades on her report card," he said.

"Tenth or eleventh grade?" Michael shrugged. I continued, "She went seventeen weeks without doing homework, and no one called us from school."

"I never understood that. Two full report periods," he said, as he pulled into a rest stop. "Are you hungry?"

"Yeah, I could eat," I said. "She told me she realized her grades would show in the final marking period, so she fessed up. Then I did a

Pontius Pilate routine." I motioned washing my hands. "I told her it wasn't my homework, and I was never going to ask about her homework again. That year counted for college, and if she didn't get into school, she'd have to work and pay rent. Now summer school was the only way she could bring her grades up for college." I looked out the window as the parking lot came into view. "She kept me hopping, that's for sure! I think that was the second time we grounded her for a month."

Michael gave a wry shake of his head. "But, you know, she fixed it! She worked so hard in summer school, she pulled her grades up and got into Florida Tech. Unbelievable!"

We got out of the car, stretched, and had a bathroom stop before lunch—a nice break before we hit the road again.

Michael asked, "So, what is *your* favorite Jessica story?"

"When she was sixteen or seventeen and we trusted her alone overnight. We went to Shaun's wedding in western Pennsylvania," I said.

"Oh, yeah. That's when I found the bag of beer cans in the woods."

"That's not *my* favorite part of the story," I laughed. "When I saw my trampled gardens and overturned orchids, I asked her what the heck happened. She said *a tornado* went through while we were gone. I said, 'Oh really? Well, that tornado had feet.' That was the third time we grounded her for a month."

"She didn't really invite all of those kids, did she?"

"Nah. She only invited a few, but word spread, and a whole bunch crashed the party. Actually, she protected the house."

"How'd she do that?" Michael asked.

"She came in and found a girl she didn't know sitting on our living room couch with a lit cigarette. She knew cigarette smoke would be a dead give-away. Plus, she got worried about the house being trashed if any drunk kids got in. She chased everyone outside and locked the doors."

"That was good thinking in a bad situation."

I agreed. "But my favorite memories are working at the barn, riding, and going to her horse shows before I got Lyme."

"What's your favorite 'after Lyme' story?" he asked.

I thought for less than a minute. "I was always so exhausted with those spirochetes attacking my brain. All I could do was go to work, come home, and crash. One Christmas, we had the tree in the stand. I don't remember if we put the lights on it already. I was too tired to do anymore; I had to work the next day. Anyway, I came home from work the following day, and Jess met me at the door. As I came in, she said, 'Ta-da!' There was our Christmas tree, completely decorated! It was perfect! That's at the top of the favorites list for me. I was so grateful, and she did an incredible job."

Michael smiled. "You're better than you were back then."

"Oh, hon', I'm so far from the health I knew before; but it's 1998, and I'm still learning!" He rubbed my shoulder in affectionate understanding, as we continued north. Our new life as a couple started on the way home. Successfully out of the nest, our chick became a faraway, treasured blessing.

So many memories beyond Jess came to mind, not all of them good. God allowed the sad, difficult, over-the-edge times to occur.

His ways are not our ways, yet He has not deserted us. He gives us the choice to desert Him. We are His children; desertion must be terrible for God who gives so much. Without Him, we are dust in the wind. And some choose dust...

4 0

FANFARE

"To everything there is a season,
A time for every purpose under heaven:
A time to be born, And a time to die..."
— Ecclesiastes 3:1–2

"THE GROWTH around the kidney is cancerous," the surgeon said. He paused, familiar with stricken faces like ours, his explosive words reverberating in our hearts. I held Mom's hand a little tighter as the doctor continued. "It's well encapsulated, and I think we got it all. His lymph nodes are clear. With radiation and chemotherapy, he should do well with one kidney."

I hugged Mom hard before she left to be with Fell after he came out of recovery. As always, Michael and I held hands leaving the hospital; but we walked closer together, the full length of our arms touching down to our wrists, fingers interlaced. Our stark understanding of the situation choked us, as heavy silence wrapped each of us like a shroud. Mutual professional knowledge made silence preferable to speech. We had treated debilitated cancer patients, listened to their complaints about radiation and chemotherapy, watched some make it and others fail, pound by pound. I thought of dear Ruth, my best friend, gone but unforgettable.

At home, Michael mowed the lawn—a four-hour job since grass grew on most of our hillside, with only a tiny strip of woods at the northeast end of the property. Navigating the riding mower over steep terrain, cutting in a practiced pattern, his mind lulled by concentration on a normal activity, Michael decompressed.

Incapable of any such activity, I curled up on the couch, Copeland's "Fanfare for the Common Man" filling our living room with majestic French horns and kettle drums. I hit the repeat button over and over, my face washed in the sickening overflow, the terrible thought of life without Fell. This soaring music captured Fell's essence; it lived as his song, in my heart. I grieved the distinct possibility of his loss. I grieved for our whole family. I pushed the dampened couch pillow away, gathered myself, sat up, and folded my hands in prayer.

Michael and I pampered Fell and Mom whenever we could. When Daddy came to Eden Hill after his cancer diagnosis, he sat in the summer shade on a lawn chair near our driveway and gazed, contented, over the front yard landscape. Woods behind the house to his left, the pool downhill in front of him, and the grassy hillside dotted with trees on his right. Our home had to remind him of his joyful gifts to his biological daughter and three stepdaughters: down payments on each of our first homes. He told us the only thing that could make this view better was a good hot dog and an ice-cold beer.

Ever since they had married, he and Mom traveled once or twice a year. They didn't stop traveling after the diagnosis, but we missed them a little more when they were out of the area. Birthday celebrations always landed at Café Le Grande for brunch, everyone's favorite buffet.

Fell's daughter, Leigh, and her husband, Dick, drove from New Mexico with their two children several times over the twenty-five years we had Fell in our lives. They came Thanksgiving week, in the summer, and a couple of other times throughout the year. I never called Leigh my "stepsister" when introducing her to other people. She rated the title of sister in my eyes.

With the news of Fell's diagnosis, calls flew back and forth to Leigh in Illinois. Mom, Gay, and I kept her up-to-date on Fell's condition. All of us, including Lynn, who lived a little farther away toward Philly, loved Fell. Everything about him sparked of honesty, love, generosity, and laughter. Leigh had had him all to herself as an only child. I shared with her what he meant in my life during some long, sister-close, phone conversations.

Looking back, Fell usually had a humorous glint in his eye. When he wanted to comment on a screwy situation, he made a comedic, high-pitched noise, like flustered Cary Grant in *Arsenic and Old Lace*. He had pretended with four-year-old Jess, "Look, Jessica. Look at the pretty purple leaves on the trees!"

"*Grandpère!*" (Grandfather in French, instigated by Mom whose chosen name indicating grandmother was Grand'Mere.) "Oh, Grandpère," Jess said, horrified, "Those leaves are green!"

"Oh, they are? I thought the sky was green."

"Grandpère, the sky is blue!" Jess turned, as I hid my smile. "Mommy," she said with sadness in her voice, "Grandpère doesn't know his colors."

"You'll have to teach me, okay?" Jessica smiled and nodded, took him by the hand, and "taught him his colors."

Daddy often took our collie, Brandy, for chemotherapy, since Michael and I both worked during the day. He said it *made him feel hopeful, as long as Brandy lived and fought lymphoma*. I counted on his sage advice. Every one of us softened around Fell. The family drew close and loved on him at every opportunity.

During the ten years that Daddy had cancer, I missed one Thanksgiving with our family when Leigh and her family visited. That November day, traveling for work, near freezing temperatures turned big raindrops into fat, white, snowflakes. Late as usual, I finished my last home care patient for the morning. Mom, Fell, Michael, and all my sisters, nieces, and nephews were meeting at

285

Café Le Grande to celebrate Fell's birthday and Thanksgiving with Leigh and family. We knew we didn't have unlimited time with Fell and loved to shower him with things he enjoyed.

The roads posed no problem, until I rounded the corner across the Schuylkill River bridge in Phoenixville. At a 90-degree turn onto the bridge, I tapped the brake. The rear end of my little, blue, 2003 Forester fishtailed, as the wheels slid on a sheet of ice. Halfway across the bridge, I lost control.

"Oh GOD!" I screamed. The car's tail swung 180 degrees; the passenger side whipped toward the curb with a crashing impact and quick levitation, before the car and I landed in a small park, facing the icy bridge.

I sat still, breathing hard for a moment, puzzled at the car's position. It should have flipped. With slow, deep breaths, I calmed my racing heart and thanked God for answered prayer and another grace-filled miracle. The car had to be maneuvered farther away from three stainless-steel posts that marked a pedestrian park trail. "Come on, sweetie," I coaxed as it limped but responded to the gas pedal. Out of the car, I took a minute, balanced myself, and began damage inspection. *No blood noted; glasses still intact on my face; my left hip a little sore, but no big deal.* My car told a different story.

The car's condition sent a wave of disbelief and shock through me. The passenger-side wheels had slammed into the curb, the rear wheel hitting first with its alignment skewed to a 30-degree angle. The front wheel angled in 15 degrees, ruling out any kind of celebration with my family.

I phoned Gay and then Michael to let them know the situation. I asked Gay to hug Leigh, Dick, and the kids for me. Michael would meet me at Roberts Subaru in Downingtown. Daryl Fling Towing came within twenty minutes, but the driver couldn't get the flatbed lined up to use the winch on my car.

"Can you drive it two hundred feet, to that open area past the bridge?" he asked, pointing.

"We'll find out," I said, asking for further grace from above. He smiled and nodded.

The faithful, little car lumbered through the field and loaded with ease using the winch. Half an hour later, we arrived at the dealership.

The manager watched as the flatbed, with my car, passed the floor to ceiling windows. One fleeting look at the car's damage was enough. "We don't do body work or replace axles. Here's the address, just a block away, for a body shop we recommend," he said as he handed me a card. "We'll get the car over there for you."

"Thank you. I'll call them tomorrow."

By the time Michael came to drive me home, a large, black-and-blue, circular bruise covered my left hip. Even with a snug seat belt, my hip must have hit the door.

"Honey, my car should have flipped. With the way the car wheels hit the curb, there's no earthly reason that it stayed upright." I described the impact and angled wheels as we headed for home.

"I guess from a physics standpoint, you're right," he said. "What do you think happened?"

"*Angels*," I said smiling with gratitude. "Jesus said we 'little ones' had angels who saw the face of His Father in heaven. I don't see any reason to think they give up on us as adults. I think my guardian angels kept the car from flipping." I put my hand on Michael's thigh and slid my hand up and down its length, a maneuver I frequently used in the passenger seat when he drove. He glanced at me and smiled, his grip light yet firm on my upper arm, telling me he understood my miracle.

I had called out to God in the midst of the accident; He and His angels were there for me. *If only they will take care of Fell*, I thought. Yet, I knew: *Angels are messengers and warriors, under God's authority. Your will be done Lord; but, please, could we keep Daddy a long time?*

"Hey, Mom, how's our guy?" I asked.

"Wait, honey. Let's see if he can tell you. It's Violet, Fell. Do you want to talk to her?"

"Hi."

"Hi Daddy. How's it going?"

"I'm being turned into a pincushion with vitamin C IVs. Now I know what your collie, Brandy, goes through with her chemotherapy. I'm okay. Here's your mom."

Never one to spend time on the phone, Fell turned it over to Mom.

"Mom, go in a different room so you can talk to me about Fell."

"Okay, I'm in the bedroom. He sounds different, doesn't he?" Mom said, more of a statement than a question.

"Yeah. What's going on?"

"Oh, I'm going to cry," she said, blowing her nose.

"Aw, Mom, I'm sorry. What is it?"

"I'm starting to see some changes in Fell's walking. There are times he doesn't quite have his balance. He's fine mentally. You know that Dr. Grace, his oncologist, uses both traditional and alternative medicine. He may have Fell take radiation if there is deterioration."

"Is he actually losing his balance, Mom? I'll want to teach you fall prevention and how to lower him to the ground if he's going to go down. He's too tall and heavy for you to hold up if he starts falling."

"No. He just sidesteps every once in a while. He didn't do it in the doctor's office. Dr. Grace is a friend of the family after all this time. Fell is his longest surviving cancer patient—ten years after diagnosis."

"Does he have any idea how much time we have?"

"He doesn't talk about it. He says if Fell quits on him and dies, he's retiring. He had us both laughing at the last appointment. I'm starting to take him to the doctor visits. He never let me go in with him before... Oh, honey, I must go. He's calling me."

"Well, I love you to pieces, and give Daddy an extra big hug for me." Mom drove Fell everywhere after that.

Soon after that conversation with Fell and Mom in February, Mom told me he was in the hospital. He couldn't sit up in bed or move his arm and leg on one side. Fell went by ambulance to Paoli Hospital. The doctor told Mom he had "terminal kidney cancer with metastases to the bone and brain." His cancer had spread. To our surprise, Daddy gave permission for radiation treatments.

Mom had three weeks of practice at being alone, handling mail and bills, until his discharge home.

Daddy came out of the Bryn Mawr Transitional Unit mentally sound. He answered all Mom's questions as to the whereabouts of paperwork and checking account balancing. His physical problems kept him home, but he stayed mentally sharp.

"Come on, Vitterette," he joked with an affectionate nickname for Mom. "Go get the checkbook and pay these bills with me. I watched over several visits as he helped Mom become independent in the paperwork and contacts that daily life required. After nearly twenty-five-years of marriage, they still looked at each other with love-filled eyes.

41

OUT TO DINNER

"For this corruptible must put on incorruption, and this
mortal must put on immortality."
— *1 Corinthians 15:53*

THE PHONE CALL came in mid-April. "Violet, Fell can't get out of
bed. Can you show me how to move him? I'd like to change his sheets
tomorrow. A fresh bed always feels good."

"Mom, I can arrange for home care with my company."

"No. I want to take care of him. No one else is going to give him a
bed bath. He wouldn't like that."

I understood; I would feel the same way about Michael. But
when I called Mom the next day, Dr. Grace had arranged for home
care and already scheduled the physical therapist. Mom cared for
Fell with some nursing help, after her crash course with the PT in
safely moving a bedbound patient.

In the beginning of May, I arrived and found a hospice nurse
with Mom. I sat with Daddy while Mom and the nurse scheduled
visits, discussed medications, and worked out Daddy's care.

Mom phoned me later after I got home. "Dr. Grace told me I'm exhausted. He ordered hospice services for Daddy; you saw the nurse today. I'm sorry it took so long, and we didn't get to talk." Hospice came at the time when Mom could no longer deny her depleted state. But she never let anyone give him a bed bath.

When the phone rang at eight o'clock in the morning on May 7, my heart jumped in my chest.

"Honey, I have some bad news. Fell told me he loved me as I was walking out of the room. I went back, kissed him, and told him, 'I love you more,' like I always do, and we laughed. I was gone just for a couple of minutes. When I came back, he looked frightened. He can't move at all. He's completely paralyzed. He can't talk either," Mom cried. "Now, medically, nothing more can be done. Dr. Grace gave me instructions to keep him comfortable. Then we cried together. Violet, Dr. Grace told me he's going to retire."

Mother's Day crept up on us. The three East Coast sisters—me, Gay, and Lynne—had planned to take Mom out for a Mother's Day luncheon. But she spent every precious second with Fell while he could still respond at all. I asked Mom, and she wouldn't leave him in the daytime, when he was awake.

As May 10 drew near, Daddy weakened. We didn't want his death to be her only Mother's Day memory. My youngest sister, Gay, and I made reservations at Ludwig's Inn and Oyster House for the evening of May 9. Michael volunteered to sit with Fell. Our middle sister, Lynne, didn't drive at night; but we had no choice. Mom wouldn't go in the afternoon. At first, Mom agreed to go just for a much-needed break. Gay and I talked her into dinner.

By the time Michael and I arrived at their home, Daddy could only make a sound acknowledging that he had heard us, but he could not speak in return.

"Daddy," I said, holding his hand, "It's Violet Junior."

"Hmm," he responded.

"I want to tell you how much I love you. Without you, I wouldn't know a father's true love or how amazing the relationship can be between a husband and wife. I learned watching you and Mom. We wouldn't have Eden Hill; and I wouldn't have another sister. Do you understand how precious you are to me?"

"Hmmm," he said as he tried, but failed, to open his eyes.

I told him I loved him again and put my face next to his. He pressed his face into mine and gave a gentle moan, the closest gesture to a hug he could manage.

Since he couldn't speak or move, all of us were able to love on him, admiring him with words. Before this—when he could move and speak—his strong, innate humility waved us off.

"I know how much you love me—how much you love all of us! I know how much you love Mom. We're going to take her out for Mother's Day, and we want you to come with us."

"Hmmm," he said.

"There's only one catch: you can't bring this body with you. We're going to your favorite place, Ludwig's Inn. Can you do that? Be there with us?"

"Hmmm!" Weak, but fully present, he opened his eyes and squeezed my hand. We missed Lynne but I heard Gay talk to him as I had—a declaration of love and appreciation. Mom spoke to him softly, as Gay and I moved away to allow her some privacy. She gave him a dose of medication, held his face, and kissed him.

I kissed Michael and thanked him. He smiled, his eyes sad, and gave me an extra hug.

The medication had taken effect, and Fell had fallen asleep.

During the last several visits, all of us had given Fell permission to pass on when he felt ready. He understood.

In the car, we told Mom we wanted her to have something good to remember this Mother's Day. We talked about Fell and why all of us kids called him "Daddy."

"You know, Mom," Gay said, "We're not just celebrating Mother's Day. We're celebrating *Albert and Violette Fell*."

"I told Daddy to come with us in spirit," I said.

"I heard you, Violet, and Gay too."

Once at the table, we ordered champagne to toast both Mom and

Daddy. As we perused the menu, Fell's sudden presence charged the atmosphere—his essence palpable and sweet. We told one story after the other and laughed with no sadness or grief. We all acknowledged we could feel his presence—joyful, attentive to our words, and comforting—as we ate, swapped "Fell stories," grinned, and reminisced.

"Do you remember when Daddy hid my car?"

Mom turned to my sister and laughed. "I remember! You were late for work that day. He wouldn't admit he hid it; but you knew him, Gay, and hunted until you found it behind the pine trees!"

By this time, people at the next table laughed with us.

Mom lowered her voice. "But he pulled the best one on me."

"What did he do?" I asked.

"I used to go to the bathroom in the dark at night. You two know how your father hated wasting electricity! We always walked around in the dark, and I never broke the habit."

Gay and I looked at each other and nodded. "I still walk around at night in the dark!" I said.

"Me too," Gay agreed.

Mom continued, "One night I went to the bathroom. I twirled the toilet paper, and I twirled it, and twirled it again and again— trying to find the loose end to pull from. Then I heard Fell laughing. I got up and turned on the light. He had taped the end of the toilet paper to the roll; he laughed into his pillow until he cried!" She smiled at the memory.

As dessert came, I looked at my new watch. It read 8:35 p.m.

"Hey, what time is it? This is a new watch, and I think it stopped!"

"Nine-fifteen," Mom said. "I didn't realize it was so late! Thank you, sweethearts, for a delightful evening. We better get home and relieve Michael."

On the way home, Mom told us one more story I had never heard. "Leigh and Dick were visiting between Thanksgiving and Christmas. Duke and Brianna were, oh, about three and four-and-a-half years old then. The grands stayed overnight with us as a treat. Dick and Leigh were going to have a rare night alone at the hotel. Fell loaded us all into the car and headed for Valley Forge Park, just after dark. He told the kids we were looking for something very special."

"He handed me a spotlight to hold while he drove. When we got into the park where there were rolling hills and woods, he stopped every so often and shined the spotlight at the edge of the woods. Snow flurries started drifting down lightly—a December Christmas scene. By the fourth stop, he found what he was looking for."

"'Look, kids,' he pointed to the edge of the woods. "Can you see them?'"

"There at the woods' edge, a herd of deer were bedded down for the night. Their eyes glowed in the spotlight."

"'There are Santa's reindeer,' Fell told them.'"

Both "oohed" and "ahhed." They could see the deer clearly. Leigh told me this night drive stayed with the kids, still the age to believe in Santa Clause, to the present in 1998 as a Christmas reminiscence." The scene hung in the car, thick with Fell's caring ways and memories, as we turned into the condo parking lot.

Michael sat near Fell's bed in dim light. He rose and put an arm around my waist as I drew near. Fell breathed in and out of his slack, open mouth. His cheeks had a sunken look. He truly had come to dinner with us. His body appeared vacant but still breathed, as it wound down toward death; his spirit stayed tethered until life surrendered.

"How long has he been this way?" I asked.

"Since about 8:30." He pulled me closer to him. I held him; the touch comforted me. Michael's eyes, guarded at first, betrayed his deep sadness as we stood together, leaning on one another.

"Honey, my new watch stopped at 8:35." I looked at Michael, then at the still watch.

"That's when this happened," he said, gesturing to Fell's body. Fell's irregular breathing told me he would be gone tomorrow.

We said our goodbyes. Mom's peaceful face reflected memories and acceptance, an unforgettable dinner with a very special guest. Michael and I drove home, holding hands. Not wanting to be apart, we went to bed, cuddled close, and celebrated our lives together in the union of husband and wife. We couldn't get any closer than that. Sleep came only after whispered acknowledgment *that during our time together, we must love each other, with all of our hearts spilling over into words and embraces throughout our lives.*

My mostly silver cross collection displayed for my readers. 1st cross bought the day Fell died. I wear the Celtic knot cross most of the time (below). The two Middle crosses were Christmas gifts from Michael—gold for special occasions.

Fell died the next day, at 3:30 in the afternoon. That day, I bought a Celtic cross necklace. I've worn the cross of Christ's resurrection, in its many forms, ever since. Our collie, Brandy, died of lymphoma a month later.

We know Jesus is coming back on a white horse, so, I'm banking on the existence of animals in heaven. Perhaps Fell and Brandy go for long walks there. We'll know someday. But for now, we have a forever memory of his goodbye attendance at a dinner, filled with love and laughter, the night before Mother's Day 1998—a tender miracle from God.

Ever since Fell died of kidney cancer, I phoned Mom every night. Gay, Lynne, and I adored him—as did Leigh, our stepsister. We had no true blended family experiences, since all of us were adults when Mom and Fell married. Leigh had her own life in Illinois, and the rest of us lived in Pennsylvania. Even so, Leigh is a sister of my heart. Fell's passing left a massive hole in our lives, but Mom's most of all. We all touched base with her more frequently, and she did well with her many friends and family giving her extra love. Mom's terrible acute pain healed over time. We will always miss him until we meet again with the joy of eternity in our spirits.

"He made the Pleiades and Orion;
He turns the shadow of death into morning
And makes the day dark as night;
He calls for the waters of the sea
And pours them out on the face of the earth;
The Lord is his name."
—Amos 5:8

My favorite picture of Mom and Fell.

42

YOGA

"Let no one deceive you by any means; for that Day will not come unless the falling away comes first, and the man of sin is revealed, the son of perdition..."
— *2 Thessalonians 2:3*

THE SUN WAS HOT, but not enough to make me lightheaded. I only walked a quarter of the mile track. My rubbery legs made me sit down before I fell on the cinders. Any exercise requiring endurance exhausted my Lyme-damaged body in short order, which seemed totally unacceptable as a physical therapist.

One of my patients raved about yoga at a nearby studio. I arranged to try a class with the instructor—a soft-spoken, attractive woman near my age.

Callie showed me how to use my yoga props for the first, restful pose—on my back with my legs resting on the folded, fringed, plaid blankets. The position produced quiet throughout my body, almost sleep-worthy. Callie came to each person and lengthened one arm at a time. I felt like part of the floor when she finished with me. Hindu music chanted in the background.

In the dimly lit room, with hypnotic music and restful position-ing, my body sank into relaxation. Each basic yoga pose progressed through the routine with an increasing degree of difficulty, benefit-ting strength and movement. Callie's soothing voice and light touch guided our class of fifteen people. At the end of the hour-and-a-half, my body felt lighter, my shoulders lower, without tension. I hadn't felt like this in years. That night, I decided to join the classes two nights a week.

I never missed class, each one different from the last. Gradually, the Hindu words for each pose rolled off my tongue naturally, and each pose became less effortful, as my muscle strength and joint range of motion improved. In six months, I could walk around the entire mile track.

My "prayer room" became my yoga room, complete with blankets and my own quiet music. Callie hinted about courses to deepen the experience, enhancing the spirit along with the body, while calming the mind. I asked Callie about the courses she alluded to in class.

"There's a certification process called yoga teacher training, if you're interested in teaching yoga. There's also a specialized scoliosis program. If you go online, there're many classes available. Are you interested?" she asked.

"Yes, I am. I've never been this well since several bouts of Lyme Disease. I live in the middle of a herd of deer and white-footed mice; and don't forget birds of every variety. All of them carry deer ticks, which carry the Lyme spirochete."

"I've heard of Lyme, and I'm not surprised yoga is helping you. Have you had Lyme long?" Callie asked

"Well, I've been bitten multiple times but never had a bull's eye rash. Consequently, I wasn't diagnosed for two full years. One of my patients who had Lyme actually told me that's what I had." I paused, but Callie still looked interested.

"What were your symptoms?" she asked.

"A physician from New York listed thirty-four symptoms in his literature. I had thirty-two of them. It ruined a very pleasant life. You know, it's a lot worse than the typical, arthritic joint pain people usually think of when they hear 'Lyme Disease.' My ability to think and sequence couldn't be trusted. And my memory," I stopped to roll my eyes, "went south. I got lost in familiar places and couldn't drive for a year."

"My word!"

"If I exercised, even walking, exhaustion set in very quickly and could take out the next two or three days with fatigue and cognitive deficits.

"Have you stopped working? Did you say you were a PT?"

"I never stopped working. I own a private PT practice with my husband. Isn't that crazy? But I can't do anything else; I come home from work and crash."

"That sounds awful! Psychologically it must have been devastating," Callie exclaimed.

"My life became so difficult that Dr. Toren, my Lyme specialist, asked me if I considered suicide." I raised my eyebrows and nodded, as Callie drew back and made a horrified "O" with her mouth. "I told him, 'I imagine it would be easier to be dead. But I have a fifteen-year-old daughter, a husband, a job, and a house I love that keep me here. Even more important than my ties to the world, my deepest Christian, biblical beliefs tell me I cannot snuff out what God has given me: the gift of life.'"

"It looks like you're getting better," Callie said.

"Yoga is changing everything. I'm better than I've been in every way, even driving. And I love to teach. When is the first course?"

Over time, I traveled to New Jersey, Delaware, and Pennsylvania for Yoga Teacher Training. Each time, when we were given chant music to sing in Hindu, I made up my own Christian words acknowledging the God of Abraham, Isaac, and Jacob: Father, Son, and Holy Spirit. Yoga fascinated me; and though not fully healed, significant improvement led to my being fully convinced I had found a road to health, with God's help.

I not only practiced yoga at the studio, in my home and taught beginner's yoga at Callie's studio. I also brought it into West Chester Physical Therapy as part of my PT practice. I used both the energy skills and yoga sequences to work with patients. I even talked Mom into coming to one of my beginner's yoga classes.

Michael told me later he disagreed with my path of pursuing yoga, but said nothing. My sister, Gay, thought I'd lost it. She kept that opinion to herself at the time.

When I asked Michael why he held back, he said, "You know you would have said I wasn't supportive of something that was a tremendous benefit to your health. You were obviously better physically than you had been in years! But in the business, it just didn't feel right. I think it turned off some of the patients. Gay's well versed in alternative therapy in her practice, and she thought it was over the top. We talked about it and both came to the same conclusion: don't poke the bear!"

And they had been right. That's exactly how I would have reacted. So, on we went with a small treatment room floor covered by a futon mattress that cushioned the hardness, and a great space to do yoga poses and yoga-based healing.

The change in yoga teacher training curriculum came gradually. Little by little I experienced growing dissatisfaction with class modules like yoga accounting, yoga ethics, and yoga service—which included washing all Callie's yoga blankets and cleaning her studio as "a service" required for training completion. The gravest sign of wrongful spiritual ownership of yoga came at a course taught by the originator of this form of kundalini yoga.

Rama had left her husband and took her children to an ashram in India. She studied under famous yoga masters and became a master herself. When I met her for the first time, her coldness struck me, along with the altar to kundalini in the corner of the studio. She stressed that each yoga pose must be done in sequence to draw kundalini energy deep within, ready to infuse each participant who performed the sequence correctly.

Rama continued, "Kundalini comes from the root word *kundela*, meaning coiled, and is personified in Hindu mythology as a goddess, sometimes with the aspect of Durga, creator, sometimes Kali, the destroyer, or Bhujangi, the serpent. Kundalini lies coiled at the base of the spine until aroused. Only then does this *life force* ascend to the head and trigger enlightenment!" Her eyes widened, almost hypnotic with intensity.

We paired with another trainee for an exercise in assisting kundalini energy. My partner—a petite, brown-haired woman, nearly my height—gazed at Rama with a reverence I did not feel. She wanted to be a master someday in Rama's form of yoga. As I performed the prescribed exercise on her supine form, her face shifted. Her body arched, as her eyes rolled back in her head. Guttural speech in a deep, dead voice came from her mouth. I flagged Rama down and pointed to my partner.

Rama's face transformed with delight. Ear close to the girl's lips, she said, "She's speaking in ancient Sanskrit! Kundalini has claimed her!"

As my partner relaxed slowly amidst the class that surrounded her, she regained full consciousness. Still slightly dazed, she looked at Rama who said, "Welcome, servant of kundalini. You have been chosen." Tears filled my partner's eyes as she smiled broadly in exultation. Members of the class congratulated her as one of the chosen.

The scene continued, but I shut down in my mind. To my observation, I had just witnessed a demonic possession.

One would think *that* experience would change the course of my life immediately. But yoga had made me *feel wonderful*. I continued, defying the Scripture that states:

> "For whoever desires to save his life will lose it, but whoever loses his life for My sake will find it. For what profit is it to a man if he gains the whole world, and loses his own soul?"
> —Matthew 16:25–26

43

DREAMS AND VISIONS

"You shall have no other gods before me."
— *Exodus* 20:3

"AND BREATHE," I told the beginner's yoga class, as they slowly came back to reality at the end of class. Mom had tried my yoga class for the first time tonight, but remained on the floor as the other students began leaving the studio. "Mom, are you okay?" I asked.

"Oh, honey, I can't get up! I feel like a turtle on its back!"

"Here, let me help." She couldn't roll from her back to her side without a big helping hand on my part. We joked about beached whales, but I knew something was wrong.

Mom phoned two weeks after the yoga incident. "Violet, I saw my family doctor and she sent me to a neurologist."

"How did you make out?" I asked, wary at her somber tone.

"I have Parkinson's disease, and he gave me medication. My hand is starting to tremor. He says it won't kill me," she said in a wry voice.

"Well that part is good news," I said with a laugh. "Do you like the doctor?"

"Yes. He explained some things and gave me a pamphlet to read.

He did say it's affecting my balance a little, but I think I'm doing all right. I just won't be coming back to yoga class. That's why I couldn't get off the floor."

"Well, Mom, falls are a real problem, from what I've seen with my physical therapy patients. I think you should get a medical pendent or bracelet, so you have a button to press for help if you do fall."

"That's a good idea," she said.

My calendar prepared me for a Black Rock Retreat weekend with my friend, Priscilla, one of my mentors in Christian living. She had a past as a Presbyterian minister and co-ministered a church with her husband. As an artist, Priscilla paints pictures the Lord shows her. When I reached Black Rock, exhausted as usual from my work and yoga schedule, I pulled into the circular driveway at Whippoorwill Lodge, one of the houses for rent on the Black Rock Retreat grounds. It was used as housing for programs like the Silent Sanctuary Retreat that Priscilla and I had come to attend. After unpacking, I complained to Priscilla, "I am so annoyed with the additions to my yoga courses for teacher training. I'm so tired, I could drop right here!"

Priscilla took a few seconds to scrutinize me and asked, "When was the last time you prayed over this training?"

I stopped in surprise. It should have been an obvious question, but it hadn't occurred to me. "A long time ago," I said as a mental red flag went up.

"Go take a nap, and pray before you sleep," she advised.

I prayed, thirsty for His advice before my grateful body let sleep take over. Indelible dreams—vivid, living-color-real—came clearly, with no doubt as to their meaning.

In the first dream, a lovely home had buyers ready to give a down payment. The sale would fall through because of a slovenly addition tacked onto the side of the house. It had boards missing, was not plumb, and looked completely out of character. The addition was stuck on the house like a cancerous growth that needed excision. I knew it had to be torn off so the house would sell.

The second dream evolved with more complexity. I saw a man and laughed while I dreamed, because he looked like Snidely Whiplash—a thin man in black, with a handlebar mustache and shifty eyes—a classic cartoon villain. He talked, in an animated way, to a dark-haired, shapely woman who seemed enamored with him. She continued their conversation, as he motioned with his hands and levitated her from the ground, moving her wherever he liked. She smiled, oblivious, as he turned her upside down, then horizontal to the ground, rotating her floating body around and around. She kept on smiling and talking.

The scene changed as the dream continued. I walked past the Snidely Whiplash character and the same handsome woman; but this time, she said to him in sharp tones, "I know what you want. You want my inheritance, but you can't have it!" He could no longer manipulate her as he had earlier. Now, she controlled herself.

When I awakened, I immediately knew *my* inheritance was in jeopardy, and *I* had to tear the growth nailed to *my* spirit off *my* house. Stunned, I tearfully told my retreat friend what the Lord had given me. She advised me to give up yoga immediately and confront Callie with this newfound truth.

On the hour-and-a-half drive home, I pondered how Callie would respond to me. I stopped on the way and bought a red-letter edition Bible for her. I knew the Lord had a plan.

As I expected, Callie was not open to biblical context.

"You want me to give up yoga? My livelihood?" she asked in astonishment.

"It's better than losing your soul," I replied. "By engaging in yoga, we are worshipping other gods, Hindu gods."

"That's your belief. I don't believe I'll lose my soul," she answered. "But thank you very much for the Bible. Will you still teach the beginner's class for me?"

"Let me try and see how it goes." Why I thought that was possible, I'll never know. But *something* pushed me to acquiesce.

Two days later, I came prepared to teach, but I held reservations. I knew the Lord would show me something special that I had missed about yoga. Why else would I be led to teach after my retreat experience and the possession I witnessed at Rama's course? To my surprise, Callie was there.

"I'm going to teach tonight. Why don't you just participate," she said.

As I stacked yoga blankets with a feeling of unrest, the chant music began. I stopped, jarred by the sound. A realization dawned: *the chant music had a different quality, one of discord, with an underlying screeching tone I had never heard before this class.* I approached Callie and whispered, "I can't stay. The chant music has a different frequency. I can't listen to it!"

She looked surprised, and then dismayed. "Yes, it is a different frequency from other music. How did you know that?"

"I can hear it; I know it is. I won't be able to teach or participate. I'm sorry," I said. By "sorry," I meant I felt sorry for Callie and the class who were performing a yoga discipline designed to increase spirituality in the Hindu practice—in this case, power that changed forms, sometimes to a feminine figure, while bathed in the sound of Hindu chant music worshipping Hindu gods and goddesses. All the poses, designed for relaxation of mind and body, masked a Hindu spiritual connection to another god.

"I'm sorry you're leaving," Callie said. "You were a good teacher."

Amazement engulfed me. I had never thought of the chant music as worship of Hindu gods, like a Hindu hymn. The same Hindu chant music played during this class as all of Callie's other classes; the music had always been a *different frequency*—different from other music—a frequency to attract kundalini. I cringed as I thought of myself deaf and blind for years. Tonight, Holy Spirit interceded and opened my eyes and ears.

I said goodbye. Callie returned to class, and I left fifteen to twenty souls on the floor, unknowingly participating in kundalini 'enlightenment.' My heart broke for them, blind and deaf as I had been. But, tonight, I saw *and heard* the truth. I turned, stepped out into the cool night, thanked God, and walked toward my car.

Michael didn't say much as I shared my experience with him; I crossed all the yoga classes off my schedule. Unreality swirled about me; I felt like a boat loosed from its moorings, adrift. Fear engulfed me, as I thought of my lack of endurance before yoga. *How would I replace this efficient exercise?* I went into my yoga-ravaged prayer room. I lay in darkness, on my back, supported by yoga blankets. I prayed to relinquish the lifeline that yoga had become and find another form of exercise. I rested and willed my body to let go, a well-practiced move learned in the yoga classes. *That isn't worship,* I thought. I breathed rhythmically, exhaling longer than I inhaled to enhance my connection with the Lord and cut through anxiety.

A smoky vision began with indistinct, hazy colors and lines. It cleared, as I breathed and came into sharp focus. A life-like, brilliant, striking woman with scarlet lips, rosy cheeks, alabaster skin, and long, resplendent black hair spoke to me, softly at first.

"Come, my dear! You will not give up your health and all you have worked so hard to achieve!"

"I will give it up," I said, firm in my conviction.

"You can't mean that," she exclaimed.

"My Lord is very clear. I will not do anything to worship or bring kundalini into my being. I worship the Creator of all things, Jesus Christ."

The beautiful woman's face screwed into a screaming mask. "You fool! You are giving up the whole world! It's at your fingertips!"

"I believe Christ is my whole world, not just the temporal world of which you speak. I am His, and He is my shepherd! You will not have me, kundalini!"

The screaming face distorted until it peeled back and revealed a leather-skinned, craggy, dragon-like serpent, hideous beyond description. With my spirit resolved to take what the Lord would give me, I said, "I don the full armor of God against you." I breathed long and slow, resting in my Mighty Fortress and His armor. With a last howling shriek, the dragon-snake dissolved into nothingness.

I lay there, alone with the Holy Spirit. He covered me with love in the velvet dark. Deep, abiding peace surrounded me; this knowledge, deep knowing, told me that although evil existed, Julian of Norwich said it best: "...all shall be well, and all shall be well; and all manner of thing shall be well." In my heart, I added, *No matter what.*

I thought perhaps just *this* form of yoga created the conflict of having *no other Gods before Him.* After a superficial online search, I realized this is not true. In traditional understanding, yoga is *itself* a religious act. The postures themselves lead the practitioners to Hindu Gods, whether they intend this or not. Rama explained that concept very clearly in yoga teacher training, but it was *never* explained or addressed in any regular yoga classes at Callie's studio. Yoga cannot be separated into religious and secular. Some American Hindus find that the way popular culture treats yoga as a personal gym routine is actually quite offensive. There is great debate on this topic, and I can certainly understand the temptation to say *I don't believe that way; it's just exercise.* The historical fact is, yoga was created to be a religious practice of Hindus. There is no such thing as "Christian yoga."

My physical health did not fall apart after I left the yoga practice. I thought that chapter of my life had closed; but the Lord has a sense of humor. He created humor, so I shouldn't have been surprised when He decided to use it in my life; I didn't expect irony...

My route on the way to work, chosen to avoid traffic and stop lights, wound around quiet back roads and residential areas. One morning, my trip to work was interrupted by a newly occupied, small home-turned-business. The large sign read, "YOGA." I slowed, looked more closely, dismayed to find it housed the same form of yoga that brought me to the edge with God. Rama had planted another studio that I would pass every day on my way to work.

That day, I prayed for the Lord to defeat the attempt to spread this under-the-radar practice that stole the soul. I prayed for the Lord's will to be done. Every week, to and from work, I prayed as one who knows this spiritual devastation. Less than a month later, I stopped electrified. A burned-out shell marred the site where the pleasant-looking, deceptively inviting yoga studio once stood. The studio was never rebuilt. In awe, I recognized, once again, *He is an awesome God—and prayer, sent winging to Him, is a powerful voice when it coincides with His will.*

Solomon said it best:

To everything there is a season, A time for every purpose under heaven:
A time to be born, And a time to die;
A time to plant, And a time to pluck what is planted;
A time to kill, And a time to heal;
A time to break down, And a time to build up;
A time to weep, And a time to laugh;
A time to mourn, And a time to dance;
A time to cast away stones, And a time to gather stones;
A time to embrace, And a time to refrain from embracing
A time to gain, And a time to lose;
A time to keep, And a time to throw away;
A time to tear, And a time to sew;
A time to keep silence, And a time to speak;
A time to love, And a time to hate;
A time of war, And a time of peace.
— Ecclesiastes 3: 1-8

44

DEATH OF A DREAM

"We are of God. He who knows God hears us; he who is not of God does not hear us. By this we know the spirit of truth and the spirit of error."
— 1 John 4:6

Michael and Jessica on her wedding day.

ON A SWELTERING, 90-degree day in July of 2010, our only child, Jessica, married Anthony—Tony to us—in Hibernia Park, Coatesville, Pennsylvania. They chose to combine their last names, which I thought a lovely beginning of a life together. A wooded setting with a picturesque stream surrounded them as they exchanged vows with Gay officiating—their legal marriage already signed and sealed. Mom, eighty-two and overweight, usually heat intolerant, perspired a little but had no real problems further blessing the important event.

After a little fairy-tale-like story written by the groom, Gay pronounced them husband and wife. I waded in the creek with Tony's mother and took pictures. When no prayer blessed the food, in the outdoor pavilion reception, I commandeered the microphone and blessed the bride and groom and food *in the name of the God of Abraham, Isaac, and Jacob*, with my daughter's eyes warning me off—that short blessing the only mention of God that day. Like many of the next genera-tion, and even my own, Jess and Tony seemed to feel no need for Jesus Christ and spoke of "the Universe" as the guiding force: a worship of the creation rather than the Creator.

Dad walking me down the aisle.

Equally misguided, my introduction of yoga into West Chester Physical Therapy and Fitness Center had taken root over several years. Before I learned the truth about yoga, I had planned to have a private yoga studio as part of our office site for classes two nights a week. Plans marched toward a basement face-lift for the studio. Two weeks away from having the studio bathroom refurbished, sewage backed up and ruined the entire, carpeted, base-ment area. With the knowledge that this could happen again, I shelved the plans permanently.

Michael handled all the West Chester Physical Therapy billing. One by one, insurance companies raised their copays from $10 to $25, to $30 dollars or more. We usually treated patients three times a week; but no one could afford that kind of a schedule now. Michael laid it on the line one afternoon after we finished patients for the day. "Honey, I know you love this place and practice. But unless more patients come through our doors, we won't be able to pay our bills."

As time progressed, Michael proved correct. Our profits shrank, and we used our business and personal credit cards to pay for purchases. I believed the Lord had given us the business, and He would turn it around in His time. More practical, Michael took a position with Mercury Home Health, a large home care organization which employed a full spectrum of rehab professionals.

He came home from the interview and told me, "Well, this is the right job!"

"How do you know?" I asked

"I was sitting in the waiting area and looked up at the wall across from me, and there was a picture of Jesus," he said with a genuine smile after months of a worry.

He took the job and worked daily with patients and a team comprised of nurses, occupational therapists, speech therapists, and social workers. Michael treated each patient for forty-five minutes in their home. We began paying bills with his salary. Although the light of reason began to dawn, I still clung to my job at WCPT.

Finally, Michael sat me down, and opened our personal and professional ledgers. He highlighted the seriousness of our financial situation. Only a fool would ignore the financial shambles. My job search began. I missed his presence desperately each day at WCPT. His void throbbed like a dull headache in the atmosphere of the clinic. Saddened by the separation, I settled into finding another place of employment.

Job hunting had never presented a problem. I had a great resume, so I wasn't worried.

My job search turned out to be a surprising affair. Each hospital said the same thing: "You are overqualified for a staff position." The rehabilitation center I hoped would be my employer gave me an interview with the director of physical therapy. I felt assured a job with my experience.

"I see, by your resume, you have worked in all areas of physical therapy, including as a director and private practice owner."

"Yes. I should be uniquely qualified to fit into the rehab setting," I replied with confidence.

The slender, blonde director pursed her lips and shook her head. "You have more experience than I do. You are overqualified for a staff position. You should be looking for a directorship, or at the very least an assistant director's position."

I felt the bottom drop out of my confidence at the finality of her words. "But I don't want that kind of responsibility! I really want to be a staff therapist," I explained.

"I'm very sorry," she said and ended the interview.

No one expressed any interest in me as a staff therapist after forty years of experience. The dried-up job market didn't resolve our outstanding bills and Michael's legitimate concerns. We had a mortgage on our home and on the West Chester Physical Therapy property—two households with two sets of bills for everything. My work at WCPT continued, since I had no other income. I felt my world sliding into an abyss.

In desperation, I called Mercury Home Health. They had an opening for which I scheduled an interview. With hope and a prayer, the day of my interview came, graced by a cloudless sky and no traffic problems. I arrowed north on Route 202.

No picture of Jesus hung in my waiting room outside a busy office in Norristown. I waited ten, fifteen, twenty minutes as people buzzed in and out, where a nursing supervisor who was scheduled to interview me continued her workday. Finally, during a brief lull in the activity, I poked my head in and asked, "Did I come at the wrong time for my PT interview?"

The blonde, middle-aged woman turned surprised eyes in my direction. "Oh, I'm so sorry!" She laughed. "I forgot!"

No interview actually took place. Laura, one of two nursing supervisors, spoke to me as if my employment approval existed already. She gave me my team assignment and said with a wink that she would be my boss. The job hinged on the pre-employment physical, scheduled in two days. If the physical went well, orientation for the job and computer system required completion, and then I'd get orientation in the field with a seasoned PT. I walked out confused, unimpressed—but with a job.

My pre-employment physical was at Urban Hospital in Norristown. The physician—fit-looking, thirty-something—had dark hair and observant eyes. He did the usual physical exam and went a little further than most physicians. He tested my muscle strength and then asked me to touch my toes. I responded by placing my palms to the floor.

He looked at me, a quizzical expression on his face. "How old did you say you were?" Glancing back to the chart in front of him, he turned a page and checked my date of birth.

"I'm sixty-two years young," I grinned. "I've always been hyper-flexible and strong."

He laughed and closed the chart after he wrote a brief note. "You're in better shape than some of my twenty-year-olds! You passed with flying colors." Signed, sealed, and employed, I didn't think about orientation. I continued treating patients as long as I could until completing orientation.

Michael and I planned together, now that I had a secure job too. We put our office property on the market; our finances were reaching critical condition. We spent every weekend packing up our belongings and clearing the space for sale.

But our beautiful, double condo did not sell. We heard the same thing from everyone that came and looked at the site: "It's too big."

After fruitless months, we restored the site to two condominiums. Construction took six weeks. I watched the grotesque and unwelcomed "reconstructive-surgery" transformation. I felt like I had walled off something beautiful, flowing—and chopped it in two. In my journal, I wrote: "The two units are separated, like identical twins sent to different adoptive homes." Already grief-stricken, I felt the fatal blow fall on something I had cherished.

Mom's falls started the same year I switched jobs. The first fracture—a shattered elbow at her Chesterbrook condo—necessitated her move to a magnificent assisted living facility, where she chose a two-bedroom apartment and rented out her Chesterbrook unit. She regained near independence but still needed assisted living for her medications and meals. The next fracture wreaked havoc with Mom's life.

Emergency room cubicles always seemed to be the same: chilly in temperature; green, white, or blue painted walls; and filled with the usual assortment of medical equipment. Mom lay in a specialized hospital bed with a probable fracture of her right hip.

"Oh, Violet, I'm sorry about this. You know how I hate being waited on. I thought I could make it from the TV room to the kitchen where I left my cane, but I fell. I'm pretty sure my hip is broken. I can't move it without screaming."

I nodded with sympathy as a dark-skinned, foreign resident dressed in green scrubs came in, clipboard in hand. I guessed Pakistani from his accent.

"I'll be taking your medical history," he said before he peppered her with questions. He didn't ask if she had a living will or advanced directives. At last, he said with certainty, "And of course, if your heart stops, you would want us to use all measures needed to save your life."

Mom paused only a second before replying, "Absolutely not!"

The resident's eyes widened with surprise. He tried his best to convince her to agree with life-saving measures. He looked to me for help, but I also had a living will and advanced directives. He repeated himself several times, not knowing how else to deal with the situation.

Finally exasperated, Mom stopped the flustered resident and said, "I have a living will. Don't you understand? I would just have to do it again!"

"Do what again?" he asked, a confused look on his face.

"Why, *die*, of course," Mom said. "Once is enough." She

promised to haunt anyone who kept her on earth by artificial means. I had a copy of her living will. Anyone close to her knew her wishes.

Parkinson's Disease and the fractured left hip ended her second-handing career. Her raven hair had faded to wavy, snow white—which made her startling blue eyes even more pronounced. Her face, almost unlined, shone with clear, pale skin and rosy cheeks. But now, she looked a bit more like a roly-poly Mrs. Santa Claus, with her "divine" sugary desserts always accepted in the assisted living dining room.

Mom had surgery at Paoli Hospital to repair her fractured hip. Even though allowed to put all her weight on the leg, she complained of terrible pain in her hip, crying out, as pain stopped her from walking after the first step. Pain medication added confusion and lethargy to her already compromised state.

Parkinson's Disease made movement difficult. One aide couldn't safely walk with her alone. Sufficient help seemed rare at the rehab. In bed most of the time, Mom deteriorated, while Medicare paid. By her discharge, she could not walk twenty feet to the bathroom. She returned to her stunning, assisted living apartment, decorated with all of her beautiful secondhand furnishings and yard sale finds, elegance and frugality.

Gay and I coordinated Mom's care after discharge. With home care and one-on-one therapy, she began walking with a rollator and assistance—still in pain, but encouraged by Gary, the male PT she called a "good looking guy," from Mercury Home Health, of course.

"So, Mom, you wouldn't walk for the aide in rehab, but you walk for Gary. I think you're flirting with him because he's cute," I teased.

"Well he is! I just can't let him down. This damn leg hurts like the blazes, but I'm putting up with it. I have to walk again."

Mom's sporadic confusion became more regular and worrisome. I conferenced with Christine from Mercury Home Health—a nurse I highly respected, although all of them were good.

"Violet, looking at her post-fracture pain meds, the only thing I see that might be problematic is tramadol. It can cause lethargy, and confusion is one of the rarer side effects."

"Chris, if I stick around after she's taken her meds, I should be able to see the change in her behavior if it really is the tramadol, right?"

"Yes, you should. That will show cause and effect if medication is the problem."

I thanked Chris and set off for the med nurse's station. Once I knew when Mom received her dose of tramadol, I could observe her reaction to the drug, which some minor research indicated is considered an opioid.

Sure enough, Mom showed signs of slurred speech, confusion, and sleepiness twenty minutes after she ingested tramadol. I let Chris and the facility nurses know. Chris conferenced with the facility physician. The resulting change in medication erased all the concerning side effects, one major hurdle overcome.

But, although her assisted living apartment rivaled a *Better Homes and Gardens* layout, the facility that seemed so promising for Mom's care became a very expensive failure. I checked Mom's medication list and found potent drugs for dementia, also listed as a diagnosis in her chart. On questioning, the director of nursing explained the inaccurate diagnosis.

"All our patients have that diagnosis on their charts. It doesn't mean anything. It allows us to medicate each patient when necessary, without phoning their doctor, who might not be available if and when the meds are actually needed."

"But that means "dementia" will be in Mom's chart forever. If she would ever leave, that chart follows her even though she has no real dementia diagnosis."

"Why? Are you planning on moving her?" she asked.

"You never know," I said to keep her guessing, hoping Mom would get better care to please us.

That never happened. Her care deteriorated until Gay and I had words with the director.

One final battle set Gay and me into motion. We were to have a family-staff meeting with Mom. Gaye, me, the team from Mercury Home Health, and the director of nurses were gathered, waiting for someone to bring Mom to the meeting room. After ten minutes went by, I opened the door and saw Mom parked in her wheelchair in the empty dining room. "Mom, what are you doing out here?" I asked.

"Oh, hi sweety! I didn't know where the meeting was being held. This's where they dropped me off."

"It's in this first-floor conference room," I said as I wheeled her in the right direction.

Once in the meeting room, Mom greeted everyone and explained she didn't know where she was supposed to go to meet us.

The nursing director said, "That's alright, Mrs. Fell. You were just a little confused."

Gay and I exchanged astonished looks. "My mother was not confused," Gay said to the director. "She was brought to the wrong place."

I nodded in agreement. This typical gaslighting, to take any onus off the facility, became more familiar to us as time went by. At the meeting, the occupational therapist noted Mom needed help with cleansing after toileting. Her Parkinson's Disease had accelerated, making her unable to wipe herself after a bowel movement. At the end of the team meeting, a consensus of opinion became obvious; Mom needed more help than the assisted living facility provided. She would need personal care aides in addition to the present, expensive care.

Gay and I talked later that night. The expense of the facility apartment would eat up Mom's finances if we had to add personal care aides to the cost. We decided fiscal responsibility meant live-in aides, so Mom could move back to her Chesterbrook condo.

Mom agreed to move, but fear hovered in her eyes. Change can confuse and frighten even the best of us; Mom was in her mid-eighties, not an age when change would be particularly welcome. But it needed to happen.

I called the realtor who handled her condo rental and asked him to give the tenant notice. I started the hunt for an agency that would supply aides on a full-time basis, around the clock. Interviews proved insufficient to find the right aide and company.

It took acrobatics and the hand of God to pack and move Mom from the assisted living location to her condo in Chesterbrook, after the tenant moved out. And the move with live-in help took months to perfect. We went through three agencies before finding the right one. Even so, one live-in, day-shift aide turned out to be an abuser.

Two months elapsed before Mom admitted she lived in fear of the woman caring for her. When I reported the aide, and our agency contact person talked to Mom, the agency responded immediately with support and no break in care. In time, live-in aides who fit Mom's personality and needs became her regular team.

I watched a glow develop about her smile, as I heard bantering between the aides and Mom. They asked me questions, designed to improve her life. They cared, and I began to relax with this major hurdle behind me.

Gay took Mom to all her doctors' appointments and pitched in wherever needed. We asked Lynne to lend a hand and offered to teach her everything she needed to know about Mom's needs, if an aide was absent. Lynne told us she had no special training in care for individuals with Parkinson's disease. She expressed discomfort with her level of competence, and no amount of discussion moved her from her false premise. She had never been comfortable around illness or debility. Gay and I let it go and substituted when aides weren't available. Gay kept Lynne up-to-date. I dealt with the aide's agency, managed the live-in aides, paid bills, and filled Mom's medication box. In between, Gay and I visited—getting pleasant quality time with Mom.

We did have some happy news during the tumultuous time with Mom and WCPT. Jess became pregnant in 2012 with a little girl. Unlike my pregnancy, she didn't feel well and gained more weight than she hoped. The call came on February 24, 2013; Jessica was in labor—our granddaughter, Katherine, on her way. Excited, I gathered all I would need for a long siege that usually accompanied a first baby. I was about to become "Nana."

We left later than I wanted but made good time on the way to the Main Line birthing center. Anxious to join Jess, I let the nurse know who I was. She returned in a few minutes. The look on her face alerted me that something was not to her liking.

Apologetically, she said, "Jessica's husband and her mother-in-law are with her. There would be too many people with three family members in the room. She would rather you wait here."

I nodded, unable to speak at that moment. There were choices to be made quickly on how I handled this stunning blow. "Thank you," I said to the concerned nurse. "I'm sure she's in good hands." The nurse returned to the delivery room, a relieved look on her face.

I don't remember how I told Michael, but I talked to no one else until I prayed. I needed to be solid in my conviction to refuse making a fuss of any kind; no negativity would color my granddaughter's arrival on Earth. I knew Jess had wanted me with her; I didn't know why that had changed.

The Lord's presence surrounded me. I knew what my birth experience had been like; I only wanted Michael there. Mom sat in the waiting room. *How did this differ, other than Tony's stepmom sat at my daughter's side?* A sweet, kind, musical lady, she exuded peace. *What more could I ask for my daughter and son-in-law, as they brought their first child into the world?* I vanquished selfish pouting, before it got a toehold. The Holy Spirit saw to that. I prayed. A lemniscate came to mind, a horizontal figure-eight signifying infinity, between my heart and baby Katherine's heart.

After she was born, when I held her, the infinity image became a palpable bond between her heart and mine. I remembered the difficulties of life with a new baby. *No need for sour grapes now, and no need later.* Katie had arrived safely, and all was well with Jess. *All will be well with me. I promise, Lord.*

By the end of April in 2013, Michael and I had each of the WCPT units under contract, and both settlements went smoothly. Grateful we were out from under the terrible financial burden, I grieved just the same; it represented the death of a dream. Mercury Home Health saved our financial necks. Michael liked his job. But my dream job would not be replicated. It was gone.

> *"The Lord gave, and the Lord has taken away; Blessed be the name of the Lord."*
> — *Job* 1:21

45

THE BUTTERFLY

"How great are His signs, And how mighty His wonders!
His kingdom is an everlasting kingdom,
And His dominion is from generation to generation."
— Daniel 4:3

THE COMPUTER SCREEN GREW MISTY. *I have to finish this work.*
My eyes focused again. *Which screen am I in?* I wondered. *I've got to
get this note done—it's already midnight,* I thought, nodding with
drooping eyelids. When I woke up, chin on chest, the clock read
12:30 a.m. Refreshed by the cat nap, I finished by 1:00 a.m. Backed
into a corner, cortisol kicked in with energy and focus—a sizable
reward for procrastination, one of my infamous, learning disability
antidotes.

My learning disabilities had never compromised my job capabilities as a physical therapist. In self-defense, I contrived ways to
improve my ever-present distractibility and difficulty with memorization, sequencing, and processing auditory information. I could talk
my way around most of my deficits; pen and paper solved some of the
memory issues. Having successfully achieved my Bachelor of Science

degree at Temple University, even recalling the terrible chemistry and statistics courses, I expected the positive pattern to continue. But computerized progress notes with multiple screens were splintering the body of patient information and challenging me to the brink of inability. Sequencing and memory claimed premium importance on the work computer and I owned little of either.

In February of 2012, Mercury Home Health orientation consisted of a never-ending information parade of computer screens, forms, icons, and sequences, all given at breakneck speed with no written information or ability to take notes. The orientation instructors stated it would take six months to get comfortable with the computer work. My learning disabilities made me a slow student, with computer sequencing demands, a problem even before my ability to sequence diminished further due to Lyme Disease.

Orientation proved a wrestling match, and I spent most of my time pinned to the mat. My saving grace: *all things were possible with God*. I knew I had to trust Him to help me handle the computer work. In my present situation, trust proved to be head knowledge, with heart knowledge progressing at sloth-like speed. According to our pastor, the longest distance is the eighteen inches between your head and heart. My head knew. My heart struggled.

In desperation, I asked for prayer from my church family: for memory, strength to smile and keep on going, organization, and time management skills. Terror whispered chilling thoughts: *I would be fired, have no job; and we would lose our home to the mortgage company*. Prayer time—along with meditation on Psalms and the Lord's faithfulness—would have been time well spent. Formal Bible study became impossible, because of my note-writing time after work. A storm of emotions broke over me; a poem flowed from the Spirit to my pen, like a dike's protection against the sea: Keep Your Eyes on Him:

Keep your eyes on Him
The water's cold and deep

You have no chance to live
Unless He has your soul to keep

Peter looked away
The raging sea laid claim
Fear took hold and ravaged faith
But Jesus called his name

It became so clear
Where his faith must be
Only through his faith in Christ
Could he be truly free

For God so loved us all
He gave His only Son
To pay so we'd be cleared
To walk with Christ, our sins undone

So keep your eyes on Him
The water's cold and deep
You have no chance to live
Unless He has your soul to keep

My pastor read the anonymous email I sent to the prayer team. Somehow, he knew my cry—an obvious conclusion, perhaps. He knew I had recently started a job. Pastor Chris, Michael, and I had developed a closer relationship on a trip to Israel with fifty-seven church members in 2011. He knew about my problems with Lyme Disease. He had baptized us in the Sea of Galilee and asked for continued healing for me, as we stood in the water, where Jesus had walked, with fish nibbling at our ankles and toes. Without my church family, my faith in God, and my husband, Mercury Home Health would have buried me. Unlike me, Michael usually finished all the notes before he came home. I relived second and third grade, when I couldn't read. I flashed back to being gut-sinking-terrified during second grade addition and subtraction flashcard tests. The minute I saw those flashcards, fear took over. Reason and knowledge fled, leaving my mind blank.

To this day, I count on my fingers to add and subtract, although I'm fine with multiplication tables. *Odd.* I made it past orientation. My "incompetence" at documentation never showed officially, because I took all evening to complete the notes. During the swirl of activity and changes with Mom, my job, and household activities, my patient care documentation time rarely balanced out with a free evening. Michael helped me as much as he could with household chores, grocery shopping, and little kindnesses that saved me time and energy. Sometimes he helped me with my computer work. His sweet help generated guilt and inadequacy in me when I added my notes to his. He needed time off from work. I chose to struggle instead.

Spring grew warmer and bloomed. I came outside, so nature could soothe my frightened soul. Our butterfly bush buzzed with bees, moths, butterflies, and the occasional nectar-drinking insect.

Nearly a year passed, with my evenings married to the computer five days a week. On a clear August morning, a lounge chair beckoned. After collapsing in the sun, I prayed and pondered over my life. My body felt crispy-around-the-edges tired from computer work late into the night. But that took up only part of my life.

Mom continued a slow decline physically. I watched as the devastation of Parkinson's Disease stole the bold, independent mother I knew. She gave her car to Lynne's son when she could no longer drive. She started having minor swallowing difficulties with meat. She needed more help getting out of a chair and dressing, but still enjoyed a good novel. She still had a mind 'like a steel trap.' When her medication box needed filling, I savored a once-a-week visit. We had great conversations with Mom's feisty, observant nature intact.

"Are you still doing notes?" Michael asked. "It's midnight. I'm going to bed."

"I have another hour to go," I said, yawning.

"What takes you so long?"

"What I write has to be refined. It doesn't come out like your notes. You actually write more than I do but your notes are good without any rewriting. I didn't start until 7:00 tonight, and my mind drifts. I have to look up patient information, and sometimes I can't remember where it is in the blasted chart. Honey, it's just the way it is. I wish I could be more like you!"

"I know; but Violet, it's not worth losing that much sleep. Come to bed!"

"Night, hon'. I'll try to finish soon."

When we owned West Chester Physical Therapy, the patients came to me, often for pain relief. In home care, I traveled to home-bound patients. They needed treatment for safe function in their homes. All the specialized techniques for neck and back pain I had cultivated over years and had used daily at our private practice languished, rarely ever needed in home care PT.

Now, nearly a year later, in August of 2013, I thought, *I am not cut out for this job. Holy Spirit, did I read You correctly?* True, Mercury proved the only employer willing to hire me with my level of experience. *Was I wrong, Lord, to assume, when Mercury accepted me for the job, I had Your approval?* Fatigue clung to my thin frame.

Too tired to do anything else, I sat in the morning sun by the pool. Fluttering motion about the butterfly bush drew my attention. I left my chair, cell phone in hand for video and photos of the colorful moths and butterflies. One butterfly-like moth, tan with orange spots, had tiny white knobs on its antennae. Shy and lightning-fast, the small, winged creature evaded my camera. It was too pretty to call a moth, from my experience, with the typical solid-colored moths much smaller than butterflies.

I flopped back on the chaise lounge. My Bible lay open to Ephesians 6, "The Whole Armor of God." Feeling exhausted after photographing the butterflies, I came to "the end of myself." My internal critic called me *inadequate, disorganized*—not able to handle the work schedule, documentation, and help that Mom needed—all at the same time. After that scathing and mostly accurate review, I gave up thinking and drifted into a quiet zone. Eyes closed, sunbathing, a peaceful lethargy stole over me.

Matthew 7:7 drifted through my head: *Ask and it will be given to you; seek and you will find; knock and it will be opened to you.*

Gideon had actually asked for a sign from God—not one sign, but two. He wanted to make sure he followed God's will. *I've got the same problem,* I thought. I prayed, then read Judges, Chapter 6; summarized, it explained that the Lord answered Gideon's request, and he received signs which left no doubt that the path he traveled fulfilled God's will.

"Lord, I want to know Your will as Gideon did. If it is Your will that I stay in this job, please let a butterfly sit on my leg. I'm asking something almost impossible, so I can't mistake Your answer." Meditating on the Lord's faithfulness, I closed my eyes and waited.

In the next few minutes, the littlest butterfly that dove and glided like a barn swallow—the shy one—sailed toward me. I felt it touch down on my left leg. Awed, I aimed my phone at it and hit video. It crawled up my leg and flew onto my red Bible marker.

"Thank You, Lord," I breathed. The joy of such a gift pulsed through me. Video kept recording, as amazement rippled through me. Time's tyranny halted as the butterfly perched, its proboscis probing the red, satin ribbon for nectar.

When time started moving again, I followed Gideon's example and asked for the second sign. "If you really want me to stay in this job, Lord, let the butterfly jump onto my hand." I rapidly swooped my right hand to the pretty insect. Instead of fleeing, the large object speeding toward it, the butterfly hopped onto my hand. It appeared on my cell screen, the video still running.

I moved my hand about, and held the little winged creature at different angles for the camera. Michael rode back and forth on the tractor, mowing the lawn in the distance, with the butterfly on my hand in the fore-ground. When Michael took a break and  stood on the deck above me, I got up and called, "Honey, look, a butterfly!"

"I see it," he said, stopping to watch for a minute on his way into the house.

Opening and closing its wings in a slow rhythm, it didn't seem in any hurry to leave; but my time was up. I had to go in. I raised my hand and fingers upward, and with a gentle flick of my wrist, it fluttered into the air and away.

I've never seen another like it. During a discussion with an acquaintance about signs from God, I used the butterfly video as my best example. The woman listened to my explanation, watched the video, then said, "You know, that's a *moth*, not a butterfly..."

In the end, I had my question answered: *Yes, I'm supposed to be in this job.* Coping with the answer remained a serious challenge. All the problems that led me to the question still existed; but now I knew, without a doubt, that the right path included this job.

Faith makes all things possible, but not necessarily easy.

My weekend break, with God's gift, enabled me to return to work with newfound certainty and perseverance. In the afternoon, our information specialist, Sarah, texted me.

"Violet, I wanted you to know, two of your charts were chosen for audit by the Medicare reviewer. The chart compliance testing came out to 100 percent. She said she'd never seen such complete, well-documented patient care. I thought you should know. I've never seen this happen either."

I thanked Sarah for the encouragement. Praying once again for the Lord to balance my life so I could rest didn't change my distractibility, perfectionistic streak, or computer slowness. I couldn't fix the innate problems. I simply did the best I could.

On a retreat weekend, I used some myofascial, stretching techniques on my friend, Priscilla. Her neck and shoulders cramped, after long periods of painting one of her prophetic art pieces in front of an ever-changing group of participants. As I worked on her with my eyes closed, I saw and felt angels—not like well-defined pictures, but abstract, colorful, impressionistic angels that moved me to tears. Warm, healing sensations flowed through me.

As I led Priscilla's tight muscles toward relaxation, more tears spilled down my face; I recalled how often I had used these techniques at West Chester Physical Therapy. I missed the specialized work I used to do. Tears washed, cleansed—helping me say goodbye and accept the loss of a dream—in a final baptism of grief. There had been no time to cry about the loss of my practice until now. Yet, I owed the Lord *praise*; He had made that precious, private practice part of my life for seventeen years. I would always have memories to treasure.

In His infinite wisdom, God spoke to me about my homecare job with two miraculous butterfly signs. He faithfully answered my prayer. Now, trusting Him fully, I followed the path that He approved: I stayed at Mercury Home Health.

> *"...we also glory in tribulations, knowing that tribulation produces perseverance, and perseverance, character; and character, hope. Now hope does not disappoint, because the love of God has been poured out in our hearts by the Holy Spirit who was given to us."*
> —Romans 5:3–5

46

HE WANTS NONE TO PERISH

"The Lord is not slack concerning His promise, as some count slackness, but is long suffering toward us, not willing that any should perish but that all should come to repentance."
— 2 Peter 3:9

MICHAEL and I planned to celebrate Mom's eighty-sixth birthday in January. Between winter colds and schedule changes, it ended up being postponed until March. I phoned her one winter night. "Mom, Michael and I are going to take you out for a belated birthday gift. Since we already bought theater tickets for March fifteenth to see *Pride and Prejudice* as part of your Christmas present, we thought we'd take you to dinner afterward at the Hunt Room. How does that sound? You have the play on your calendar, right?"

"That would be lovely, dear! Let me look. Yes, the date's already circled!"

Mom's Christmas present never changed in the last five years: season tickets to People's Light and Theatre Company. Up until two years ago, she always treated us to dinner afterward. At the onset of assisted living, we realized her financial holdings would not last without conservation. Michael and I had convinced her to forgo post-play dinners. The evening's fun would increase with a now-rare dinner added to the planned agenda.

Three weeks before the play, Mom and I fell into a discussion about God during my medication box refill detail.

"My God wouldn't have let the Germans do what they did to the Jews! My God wouldn't let people starve," she exclaimed.

"What are you doing, Mom? Making it up as you go along?" I asked, laughing.

She smiled, but then became serious. "That's nice, dear, that you have something that brings you comfort. I know you believe literally in the Bible and Jesus dying for our sins. But the Bible was written by men and for men. I'll find out the truth when I get there."

I gave a little shake of my head. She knew the words of salvation, but didn't believe them. "Mom, all I can say is if you're dying and Jesus comes to you, don't turn Him away! Take His hand!"

After our annual, mandatory God discussion, our deep, mother-daughter love surfaced, and we parted smiling, with a hug. Our date in three weeks would be a perfect birthday celebration.

Time did its usual disappearing act, and we wheeled Mom off to the play in her wheelchair on the Ides of March. Chatting on the way to the theater, laughter filled the car, as jokes and stories about work and family ricocheted back and forth.

Front row seats in the center accommodated Mom's wheelchair. As usual, the acting, costumes, set, and script rated top drawer. Michael, Mom, and I laughed and applauded. At the end, we helped Mom out of her wheelchair for a standing ovation.

We lauded the play all the way to the Desmond Hotel's Hunt Room. The restaurant reminded us of Fell, who often took us there. We still loved the place, filled as it was with sweet, undying memories. Seated at a table off to the side, Mom pushed her menu away, unopened.

"I know exactly what I want! I'm dying for a big, juicy filet mignon and a Gibson martini."

"You're kidding, right?" I asked, eyebrows raised in consternation. "Whenever you choke, it's on beef!"

"I'll cut it small and chew it well," she promised. "Besides, it's *my* birthday dinner, right?" I sighed in resignation.

Mom's big, juicy, rare filet mignon came out sizzling on a platter. Michael ordered his medium, and I broke ranks with an order of crispy duck, no sauce. Only cutlery against ceramic sounded, as we dug into the well-prepared food.

"Mom, you have to see this video of your great granddaughter," I said and showed Mom the video of Katie screaming with delight and running from Jess. After all the "Katie videos" were enjoyed, the subject switched to pets. Dessert popped up in the conversation, as I looked for a funny video of two dogs that "shared" an ice cream cone.

A minute or so went by, before I noticed Mom had stopped talking. I looked up. She had a bemused look on her face and sat unusually still.

"Mom," I said to get her attention. She looked at me as if I had interrupted something important, but she said nothing. "Mom, can you talk?"

She gave a little "No" shake of her head, the surprised look still on her face.

"Mom, are you choking?"

With the same "I'm-busy-over-here" look she nodded "Yes," as if choking rated as a minor inconvenience. Her eyes remained on me, while looking through me—calm, surprised, without pain or fear.

Michael sprang into action, but Mom—with Parkinson's Disease and 186 pounds—couldn't stand. He struggled for an effective Heimlich Maneuver, impeded by the broad-backed Windsor chair in which she sat. I watched her face. A blue tinge crept across her lips, a harbinger of grave trouble; but the expression of awed surprise never changed. No signs of panic, air hunger, furrowed brow, or hands clutched to her throat.

She gazed at me and elsewhere at the same time with those surprised, blue eyes opened just a little wider than usual. After a few minutes, without any change of expression, she slipped into unconsciousness.

Someone called 911 when Michael started the Heimlich Maneuver. We lowered her to the floor as gently as possible and continued working on her. The invisible, offending piece of meat could not be extracted.

In ten minutes, the ambulance crew arrived. By then, a nurse who had been at the restaurant had taken over CPR. I monitored Mom's radial pulse, and cued the RN confirming effective chest compressions.

"Mom! Come on, Mom! Mom, open your eyes," Michael pleaded.

Detached, watching CPR, conscious of the crowd, I took in and stored the surreal scene. It didn't feel real. I felt outside myself looking on—not fully aware, just there, doing, being numb, and recording all through my eyes. I monitored the pulse at Mom's wrist, showing that the RN's effective cardiac compressions were pumping her blood, giving her brain oxygen.

"Where's the emergency?" an EMT called from the doorway. The crowd made a path, and he threaded his way to our table followed by two other crewmen with a stretcher. "What happened?" he asked as he assessed Mom.

"She's choking," I said from my helpless, onlooker state, "on steak."

He pulled a long tool out of his medical box. One of his partners positioned Mom's head. I knelt by Mom and watched the lead EMT as he worked to clear her airway with the tool. The third, a police officer, tapped me on the shoulder. "Come over this way, ma'am, and let them do their job. I need all her information."

With my help, he filled out Mom's forms with past medical history, medications, and a full police report. After a few tries, the EMT with the long instrument drew a large chunk of filet mignon from deep in Mom's airway. Then they moved her onto a backboard and lifted her to the stretcher as they continued CPR. Parting like the

Red Sea, the throng of fellow diners and staff allowed the team to exit. One pumped for her heart, one "bagged" her and forced oxygen into her lungs, while the third powered the stretcher.

"We're taking her to Paoli Hospital," the lead EMT called as he made eye contact with Michael and me. I nodded understanding. Then, they were gone.

A siren wailed outside, as we gathered our belongings. Michael and I left, surrounded by sympathetic murmurs from people who had dined around us or served us just fifteen minutes before.

47

FINAL DECISION

*"Most assuredly, I say to you, he who hears My word and
believes in Him who sent Me has everlasting life, and shall not
come into judgment, but has passed from death into life."*
— *John 5:24*

WHEN WE ARRIVED at Paoli Hospital Emergency Department, the
ambulance had not arrived. The likelihood of profound brain damage
or death penetrated our disbelieving haze. The magic six minutes
from health to brain death came and went. Mom, crystal clear in her
instructions to us in this type of circumstance, did *not* want to be kept
alive with brain damage, or by artificial means.

The ambulance arrived with CPR still in progress. I gave Mom's
insurance card and driver's license to the ED clerk and helped a new
EMT volunteer and another police officer fill out their reports by
answering questions. Then, Michael and I held hands, alone in our
strange bubble. We sat and waited as the ED traffic ebbed and flowed
around us. We quietly agreed it was not a good sign that the EMT
team had come in with CPR still in progress. *Mom would be brain
damaged.*

I let the receptionist know Mom had a living will. She immediately made a phone call.

About five minutes later, a slim brunette woman in a white coat came toward us. "Violet?" she asked, a stethoscope draped around her neck, a hospital ID badge clipped to her pocket. I nodded. "I'm Dr. Horvath." She motioned us into a small, glassed-in room.

Michael turned to me and said, "This can't be good."

Dr. Horvath talked to us in her warm, calm way. *Mom was gone.* The doctor explained everything in detail over the next twenty minutes. She watched us closely, until certain we understood how hard they had tried, exactly what they did, and how sorry they were that Mom died.

Through my numbness, I explained how blessed we were to have spent this whole day with Mom. The day had been filled with laughter, a great theatre production, and a delicious meal with only two pieces of filet left on Mom's plate. But most amazing, I relayed the lack of any suffering experienced by Mom, up to the time she traveled beyond feeling into unconsciousness. I told her how grateful we were for the ambulance crew, the police, and now her kindness.

I also explained how death spared Mom from further progression of Parkinson's Disease. Increased choking led to pureed foods, a disaster for the palette of someone with three pages of restaurants in her address book.

The doctor bowed her head with a small smile. "I don't get to hear stories like this very often," she said. "Would you like to see her? They can't take the ventilation tube out of her mouth until later. We had an influx of ambulance admissions that took priority," she apologized.

Michael and I nodded. Dr. Horvath ushered us through large double doors lettered in red: EMERGENCY PERSONNEL ONLY. Mom lay in a small, curtained patient room— motionless, the shell of her body left behind, her spirit gone. Still intubated, her mouth twisted at an odd angle; yet her face, eyes closed, remained peaceful, vacant. We each kissed her forehead and said goodbye—still in a dream, walking in a fog, numb with shock.

Michael started second-guessing himself: *could he have done anything more, or differently?*

My answer, "No. We did everything we could."

We drove silently to Mom's condo in Chesterbrook and broke the tragic news to her stunned, live-in aide. Our faithful agency contact came to pick her up. We hugged, cried, said our goodbyes. After a quick walkthrough check, we locked the condo and went home.

I spent three days following Mom's death closing out her earthly life. Her accountant and financial advisor led me through the sequence of contacts required. Her life and health insurance companies, family members, and close friends had to be informed of her passing. Mom's body had to be identified by me before we could arrange for cremation, using her pre-paid funeral plan. Her death notice had to be written, cleared with my sisters, and sent to agreed-upon newspapers. With all accomplished, my three days of leave from work ended. The process of grieving had no time to begin.

March nineteenth dawned—raw, rainy, and dark with thick, gray clouds. Still shrouded in disbelief, Michael and I went about our morning routine by rote, with thoughts no more complicated than *which clothes to wear* and *what to pack for lunch.* "God bless you, and keep you in your travels," I said to Michael during a tight hug, my face tucked between his neck and shoulder. I wanted to stay there, safe in his embrace. "I love you."

He held me close, cheek to cheek, before he tipped my chin up and kissed me. "I love you too. Be careful," he said, hazel eyes concerned, as he released me and turned toward the door. I watched him drive down the hill.

Still, something held me together. I didn't wonder at the nothingness, the lack of grief. There hadn't been time. But fear pulsed through me at the thought of Mom, headed for hell rather than heaven, because of her strong disbelief of needing Jesus's salvation. As a Bible-believing Christian, my faith stood on the rock of Christ's salvation.

So, driving down an empty country road on a nasty, damp day, sadness grew to flood stage as I prayed for help, comfort, and peace with her passing. Tears spilled, a dam of grief breaking, as I drove toward my first patient in Phoenixville, only seven miles away. "You have to get your act together," I said—sternly, out loud, between sobs. "You have to help patients, and you can't this way!" As I approached the Mainline Animal Rescue on Route 113 north, no sign of emotional control returned. *How could I work this day?* "Lord, help me," I wept.

Suddenly, everything stopped in freeze frame. Time stood still, although I continued driving on a main road. Steep, wooded banks on either side of the road led to a brighter horizon at the hill's crest. My body felt suffused with a glowing warmth. Strong tingling vibrated inside and outside, from the hair on my head to my toenails. Finally, "the peace that passes all understanding" descended and covered me. At that moment, the Lord gave me knowledge that Jesus had come for Mom as she choked. He held out His hand, and she took it—in repentance, acceptance, and salvation.

I would see her again. We would spend eternity together with God. Grieving ended at that moment.

On my way home from work, I bought whimsical, cheerfully-detailed change-of-address cards and mailed them to the friends, family, and acquaintances in Mom's address book. After I put my pen down, each card listed Violette Fell's "new address" in bold script as **"Heaven."**

"Surely goodness and mercy shall follow me all the days of my life and I will dwell in the house of the Lord forever."
— *Psalm 23:6*

48

NO WORDS

"Let the words of my mouth and the meditations of my heart
be acceptable in Your sight,
O Lord, my strength and my Redeemer."
— Psalm 19:14

THE MIGRAINE AURA interrupted my vision ten minutes away from a new patient's house. Already late, I didn't want to stop for the medicine buried in my purse on the passenger side floor, out of reach. I rolled the dice and waited until I stopped in her driveway before swallowing the tablet.

Jemisha, a kind woman of color, had a long history of serious medical problems. I launched the physical therapy evaluation on my work tablet, which time-stamped the visit. Then I wrote a list in my schedule book, so I could finish the eval at home without taking up her precious time.

We proceeded through all her past medical history, her vital signs and started the objective tests. I finished her strength test and asked about her endurance.

"Girl, I get so tired! Just walking down them thirteen steps from

338

my bedroom to the kitchen is a killer. It puts me away for the whole afternoon."

She explained that she tried to cook at least three times a week for her sister and family, including two pre-kindergarten-aged children.

"You'll get there," I said. "You're just deconditioned. That takes time and consistency, all fixable."

Pen in hand, I tried to write the number of times she could sit and stand from a straight-backed chair—a test for strength, balance, and endurance. My pen made an illegible squiggle, with no resemblance to any number. I looked up at Jemisha, who awaited my next direction. My mouth opened, but nothing came out as I struggled to speak. I mimed, *No speech,* with a shake of my head, my fingers opening and closing like a clam shell, my hand moving away from my mouth. Then, I gave a shrug of my shoulders and aimed an apologetic look at the concerned patient.

Jemisha's mouth formed a small "O" as her eyes widened. "Do you want me to call 911?" she asked with obvious concern.

With a smile and a shake of my head, I signaled that I could walk and think. When I saw she understood, I gave her a thumbs up. The eval had to be finished, and that took any true worry out of my immediate thought process. Yet I assessed my symptoms the whole time.

I mimed the next test: stand from a chair, walk ten feet out, then back and sit down. I showed her my timer. She understood, and I committed her time to memory. We did a few more tests before I motioned "All done."

"I'm worried about you! I still think we should call 911!"

I raised my eyebrows as I shook my head, *No,* for emphasis. I accurately judged how far things were from each other, so I could navigate safely. I knew I could think logically, and my strength remained normal. I thought I could drive safely rather than be taken to a hospital in Norristown, the closest facility to Jemisha's home.

She gave me a bottle of water, which I opened and sipped before I wrote an X sort of squiggle in the appointment book for her next appointment time. I smiled broadly after I hugged her goodbye and let her know I was bound for the hospital emergency department. She nodded with hesitant approval. I mimed that I would call her later.

Jemisha made one last attempt. "You know it's against my better judgement, letting you drive like this." I nodded understanding and placed my hand over my heart in thanks, then pointed to the ceiling, and finally, placed my hands in the palms-together, prayer position. She gave a little shrug of her own, a rueful smile and a final nod.

Once in the car, I rationalized if I could back out of her driveway and parallel park, I should be okay to drive. Successful in that test, I assessed my symptoms. I understood speech and formulated answers. I couldn't express the answers in speech or writing. I recognized a clear case of "expressive aphasia," a symptom usually associated with cerebral vascular accident (CVA) also called a "stroke." Yet, that symptom stood alone, without any other signs.

My constant assessment of my abilities left no time for fear. Besides, I pantomimed with ease and could read and understand everything. I could live with that if I had to. *God, are You telling me something, like, "Be quiet and listen?"*

As the minutes ticked by, I found I could speak a few words. My speech was coming back! I called my doctor's office and talked to the nurse, at first halting, monosyllabic. She instructed me to go to the emergency department. I gave Paoli Hospital as my destination. By the end of the conversation, I strung a few more words together.

Initially and irrationally, excitement arose: *I might not be able to do my job!* Even though I loved my patients, a stint in the hospital would be a vacation from the never-ending tablet work and constant deadlines.

Of course, my absence would not pay our mortgage; excitement died with a single, financial blow.

"Michael? I'm headed...Paoli Hospital. Aura...expressive aphasia. But walking, driving...fine."

"Did you talk to Dr. Holgado? Are you okay to drive? I can pick you up!"

"Called doctor. Finish work. Meet...Paoli...ER. K?"

"All right, Violet; as long as you're sure you can drive."

"Speech is coming back," I said in my first, full sentence. I still had word-finding problems, but it improved with each passing minute.

"Honey, get off the phone and concentrate on your driving," Michael said.

"Yup. I agree. Love you, honey! Meet me at the ER in Paoli. Pray me there," I replied in several glorious, complete sentences.

"Drive safe, and I'll pray you there. Love you back."

Driving went well. Forty-five minutes later, I pulled into Paoli Hospital's ER parking. My speech had improved, slower than usual with occasional word-finding glitches, but good enough for the ER staff to get a full medical history and an explanation of my problem. One of the residents thoroughly examined me, followed by a neurologist. They ordered a STAT MRI.

Michael appeared, as I waited for the MRI. I stood and hugged him. "I'm fine now. Just the tiniest bit of word-finding, but no big deal!" Forty minutes later, in the metal MRI tube, Mozart played on my headset as the MRI machine's magnets thumped, clanged, and banged—nullifying the beautiful, soft music. I closed my eyes and drifted, my body at peace on the thin, padded, metal surface—thumping noises nothing compared to the difficulty of completing documentation until 1:00 or 2:00 a.m.

I had called my office and let them know what had happened. They cancelled the rest of my patients for the day. Knowing that my schedule was clear, I fell into a peaceful sleep during the noisy, forty-minute test.

Several more tests, including an MRA and an EEG, assessed my brain's condition. A neurology resident came in and discussed my test results.

"When I looked at your MRI, I had to check your age," he exclaimed. "I found none of the usual markers of aging present; in fact, you have a young brain!"

"So, I actually have a brain up there! I know you've never heard that one before..."

"Yes," he smiled, "all the time!"

"Well, that's great news. I had undiagnosed Lyme for two years and hoped no plaque would be found."

"Not even a hint! The neurologist should be in to explain your diagnosis."

"I'm going to have to thank God for another miracle," I said, looking toward the ceiling. The resident smiled again and left me basking in the good news.

An hour later, the neurologist came bearing my MRI films in hand along with a packet of information. "You had a complex migraine," she said as she handed me the information. "The symptoms mimic stroke symptoms, as you described so clearly. You already know all your tests normal. I want you to spend the night at the hospital, so we can observe if any further symptoms surface over the next twelve hours. I'll see you tomorrow before you're discharged."

Michael went home and brought the "necessity list," including my journal and emergency food bars. If this had to happen, it couldn't have happened in a better way. A prayer of thanksgiving drifted heavenward from the hospital bed, and I enjoyed my freedom from the time ogre.

The neurologist caught me scheduling patients on the phone, when she came to discharge me the next day. I had finished Jemisha's evaluation from our PT session the day before and phoned the office since the midnight, day-of-treatment deadline for Mercury Home Health patient documentation had passed. The neurologist overheard me trying to schedule a patient for that afternoon and shook her head NO at me. I grimaced, but smiled at her and rescheduled the patient for the next day.

"As I said yesterday, you had a *complex migraine*." She handed me a packet of information. After explaining the contents, she said, "Make sure you take your medication right away when you get an aura. Your MRI is normal, and so are your MRA and EEG. Do you have any questions?"

"No, I don't. Thanks so much."

"I want you to take it easy for the next few days. Try not to push it," she said with concern.

"All right. We have a weekend coming up. That will help," I said.

She nodded and waved as she turned for the door.

Michael collected me after the neurologist discharged me on that windy, February day. Home never looked better. I reveled in a quiet afternoon and evening. The wood stove's heat enveloped me. One day of work remained before the weekend—when I could rest. Friday passed, slow, interminable; but I got my tablet work done by 11:57 p.m. No further auras surprised me over the next several weeks. That had to be a good sign.

This episode felt like a warning shot across my bow. I would never neglect a migraine aura again; but could I learn to get my paperwork done on the tablet—*if not easily, at least on time?* Perhaps my "thorn in the flesh" required me to find a work-around, if one existed. The Lord's lessons in my past entailed illness, miracles, signs, and whispers—all of which impacted my life. *Perhaps this time, weakness with perseverance ranks highest on the lesson list. He will let me know.*

The Thorn in the Flesh (Paul)

> *"Concerning this thing, I pleaded with the Lord three times that it might depart from me. And He said to me, "My grace is sufficient for you for My strength is made perfect in weakness." Therefore most gladly I will rather boast in my infirmities, that the power of Christ may rest upon me."*
> *— 2 Corinthians 12:8-9*

49

THIS TOO SHALL PASS

"Since his days are determined, The number of his months is with You; You have appointed his limits, so that he cannot pass. Look away from him that he may rest, Till like a hired man he finishes his day."
— Job 14:5–6

NEARLY SEVEN YEARS AGO, after a small butterfly (or very pretty moth) landed on my leg as a sign from God, I never questioned if I still belonged in my job with Mercury Home Health. The Lord's affirmation of the job as part of His will for me had been cut-glass clear. It didn't occur to me that I should pray to *end the job*, or that I should stop working there without another sign—or at least a whisper. *Had I missed a message from Him?*

Less than a year remained on our home mortgage. Continuing to work would finish off that financial burden. I loved my profession—in particular, one-on-one patient care—but any additional activities exhausted me, because of my inability to handle the documentation process in a "timely manner."

Other therapists with heavier, full-time caseloads handled the documentation well. Michael, as a part-timer, did it well. But I still struggled. "After midnight" now counted as late. My supervisor apologized when she gave me a verbal warning at my last work evaluation for late documentation. In the next year, she told me, there would be no pay increases for those with late charting.

As my fatigue grew, I began looking forward to retirement, but with no set date. I asked for guidance again, in prayer. *Silence.*

To me, silence meant *keep working.*

In November of 2018, I packed to go on one of my four-times-a-year Black Rock Silent Sanctuary Retreats. It had been a busy, exhausting week. The more tired I became, the longer documentation took. I didn't get any better at the notes, just wearier. By the time I reached the retreat center, I sat and stared at a wall, too tired to do anything else.

My friend, Priscilla, and I were in Whippoorwill—the beautiful, modern, A-frame cabin—a very special treat. On Silent Sanctuary Retreats, I always helped Priscilla set up her Art Prayer Station with art supplies of every kind imaginable. Tonight, Priscilla left after I told her I needed a little rest before starting to unpack and arrange the supplies.

But, instead of joining her after dinner, I sat—catatonic, flagged, staring into the fireplace—the leaping flames part of Whippoorwill's charm. Abandoned in this way, Priscilla set up the prayer station by herself. She needed prayer-time to hear and see what she would be painting. Instead, she set up the room while I sat in the cabin, paralyzed. By the time I could move again and arrived at the art station, the clock read 9:30 p.m., long after dark, long after she finished. We spoke little. I returned to Whippoorwill, fell into bed, and passed out.

Saturday evening, we had dinner together. Without preamble, Priscilla sat down and said, "Work is supposed to be beneficial, not kill you! You need to retire!" Blindsided by her uncharacteristic, sharp tone—compared to her usual kind, caring voice—this curt, annoyed, almost disgusted voice stabbed me. At that time, I didn't fathom what my lack of help cost her; nor did I consider how worried

346 of our home mortgage.

she may have been for my health and well-being. I didn't know this Priscilla who spoke with such harshness, when my being had fallen to rock bottom.

Even so, I only needed to hear the truth in what she said. When she returned to the art station, I called my husband. "Michael," I said, "I was so fried from work, I couldn't help Priscilla set up last night. I couldn't move until after nine o'clock, and by the time I got down to the art station, she had it all set up. Honey, I can't do this anymore," my voice trailed off.

"I saw this coming," he said in a soft voice. "When do you want to retire?" No recrimination, no judgement, only gentleness flowed through the phone. We talked about timing. A date—set in my mind, etched in white light—lit up my brain; and Michael agreed. *March 29, the day we would pay off our home mortgage.*

"Can you hang in there that long?" he asked.

"I'll make it happen," I said grimly, "if the Lord allows it." *Twenty weeks in the future.* I knew God stood beside me, even when He didn't speak. He had his reasons. Michael and I spoke a few more minutes, before we ended our conversation as always.

"I love you," I said.

"I love you too. Call me tomorrow before eight."

"Okay. Night-night, love."

When Priscilla returned, we had a cup of tea before bed. "I'm retiring. Michael and I talked about the timing tonight. March twenty-ninth is the last day of our mortgage," I said, "and I'm out of there!"

Priscilla examined my face, her expression still hard. "Not a day later, or there will be irrevocable consequences to your health." Her intense gaze seemed caring, yet I felt the palpable coldness I richly deserved after deserting her last night. "I've watched you go downhill over this last year. I thought you would recognize the danger signs." I knew she was right. I had waited for the Lord to tell me. He showed me instead.

I resigned with a month's notice. Uncontainable delight became obvious to everyone I worked with at Mercury Home Health. Many of my peers expressed good-natured, understandable envy. Each day, I arose with difficulty. Patient care, compelling as it had been for the last forty-six years, became fatiguing. This year, the forty-seventh, my worn-out body dragged through each day. I still worked caring for my patients. *One difficult year out of forty-seven is not bad!* I thought. Those last months were the hardest. The old adage, *and this too shall pass*, often came to mind during the waning days of my employment. I had started working at age fifteen and never stopped. Now, I didn't have energy to think about retired life. I wanted to finish well, and that took all I had.

On March 29, 2019, I returned my tablet and "bin" that held all the supplies I used on my job. My supervisor and I chatted amiably. Though I had been concerned the day she hired me, I was grateful to be on her team. She had been a knowledgeable and understanding boss.

"You know, there are three of you retiring at one time," she said.

"An epidemic," I joked.

"We should throw a party after things settle down here," she said.

"I'd like that." I would have enjoyed such a gathering with the other two perspective retirees and those who wished to celebrate our freedom. The party never happened.

My employment ended with smiles and well wishes. *A party*, I thought, *not necessary.* I knew my blessings came from God, not celebration, documentation, lack of sleep, or incessant striving. But part of me wanted a party. My spirit knew the Lord alone understood my heart; He alone knew gold apart from wood, hay, and stubble. *What will retirement bring?*

"Search me, O God, and know my heart; Try me, and know my anxieties;
And see if there is any wicked way in me, And lead me in the way everlasting."
—*Psalm 139:23–24*

50

CELEBRATION

*"...Jesus answered and said, '...Come to Me, all you who labor
and are heavy laden, and I will give you rest.
Take My yoke upon you and learn from Me, for I am gentle
and lowly in heart, and you will find rest for your souls.
For My yoke is easy and My burden is light.'"*
— *Matthew 11:25, 28–30*

THE EVENING I RETIRED, Michael said, "Promise me you won't do
anything this summer. I want you to rest." Although his voice
sounded stern, the depths in his eyes revealed only love.

"I promise," I said, and meant it. A limp excuse of a woman, too
tired to be herself, I had a husband who wanted his wife back—the
one with spunk, sparkle, and sass—the girl he had married. With
God's help, I intended to get her back, for both of us.

My 6:30 a.m. alarm opened my eyes each morning for medication an hour or more before breakfast. I stretched and swallowed my
pill with the bottled water from my nightstand. *I can get up or go
back to sleep*, I thought with a new, delightful sense of choice.

Mundane chores became savored activities compared to constant problem-solving, notes, and deadlines. Seven years in the desert (the time I spent at Mercury Home Health with no formal Bible study) yielded a parched spirit and battered body. I wanted to return to Bible study at our church. Though I promised Michael I would rest, I felt wired, jangled, and raw. Like gentling a wild horse, patience, a soft touch, and perseverance pointed the way to healing.

Invariably, when Michael left for work, if I turned off the TV, I accomplished chores and restful things. My orchids and African violets shot flower spikes and blooms, after a couple months of my caressing, mellow words of encouragement, regular watering, and occasional fertilizer. Poems sprouted from my pen, as my body stood down and my spirit reconnected. Journaling, not only with words, but all the colors in my three-tiered pencil box and three-by-five coloring cards, scattered rainbows through my new life while taking me back to my high school days. Kimberton Farms School's teaching from decades ago flowed through my colored pencils and paint brushes.

I napped daily that first six months, with my calico, Persian-Maine Coon cat curled up on my chest. Her green eyes glowed, as she purred and coated me with long, honey, white-and-sable hair. I prayed throughout my day—all kinds of prayers: praise, honoring, recognizing His glory and power, thanksgiving, and prayer requests for self, family, and friends. But a consistent "quiet time" did not emerge beyond our daily, morning reading in *Encounter with God*, and the associated Bible verses, insufficient, in my estimation, for the King of Kings and Lord of Lords.

After six months of retirement, my shoulders relaxed down, neck muscles unknotted, and jaw unclenched. Lighter, feeling free, my body walked with ease. Yet, leaving home felt like an imposition after I quit my job (although, I actually enjoyed grocery shopping.) I craved quiet, the sounds of nature and stillness uninterrupted by human conversation. With no demanding voices or schedule, my natural optimism and energy seeped back into my being, not overnight, but on a steady rise. Our comfortable, secluded, Eden Hill home sat tucked in the woods near the hilltop. The wooded piece looked very like where I'd been raised "in the country" of Montgomery County, Pennsylvania. At ease in my own skin, the solitary silence centered me, bringing me closer to God.

"Aren't you afraid, being here all alone with these big windows?" one of my church friends asked.

"No, never... Oh, wait! Once, in 1977," I recalled. "I'd started reading *The Shining*, by Stephen King, the master of horror novels. Michael was in New York City, taking a PT course. A bestseller, this book topped his list. I started to read and crawled into one of the characters."

"Stephen King, whoa!"

"Two hours into the novel, I imagined things moving out of the corner of my eye. When my heart started pounding, I called Michael. Talking to him did the trick. I put the book back on the shelf and went to bed. I finished it after he came home."

"Being afraid like that doesn't count," my friend said. "King's novels can scare you in a crowd, let alone by yourself." I nodded.

"But what about day-to-day?" she asked. "There's nothing up here; you can't even see your neighbors, except the barn at the bottom of the hill."

"No, I'm not afraid. Now I *can* say never. My father renovated the home my grandfather built. He replaced the rotted French doors with floor-to-ceiling picture windows. They faced south, just like the bank of windows in this house. I grew up in that home. My Dad called it "a goldfish bowl." At ten, Mom let me stay home alone for a few hours at a time. I liked it with no one else around."

My friend whistled and shook her head. "That's really different from the way I grew up!"

"No surprise," I said with a crooked smile. "*Different* describes my family." We laughed and left it at that.

One pretty, June Saturday, Michael said, "Let's go out to dinner tonight."

"Sure," I said. "Where do you want to go?"

"You know, we never really did anything for Mother's Day or for your retirement. Let's do something special. How about The General Warren Inne?"

"Really? That's expensive," I said, surprised.

"How often do you retire? And add Mother's Day to it."

"I can't argue with those facts. I'm sure we'll need reservations."

I dialed the restaurant and asked for reservations for two under Michael's name at a quiet table.

"Did you say "Batejan," Ma'am?" the receptionist asked. When I affirmed the name, I waited for a minute before the answer came back for a 5:30 p.m. seating. I wore a long-sleeved, purple dress, one of my favorites; Restaurants were usually on the cool side for me. A hand-wrought, glass pendent with violets I had given Mom hung on a silver rope necklace. Michael wore a navy-blue suit and burgundy-red tie with silver-blue dots. His Oxford-blue dress shirt created a handsome background for the classic tie.

"You look very nice, Violet."

"Thank you. And you look handsome."

I took his hand as we walked toward the car. "You know, I miss your old Chevy's bench seats." Michael smiled as I indicated bucket seats separated by the manual brake in his Forester. "I can't get close enough to you."

He gave a laugh I loved to hear, low and deep in his throat. I patted his thigh and settled back, pleased with life.

A wedding in progress almost filled the parking lot. Walking, hand-in-hand to the entrance took us around the colonial home-turned-restaurant. Sent to the North Room, we arrived to a bit of confusion.

"Oh, I'm sorry," the hostess said. This is set up for a private party."

We turned back, but the maître d' gave the hostess a cryptic look and said, "That's all right. Their table *is* in The North Room."

"Ah, of course." I watched people and took in the surroundings. Michael and I had only been there once, a memorable occasion near Christmas.

As we followed the hostess back to a room with a wall of early American glass windows, a group gathered.

"Surprise!" someone yelled as my eyes focused on people. Immediately, Jessica, Priscilla, Gay, and Lynne came into focus. The rest of the pack followed, as friends and family surrounded me.

Doing a good imitation of a goldfish, I finally found my voice. "You!" I cried, nudging my grinning husband.

Six-year-old Katie came running and hugged me. "Nana," she squealed. I had babysat Katie all day Friday, the day before, yet she never said anything about a surprise!

"Katie, you little rascal!" I tickled her and enjoyed her familiar laugh.

"Nana, I wanted to tell you, but I promised Momma and Papa I wouldn't!" I picked her up and hugged her close, as she buried her face between my neck and shoulder.

"Okay, who's responsible for this?" I looked at Michael, as Jessica appeared at my elbow.

"Jessica did everything," Michael said, looking from me to her with affection. "I just paid for it," he added.

Jessica toasted me before our appetizers, with some memories of her own and an overview of my career. She gave an eloquent toast that honored my forty-seven years of service as a physical therapist. With a glass of champagne and some hors d'oeuvres, my smile grew to encompass my whole being.

Before dinner had been served, my facial muscles complained of fatigue; still, they kept on working. Sixteen beloved people celebrated with us. Jess planned the menu with all my food intolerances in mind. We enjoyed main courses of steak, fish, or vegetarian fare and a selection of side dishes everyone relished. Friends identified people they had only heard of with actual faces. Retirement gifts overflowed: a purple leather-bound journal, African violet, plushy robe, foot massager, hummingbird feeder, tiny orchid, and plant holder, to name a few. Each gift sparkled with love and the personality of the giver. Gifts, ongoing blessings, permanent reminders of the celebration, touched my heart. Jess told me she created a retirement dinner "that would have made Grand'Mere proud."

After dessert and pictures, Michael and I thanked Jessica, whose organizational genius created an event I would remember the rest of my life. Later at home, I found a place for each gift, still overwhelmed and wrapped in gratitude. My family and friends gave me the best surprise of all: the joy of their company in celebration.

I had a feeling a broad smile graced God's face.

51

RETIREMENT

"Surely goodness and mercy shall follow me all the days of my life; and I will dwell in the house of the Lord forever."
— *Psalm* 23:6

IN EARLY SEPTEMBER, I signed up for both the Matthew and Revelation Bible studies at our church. In addition, our church requested volunteers for English as a Second Language (ESL). I always wanted to teach reading; this seemed even better. I signed up for ESL volunteer training, the last activity I could fit into my increasingly busy schedule.

My class in Revelation, a Precept Ministry International Bible Study, dug deeply into the richness of God's word—with a well-founded reputation for massive amounts of in-depth homework to fully prepare for each class. Two sets of Bible study homework proved daunting, until I worked out a system.

I savored the personal, relational aspects of the Matthew study compared to Revelation, with its intensive lecture, participation from the homework, and an instructional video at the end. The Revelation study seemed reminiscent of a college course.

At this time in my life, I wanted to make new friends and learn at the same time. For the time being, I managed both courses.

In September, after one of the *Delighting in the Lord* studies in Matthew, the class leaders, Carlotta and Dione, stopped me. "You share the most interesting experiences! That story about your mother really struck a chord with the group. It was the same last week, with the butterfly story," Carlotta said.

Dione chimed in, "You should write a book!"

I should write a book. Those words reached down deep and grabbed something forgotten—something breathed upon by the Holy Spirit then and now.

"Yes, I'd like to," I said. "I've always wanted to write a book. There's a half-finished novel at home in a box, written before Lyme Disease stopped me dead in the water."

"My husband still suffers from the effects of Lyme," Carlotta said. "That is one nasty bug!"

Dione nodded and returned to the book idea. "But this book would be true-to-life stories, like you share in class."

"Yes," I said as the Holy Spirit breathed living-color into the idea. "I'm going to go home and start it today!"

"Good!" Carlotta cheered. Dione smiled.

That week, I wrote three chapters, out of sequence. Each chapter included a memorable event where God wove His purposes into my life. I brought them in the next week for Carlotta and Dione to share. On the way to Bible study that morning, the words *Messages from God* came to mind. "That's the title of the book," I said out loud. *The Holy Spirit was at work, and I heard Him.* The title described the book I planned.

I told Carlotta and Dione the "working title" was *Messages from God* and gave them the chapters. The next week at Bible Study, Dione said, "I really like your writing."

"Could I read more?" Carlotta asked.

"Absolutely! If I'm going to do this, I need to be held accountable with deadlines. Would you ladies be interested in helping me?"

"Yes," they said at the same time. "We were going to suggest something like that. It must be a God thing," Dione said.

As time vanished, keeping up with *Messages from God*, two Bible studies, and ESL became impossible. Something had to go, but I needed help determining which activity to cut. Revelation: fascinating, deep, and compelling. Matthew: relational, full of everyday-life parallels and Jesus's parables. I loved both studies. But in prayer time, the Lord let me know clearly that *Messages from God* had to be written during the time presently needed for the Revelation Bible study homework.

I wrote a chapter a week. Carlotta and Dione became my "Book Angels." Each Tuesday, I read the chapters to them on a conference call started by Dione. Both women had different skill sets—from grammar and punctuation to good word choices and story line suggestions. We came to know each other as the book developed into a memoir of God's weaving on the loom of my life.

Each side of my life's fabric furnishes a different message—one side shows a muddied, rough, knotted surface—the other, a smooth, colorful, picture. He created the double-sided fabric of my existence, one side—lessons and learning—the other a nearly finished product.

"Violet, come here!" Michael called from the living room. He had the TV news tuned in to our favorite morning show. "As January 2020 heads for a new month, an unknown virus is taking the world by storm. "It's called Covid-19, a form of corona virus. And it kills people." By mid-March, the virus morphed into a worldwide pandemic. The entire US population, except "essential workers," followed instructions to "shelter in place," leaving home only for groceries, pharmacy needs, or emergencies. Face covers and social distancing of six feet became mandatory.

"You know that Jess, Katie, and Tony are off limits," he said, handing me a blue, pleated mask.

"It feels strange to have English as a Second Language shut down," I said, tucking the mask in my coat pocket. "I got a text message from Carlotta. They're going to use Zoom, so we can continue Bible study until summer break."

Church, deemed "non-essential," came through TV on YouTube. Calvary Chapel Chester Springs, with the praise team and Pastor Chris Swansen, brought His Word and worship into our living room at 8:00 a.m. on Sunday mornings, a light in dark times.

By the end of June 2020 in Pennsylvania, the number of Covid deaths had declined. Selected businesses reopened with social distancing and mask requirements still in force. Our churches had services outside, some under tents as the days grew hotter. Barber shops re-opened, and wrought of desperation by March's end, Michael made an appointment at Kathy's Barber Shop rather than relying on my passable but makeshift haircuts.

Not all businesses survived. On a drive down Route 23 toward Lancaster, I pointed to a whole block of empty storefronts. "There's a sad commentary on the price of no business." They were "non-essential." Many lost their jobs, businesses—and some, their homes, although the government-issued stimulus checks and loans helped people weather the storm.

I spoke by phone to all of my family. Since Jess worked from home and Tony had an essential job distanced from other people, I felt confident they were safe. Everyone took precautions, and so far, no one I knew contracted the corona virus plague.

Gay's story radiated with warmth in this sad time.

"I'm doing well," she said.

"You can't see any massage or Craniosacral Therapy clients, at your office, right?"

"Right. But the most amazing thing happened yesterday." As she paused, I could picture her shaking her head. "You've heard me talk about my client who's a friend now. She called me and said, as my 'most consistent client,' she wanted to make sure I was all right financially. She sent me money, Violet! And more than a little."

Gay received money from several clients; a few donations in large amounts, to keep her afloat. Some people kept paying their housecleaners, for the months they could not bring these workers into their homes.

The importance of *loving one another* grew, as I sat and listened when the Lord whispered. Paul spoke of learning how to live in poverty and plenty. This time of isolation shook our ordered world. It impoverished us socially, stimulated reassessment of priorities, and challenged faith. In Hebrews, Paul said, *"Now faith is the substance of things hoped for, the evidence of things not seen." Hebrews 11:1 came to life: a time for faith, for giving in new ways, for prayer, and staying connected regardless of the Satanic viral attack.*

Suicides, severe depression, and violence mushroomed in the time of isolation. Like Joseph being sold into slavery by his brothers in *Genesis* 37:12—36, good may come out of the worst circumstances: Joseph saved his whole family from starvation, because he worked hard as a slave and stayed faithful to God. He became governor of Egypt, with humble prayer, recognizing God's powerful love and using his God-given gifts. Because of his willingness to forgive his brothers, his family lived, reunited.

Enslaved by isolation, our country needed to follow his example and work in the way we were allowed by our social distancing and sheltering at home.

As my writing progressed, I wanted to publish the book that told of God's works in my life, a few major miracles, and a multitude of signs and whispers. My chances of getting published as a first-time author—the size of an electron. Elm Hill Books sent me an infomercial email that worked: I made the phone call for "the offer of a lifetime." Ready to buy their self-publishing package, I waited for a promised phone call that never came. Finally, I called my contact.

"Hey, Jim, what happened to our phone conference?" I asked.

"I'm no longer employed by Elm Hill Books, Violet. You were on my list to call. Covid-19 stopped everything like a brick wall. Elm Hill Books didn't survive the mandatory closure of non-essential businesses. It went under."

I finished my conversation and business relationship with Jim.

My interest in publishing a book, now public on social media, morphed into multiple emails from self-publishing companies. Curiosity opened most of the links, but I made no phone calls until I watched Chandler Bolt's webinar from Self-Publishing School. His well-crafted webinar taught me several interesting points. He hooked me. I made the phone call. This outfit taught writing, marketing, and sales. I did my research on Self-Publishing School: nothing else on the market seemed to compare. With the Holy Spirit's guidance, I bought a course in "The Fundamentals of Fiction, Memoir, and Story" by the end of June 2020—a Self-Publishing School student at age seventy... back to college!

With fourteen months of writing and six months of coursework, the highlights of God's guidance in my life flowed onto the computer screen. Along the way, looking for cover pictures, I found a photograph of the sun coming through a forest with intense tones of orange, mauve, and golden yellow. The trees, silhouetted in dark vertical shapes, still recognizable, bottomed out in forest floor greenery. I bought rights to the picture, knowing Who placed it in my path. Retitled, my book, *Messages from God*, became *The Forest for the Trees, A Memoir*. A couple of months farther along in my coursework, a new title whispered in my ear. *Signs, Wonders, and Miracles*, followed by *Signs, Whispers, and Miracles*. The subtitle, bounced between suggestions for months, until *Finding God in the Fabric of Life* stuck. My cover design has the title on it. No more decisions now.

From September of 2019 to January of 2021, the memoir came to life until the last sentence ended with a final Scripture. At the end of a third draft, light shone—I could see the end of the journey.

I thought of my half-finished book, *Sara's Way*. The spare-room closet cloistered future Christmas gifts, cards, paper, a box of picture frames, my scrapbooking kit, and all of my gift-wrapping supplies. On the bottom shelf sat a dusty box. It contained all of my writings from a correspondence course taken in 1990 at The Institute of Children's Literature. My final assignment, *The Conductor*, sketched out a short story about the Underground Railroad. Imagination seized the assignment and framed a modern-day plot around the 1860s story.

As I wrote *Sara's Way* starting in 1992, twelve-year-old Jess begged, and I read each successive chapter out loud. She and my friends at work waited, eager for the next installment. I entered the first three chapters in the St. David's Christian Writer's Conference "Beginner's Novel" competition, the last year I attended in 1993. It won third prize.

Lyme Disease had attacked me three months earlier. After the conference, my symptoms worsened, creating "the perfect storm"; writing became impossible, with no energy and a foggy brain. One of my favorite pastimes, reading, fell out of my life. Processing words into pictures took more energy than I owned.

Now, in 2021, twenty-eight years later, the off-white folder fell open, its contents complete with rusted paper clips.

Sara's Way
    SARA

Her eyes wouldn't open. Somewhere, distant, echoing, people were talking; but she only caught snatches of staccato conversation that drifted around her. Surfacing further, she heard the protesting squeal of metal amidst the disembodied voices. None of it seemed important, as she floated somewhere between heaven and earth. Nothing really mattered. The warm dampness seemed almost pleasant, until she felt hands poking, prodding, lifting, pulling her back to consciousness with a prolonged, wailing scream.

Pages kept turning, until I came to the unfinished end. I lost two hours of time reading. Crafting this story, that flipped back and forth between the 1850s-1860s and modern day, turned into a new goal. With three modules left in my "Fundamentals of Fiction, Memoir and Story" course, a new fiction course flashed onto my computer screen from Self-Publishing School: "Lifetime Fiction Author." The year-long course of study included planning a fiction series.

Sara's Way? Perfect for a series. All the marketing tools needed to succeed, *if* I wrote a story worth reading, would live at my fingertips with the new course. I prayed. I slept on it. I phoned... and gave the SPS contact my book account, credit card number.

So, at seventy-one, I'm back in college for another year. God willing, I think I'll be a fiction writer when I grow up.

But my story doesn't end there. Writing opened many unexpected doors.

I decided to talk to Jess about the book, including my painful experience surrounding Katie's birth. I never mentioned my feelings of 2013 to my daughter, until I wrote about that chapter of my life in 2021.

What happened that kept her from allowing me to be with her during labor and delivery? I called, and we talked—until an opening arose as I told her about my book's editing schedule.

"It's going to my editor on Friday. I wanted to talk to you about Katie's birth and make sure you're comfortable with me including the story I wrote."

"Why wouldn't I be comfortable? What did you write?"

"You, Dad, and Gay are exceptionally private people. I'm transparent. I'm taking no chances."

"You learned from your mistakes?"

I could picture her smiling. We could joke about our differences now. I chuckled, took a breath, then asked, "What happened that kept me in the waiting room while you had Katie?"

"I wanted you with me, but labor progressed really fast. Pain took over; I can't even describe how bad the pain was. You were late, and with five people in the room, I already felt claustrophobic. I didn't want anything changed with so much going on. Since I couldn't think clearly or speak with the intense pain and contractions, I just shook my head, 'No,' when the nurse told me you'd arrived. Afterward, I felt bad, but that's the way it went."

"You never said anything." I paused, thoughtful that Jessica's reasons made me feel better almost eight years later.

"I did today," she said with a laugh. I smiled to myself. Our relationship had grown warmer and closer in the last two years. She surprised me again. "After Katie was born, I never told you I had severe postpartum depression [PPD]. I'd like you to include that in your book as a conversation that might help other women with the condition."

"Really? I would have thought that was way out-of-bounds!"

"I have changed. I was so sick during my pregnancy and even worse afterward because of mold sensitivity. I withdrew. I didn't really talk to anyone."

"I had no idea! It wasn't unusual for you not to talk much. I did realize I was always the one who called you. Looking back, it makes sense."

Jess and me kissing little 'Katie-bear': Three Generations of love.

"I became anxious and depressed after Katie was born, but not with usual PPD; I didn't ignore my baby. In fact, I felt uncomfortable if she was out of my sight—off the charts overprotective. If someone else wanted to hold her, even for a short time, I got nervous, anxious, like, 'She's mine! Give her back...'"

"Well, I had no clue."

"Your writing gave us a channel to move forward."

We talked about other things, like a possible job change in May, if she could find something she liked for reasonable pay.

Life went on, another wound healed, our differences accepted by each other. We formed new bonds, as if we were brilliant stars coming out from behind the clouds—from hazy and indistinct to sparkling, clear points of light. *Precious. Miraculous. God's hand yet again—blessing, nurturing—a good, good Father.* As my life unfolded, I became more aware of His clear presence every day. As this book progressed, I shared more openly about the Lord and His blessings, in all things, in sunny times and times of shadow.

Faith has become an everyday experience. *I look forward to dwelling "in the house of the Lord forever," after I grow up, if He allows.*

What will you do "when you grow up?" Take heart! He's there for each of us. His love never ends.

52

AFTER ALL

*Beware lest anyone cheat you through philosophy and empty
deceit according to the tradition of men, according to the basic
principles of the world and not according to Christ.*
— Colossians 2:8

AFTER TWENTY MONTHS OF WRITING, *Signs, Whispers And
Miracles: Finding God in the Fabric of Life* came to a rest in my
computer. By late June 2021, the lack of expected comments from
my Beta (test) readers triggered impatience. Once received and
digested, those comments would suggest changes that elevated the
manuscript to a book-worthy level. Especially interested in my
church Bible Study friends' impressions, I caught up with Bonnie
after class one Thursday morning. "What did you think of the book?"
I asked.

"I'm sorry, I'm not going to get to it for a while," she apologized. I
didn't badger her. Life flowed by at a terrifying pace and I understood
—at nearly three-hundred-fifty pages, my book was not a short read.
By the time I asked her again, I had published the e-book format.
This time, she responded and her comment stunned me.

"It was a really good memoir, but I don't think you were saved at fourteen. Your life just didn't show the changes that come with salvation. I kept waiting for you to give your life to the Lord as an adult, but it never happened. So, I can't review the book as it stands—it's unfinished."

I thanked her and headed for the exit, my brain storming. She was right—I hadn't written about the adult rededication of my life to Jesus Christ. The second pledge of belief didn't happen until my mid-fifties. That particular memory came to mind like a movie. My adult rededication arose during an in-depth Bible study of Second Peter. This book of the Bible opened my eyes to how little I'd submitted to the Lord—especially one verse:

> *For we did not follow cunningly devised fables when we made known to you the power and coming of our Lord Jesus Christ, but were eyewitnesses of His majesty.*
> *— 2 Peter 1:16*

2 Peter 1:16 stopped me—pulled me up short. All the apostles, except Judas, believed in Jesus as the Christ, the Jewish Messiah. They all submitted to Christ and died without renouncing their faith. These men did not go to their deaths with a lie on their lips. How, then, could I still have any doubts at all?

That realization heaved my world at age fifty-five. My hardened heart broke open. "Forgive me, Lord, for my superficial faith, my stubborn will, my doubts." Tears streaked my face as I sang Rich Mullins' and David Strasser's song, "Creed:" "I believe in God the Father, Almighty Maker of heaven and Maker of Earth, And In Jesus Christ His only begotten Son, our Lord..." I *believed* at fourteen with *all* my heart and now, my belief solidified—strong, certain, immutable. The gift of salvation came in tandem with the indwelling Holy Spirit, our companion, comforter, and personal way-shower—an unfailing guide. As one of His major roles, the Holy Spirit points the way to Jesus as our Savior, our bridge to the Father. I continued singing, "And I believe what I believe is what makes me what I am, I did not make it, no it is making me...It is the very truth of God and not the invention of any man... I believe it..." In my human pride, this crucial truth humbled me as I received a minute glimpse of the awesome magnitude and majesty of God.

My recommitment to Christ enveloped me almost two decades ago. Turning back to my original salvation experience, another Bible study friend agreed with Bonnie: there could be no redemption at fourteen with the number of Commandments I had continued to fracture after my supposed salvation. Yet, even on first impression, a major element seemed to be missing from their assessment. Pondering, I realized neither of these faithful, honest women considered sanctification—for many, a long, complex process of refinement. I *had* experienced two years of salvation changes in my life, before traveling down the wrong road. Head held high, my blue eyes connected with those of the bullies as their taunts bounced off my invisible shield throughout eighth and ninth grades. This occurred only because I knew Jesus suffered far more than I ever would with my negligible trials. During that time, my words mirrored His. Beneath a smile aimed at my detractors, I directed my thoughts heavenward, *Lord forgive them for they know not what they do.*

The more we seek Him, the greater abundance He gives us. *Ask, and it will be given; seek, and you will find, knock, and it will be opened to you. Our Father in heaven will give good things to those who ask Him!* Matthew 7: 7, 11. I *had* prayed the salvation prayer from my heart in my youth. I *knew* the Lord answered with forgiveness and the gift of the Holy Spirit. That alone rendered me heavenbound. My young being resembled a brightly colored piece of new sea glass, broken, full of sharp, jagged edges—skepticism and flaunting the law, to name a few. My small sea-glass needed time in His ocean for sanding, tumbling, smoothing, perfecting.

As an adult, I prayed, after hashing about with my church friends' comments. God pointed the way. I phoned Priscilla, my best friend, my Christian mentor and explained the sanctification issue.

Her previous experience as a pastor served me well. "Sanctification is about growing trust in the One liberating us," she began. "He's liberating us to live consistently in the fruit of the Spirit—Galatians 5:22. The New King James Version reads, '...*love, joy, peace, longsuffering, kindness, goodness, faithfulness, gentleness, self-control.*'" She rattled the list off, in sequence, by heart.

"But that's a really gradual process—at least it was for me."

"Usually," Priscilla said, "I only exist as God's unique expression —born the way He chose to express me. After birth, layer on layer of man-made expression coat God's original creation of the authentic 'me'. Sanctification is the process of removing layers that block His chosen expression. Does that make sense?"

"Yes," I said. "It does."

"He cleans us up so we have more *on earth as it is in heaven*— more of His abundant life. We cannot know our authentic selves without knowing God—*He* is our Creator. His chosen expressions live as unique individuals, crafted with a distinct purpose and plan. Each of us is one of a kind, created in His image, breathing with His breath." Priscilla stopped for a breath of her own.

"That means we develop false, man-made layers that block who we *really* are as God's creation," I said.

"Right. Living in the world, crusts of man-made expression rob us of God's authenticity. Only His sanctification frees us. God gives us freedom of choice—sanctification requires our agreement. Likewise, the devil needs our agreement to activate his plans for destruction of God's design. We absorb those crusty, man-made expressions and choose to listen to Satan."

"Exactly my experience," I said. "I questioned Christ as the Savior and turned my back on Christian morals. But salvation is *not* lost with backsliding. It's not lost in our need for sanctification either. What an amazing gift."

"Yes, it is. God's redemptive creativity works through circumstances and relationships that prepare our hearts to receive Jesus and to grow through Him."

I nodded. "As my Creator, He knows the 'real' me and my life's path, right to the end. My redemption at fourteen had to include lots of clean-up, considering all the wrong choices I made throughout my life. So, I am broken, humbled and cleansed, step by step by my Creator. With my agreement He strips away each layer of man-made dross."

"Yes," she said. "Like all humans, we are each an expression of God. He wraps each precious expression in a clay pot."

"I like that! I like to think of each expression as a bright, living spark spoken into existence and wrapped in a clay pot, as part of His Creation. You know, your instruction is exactly what I needed, Priscilla. Thank you! I have to thank my Bible study friends for raising this issue." We talked a little while about family before going back to our separate lives.

I left the conversation in a reflective mood. My rich life as a flawed woman in partnership with her Lord, shined brighter through sanctification's many cracks—a woman forgiven, lifted up by Christ, and made whole. Many free-will choices turn us toward or away from sanctification. I made good and bad decisions along the way, but I always came back to Christ. I *chose* then and *choose* now to submit to the Lord's will.

It hurts my heart, my very nature, that so many choose to deny Jesus as Savior—as our only bridge to heaven. According to the Bible, they are bound for hell. Many close to me and in my family reject Christ as Savior, like my mother until minutes before her death. The trust required to place them in God's hands and pray, took decades and only developed as I learned submission to Christ.

"Submission"—here we find a charged word not even used in my marriage vows. Yet I chose a man I would submit to because of mutual love and respect. Still, submission in the Biblical sense required a learning curve. It required years of learning at Calvary Chapel Chester Springs. Maturity in Christ with His sanctification process allowed me to hear the truth.

Being a submissive wife entails love and respect without

becoming the proverbial doormat. It means Michael is the five-star general and I am under him in rank with four stars. I rank under no man other than *my* husband. This system of ordering, as our pastor explains, is not a measure of worth. Michael and I decide everything together. Because of our acceptance of Biblical ordering, he inherited the trusted role of tiebreaker which he always aims to complete in the fruit of the Spirit. Our marital ordering is a 49/51% split rather than the original 50/50 split from the beginning of our marriage—a night and day mindset change.

My view of the job title "Homemaker" drastically changed as God plucked away layers of tarnish and poor examples. I found it easier to work outside the home with an external, well organized job description—where praise came in paychecks and through grateful patients. I struggled with homemaking since I had to organize my own time, rather than the job organizing it for me. So, I claimed the job title "Author."

Through sanctification, I gradually attained an internal structure that allowed expansion. The true expression of sanctification produces increasing levels of freedom to live God's kingdom from the inside out. Prioritizing my time requires self-discipline for self-struc-ture. I'm getting better at it. Now, that I am a retired physical thera-pist, both writing and homemaking claim much of my creative identity.

Since age fourteen to the present, my sanctification curve ranges onward, sometimes plateauing or steep, often uncomfortable, if not painful. As my beloved stepfather lay dying, I chose to wear a cross pendant signifying Jesus' gift of salvation. Until his cancer diagnosis, the cross bore a negative meaning for me: not a cross of salvation, but a cross of cruel death. Not a cross of love and giving, but a cross of crushing domination and betrayal. Now, the cross means I'll see him again in heaven—the cross of forgiveness with eternal life. It's the shining cross of completed sanctification, for believers—the cross of peace and joy forever.

Even in my worst suffering, Lyme Disease did *not* claim my

ability to work as a physical therapist—God's amazing grace in action. My ability to bounce back after exercise and eat a more varied diet came to fruition after retirement—twenty-eight years after my first symptoms. Without this part of the sanctification process, Michael and I would never have bought or enjoyed West Chester Physical Therapy, something only discovered with 20/20 hindsight.

At this writing, my health glows again. The joy, as I rise from bed in the morning, refreshed and ready to go, makes me fizz inside like happy, champagne bubbles. Michael has his wife back. I have my life back—at least 85% of my original normal, and that's sweet enough to be wonderful. Overwhelming gratitude laces my daily life.

After seventy-one years—seventy-two in December—my little piece of sea glass came near to washing up on shore. The sharp edges of skepticism and other flaws had smoothed—almost polished. Yet, the still imperfect, piece of lovely, colored glass required more sanding under God's loving hand. The undertow took it back out to the ocean depths for more tumbling. God's polishing, His sanctification, continues to refine my salvation. I want my spirit to gleam when He finally takes me home.

With so many layers already stripped away, lightness, joy, and faith abound. Each day is lit with gratefulness and contentment. Yet the capability of slipping back into a man-made rut of earthly desire and foolishness remains an icy, downhill slope. So, my gaze and heart turn to Jesus and His ways through silence, prayer, Bible study, reading, and church. The Holy Spirit's promptings touch me when still and break in when busyness surrounds me. Most of the time, a strong sense of Jesus' path plants my feet, steadfast and sure, in His footprints. My times of straying become shorter and repentance comes more quickly. I yearn for a relationship with Him whose expression forms my core. Yearning for the peace of His protection, the assurance of His love holds me fast. I'm safe when I'm with Him—and He's *always* with me. Sanctification, though painful is a liberating process that brings us into our authentic selves.

Waiting with a quiet spirit for His presence, He always arrives in

His time. Patience comes too—The Lord is neither tame nor a genie in a lamp to be wished upon. I am learning to position myself before the Creator so I hear His voice. Because I ask Him, He performs creative releases from man-made expressions and teaches me as we walk together. He knows my final moment. When He calls, I will rise with glee and cherish my Lord face to face forever.

Sanctification is about liberty: *Stand fast therefore in the liberty by which Christ has made us free...* Galatians 5:1. We are not free to do what we want. We are free to line up with what God thinks, what God feels, and what God wants—a much deeper work. This internal battle challenges the chaos of man-made structures that lie within each of us. As sanctification progresses, the authentic me becomes freer to engage in deeper encounters with the Lord.

I invite you to consider what redeeming process you are in with your Creator. His heart yearns for your freedom to live out His full, authentic design.

Come! Live the unique design He created just for you and enjoy the fruit of the Spirit—love, joy, peace, patience,* kindness, goodness, faithfulness, gentleness, and self-control. *Amen.*

Following the epilogue you'll find questions for a deeper personal experience. There are also some comments from me—now that you know me better than most of my family! May the Lord bless you and keep you as you find your own signs, whispers and miracles from Him. I leave you, with a smile and a hug, in God's loving hands. Read on!

longsuffering is used in the New King James Version, quoted throughout this book (other than this passage). In other versions, patience is translated as *perseverance.*

EPILOGUE

MEMORIES ARE like fine paintings in full, vibrant color; alive, they take us back to the moment they formed, for better or for worse. *Signs, Whispers, and Miracles: Finding God in the Fabric of Life*, recreates a selection of my life's canvases. With life-changing messages coursing through my existence from past to present, each event claims a unique palette of colors, under the shadow of His wings.

Grace-filled love saw me through life, from failure to success, even with undiagnosed learning disabilities, loving but challenging parents, and painful mistakes—so many shadows. Look for His hidden grace in your life. Find Him in both sunlight and shadow, hardship and joy. He is always there, sewn into the fabric of your life. Blessings await...

> *"But seek first the kingdom of God and His righteousness, and all these things shall be added to you."*
> — *Matthew 6:33*

LIFE QUESTIONS

*"You shall love your neighbor as yourself." Love does no harm
to a neighbor; therefore love is the fulfillment of the law."*
— Romans 13:9b–10

How may I help you, neighbor? With most of my life in the rearview
mirror, with vast and varied experiences, what did you take away
from reading this book to help you in *your* life?

Here are some questions to deepen your experience using *Signs,
Whispers, and Miracles* as you take stock of your life: past, present,
and future. I pray you will find these engaging.

Six Questions for Deeper Thought with Application

1. What are some of your own defining life experiences? What might they tell you about God?

Me: My experience with "The Butterfly" miracle showed me the personal, loving God I've come to know over a lifetime. As I experienced life and studied the Bible, with the help of the Holy Spirit, I understood: He was, is, and always will be God, the Son—a Savior for sinners who accept His gift of salvation. The Father, the Son, and the Holy Spirit—our Triune God—is a God of mystery, who we have eternity to know more deeply.

2. Have you ever experienced God's signs, whispers, or miracles? If so, in what ways?

Me: If the answer is "No," you're not looking. The time I spent on the wrong path in life involved time I ignored God's signs and whispers. Miracles, harder to disregard, happened in my life; in "The Butterfly" chapter, my request resulted in a miraculous experience. Still, unless we're open to hearing God through even the smallest of signs and whispers, unless we're willing to admit to miracles both small and great, our experience with God will be limited. The Lord created all that we see and don't see; even the smallest incident, observation, and experience may be used for His purposes as a loving Father who wants none to perish without eternal life through Him.

3. What does "Finding God" mean to you?

Me: For me, "Finding God" has meant learning to see how God continues to guide my life, season to season, day to day, minute to minute. Over many years, God has been faithful and brought me to an awareness of His consistent presence. Through many varied experiences, God showed his loving intent, even in the hard lessons.

4. Do you carry a burden that makes you feel you cannot be forgiven?

Me: Have you ever heard anyone say they can't forgive themselves? If Jesus gave His life as a bridge to the Father for each of us who chooses to believe Him, who are we not to forgive ourselves? Jesus once told a mob, "You who is without sin, cast the first stone." Then He told the woman caught in adultery to, "Go and sin no more." I've never been unfaithful to Michael; but I'm guilty of fornication before I married. I was a thief, liar, and cheat. But that's not who I am anymore. Repentance, for me, means I can let go of my past and be forgiven through belief in Jesus's gift of mercy. I think of my dear friend, Barbara, who died in peace after finding out she had brain cancer during my visit. She was able to let go of anything that held her in guilt. I saw *the peace that passes all understanding* in her eyes the last time I saw her alive. How I look forward to meeting her again!

5. Do you have unhealed wounds, or have you wounded someone without reconciling?

Me: Almost eight years later, I opened a dialogue with my daughter that healed a wound, after I understood the circumstances. The key is *prayerful communication*, if the other person cares for your feelings. Deep hurts that are buried may not resolve when there is still a hurtful memory between two people who care for each other. Resolution may require professional help in addition to prayer. If one person is not willing to forgive the other, there is no reconciliation.

I have a friend I offended in 2016. Although I apologized many times, she has not spoken to me, accepted phone calls or corresponded in any way. I am dead to her. That remains hard to accept; yet I must let it go. A one-way street does not lead to friendship. Even so, I just realized I said "I *have* a friend..." My door is still open.

Traveling on down the one-way street, I texted the preceding paragraph to her after explaining her presence in the *Life Questions* portion of my book. I gave her the title, subtitle and question number five. After citing that the questions at the end of the book were to deepen the reading experience on a personal level, I wished her well and sent the text.

Within an hour, I received the following text from her:

"If you're sending this to me for review or approval you have a gold star. As long as no names are mentioned. Your book sounds like a page turner. I almost called you two weeks ago..."

We are in contact again after five years. She wants to read my "True Story."

6. Have you made peace with your future death?

Me: At seventy-one, I still feel young. The mirror disagrees, with my silver hair and some wrinkles showing. For the first time, my heart skips beats—not for love, but because of aging. Michael and I have separate sets of covers in bed to accommodate our different thermostats, one quilt on his side and multiple blankets on mine. Other than making love, sometimes he holds me as we lie there, under his quilt, and talk. One night, as I lay on my side in bed, snuggling next to him, my heart began beating rapidly and skipping. *I wonder if it's my time to die*, I thought without fear. An unfathomable, restful peace beyond my understanding came over me, as I received the gift of *knowing* I had no reason to fear. I closed my eyes and fell asleep in Michael's arms. I awakened a little later, to crawl beneath my own blankets, my heartbeat in a normal rhythm. The heart palpitations and arrhythmia have not concerned me since. We will not know the day or the hour; but for death to hold no fear, each of us needs peace with the Lord.

Now, go in peace, in Jesus's name.

SIGNS, WHISPERS, AND MIRACLES: SCRIPTURES

Prologue

Chapter 1 The Beginning
    Genesis 1:31

Chapter 2 Elementary
    Matthew 11:29

Chapter 3 Germany—Magstadt
    Psalm 137:4

Chapter 4 Germany—Backnang and Europe
    Psalm 23:2–3

Chapter 5 Trial by Fire
    Isaiah 51:7

Chapter 6 The Robe
    John 3:16

Chapter 7 Second Chance
    Hosea 6:1

Chapter 8 The Accident
    Isaiah 40:31

Chapter 9 Prelude
   Ephesians 6:1–4

Chapter 10 Evil and Good
   Mark 13:48

Chapter 11 God Is Not Dead
   Matthew 14:31–32

Chapter 12 Don't Go!
   Exodus 20:15

Chapter 13 The Precipice
   Colossians 1:13–14

Chapter 14 The Townhouse
   Romans 9:15a

Chapter 15 Busted
   Jeremiah 13:21

Chapter 16 Moving On
   Psalm 130:3–4

Chapter 17 Transitions
   2 Peter 3:9

Chapter 18 New Beginnings
   Proverbs 10:16

Chapter 19 Family
   Psalm 107:8–9

Chapter 20 Seers & Forbidden Things

Ephesians 1:7–8

Chapter 21 Life and Death
2 Corinthians 5:1

Chapter 22 Love's Spectrum
Galatians 5:22–23

Chapter 23 Wedding Plans and Reminiscence
Romans 12: 18

Chapter 24 The Wedding
Hebrews 13:4

Chapter 25 Out of the City
Psalm 24:1-2

Chapter 26 God's Timing
Numbers 14:8

Chapter 27 Eden Hill
Proverbs 24:3–4

Chapter 28 With Child
Ecclesiastes 11:5

Chapter 29 New Life Coming
Proverbs 22:4

Chapter 30 Upside Down
Matthew 19:14

Chapter 31 Valley of the Shadow
Psalm 23:4

Chapter 32 Going Home
    Hosea 13:14

Chapter 33 Oh Baby!
    Psalm 127:3–4

Chapter 34 Broken
    Psalm 91:1–4

Chapter 35 Learning Curve
    Psalm 91:1-2

Chapter 36 Fighting the Dragon
    James 5:13

Chapter 37 Deception
    Matthew 26:21

Chapter 38 Beauty for Ashes
    Isaiah 61:1–3

Chapter 39 Out of the Nest
    1 Corinthians 13:11

Chapter 40 Fanfare
    Ecclesiastes 3:1–2

Chapter 41 Out to Dinner
    1 Corinthians 15:53

Chapter 42 Yoga
    2 Thessalonians 2:3

Chapter 43 Dreams & Visions

Exodus 20:3

Chapter 44 Death of a Dream
   1 John 4:6

Chapter 45 The Butterfly
   Daniel 4:3

Chapter 46 He Wants None to Perish
   2 Peter 3:9

Chapter 47 Final Decision
   John 5:24

Chapter 48 No Words
   Psalm 19:14

Chapter 49 And This Too Shall Pass
   Job 14:5–6

Chapter 50 Celebration
   Matthew 11:25, 28–30

Chapter 51 Retirement
   Psalm 23: 6

Chapter 52 After All
   Colossians 2:8

Epilogue
   Matthew 6:33

Life Questions and Application
   Romans 13:9b–10

ABOUT THE AUTHOR

Violet Batejan grew up near Valley Forge, Pennsylvania. A graduate of Temple University, she spent forty-seven years as a physical therapist in various settings. Writing, always a first love, played an important role in her life. In 1991, she graduated from the Institute of Children's Literature. She won awards at St. David's Christian Writer's Conference, where her writing became a life-long ambition. Presently, she is a full-time writer who lives with her husband, *Michael, their Maine Coon-Persian cat and two gerbils*, in the picturesque hills of Southeastern Pennsylvania.

Always a lover of nature and "furry things," Violet has enjoyed cats, dogs, horses and many smaller creatures of God's creation. When called to save a fellow employee from a small snake, her instant response was, "Don't hurt it! I'm coming!" Married for forty-five years, Violet named their home "Eden Hill" reflecting gratitude for her surroundings and husband. They have lived on this piece of God's real estate forty-four years and counting.

My writing companion, Sasha.

Lynne, Violet and Leigh.

Jess and Katie by our wood stove (Sasha's underneath.)

Mom, Jessica, Violet, Michael and Tony.

Katie at Thanksgiving with Nana and Moshu.

Violet at Black Rock Silent Sanctuary Retreat (Silent Retreats discontinued 2020.)

Michael shoveling snow.

Sasha, the indoor cat, exploring.

Kitchen corner reminder (normally without the necklaces,)
"This [world] is not our home."

Blessings until we meet again...

ACKNOWLEDGMENTS

This book is a work of love on many levels. I thank God for the gift of writing this book and any others as His provision allows. Writing *Signs, Whispers, and Miracles* granted me a deep sense of gratitude at the richness of my life's fabric. I also have to thank God for the gift of my husband, Michael. He never complained about the hours my computer consumed and made dinner often. His humor and comradery brought me back from my deep visits to the past and into the present with a smile. Reading my own book told me, in print, that we have as near a perfect marriage as can exist in a fallen world. Thanks, my love!

This book may never have been born without Charlotte Daiello and Diane Morrow, my small group Bible study leaders and sisters in Christ. They turned into my "Book Angels" taking precious time each week to listen to the 'next chapter,' which gave me a deadline and kept me writing. Thank you to my Bible study small group, who put up with my wordy enthusiasm about God's hand in my life resulting in a book. Thanks to Mary Ann Thomas and Deb Wilkinson who proofed the copy before formatting.

Thanks to my amazing editor, Jocelyn Carbonara, who gave generously of her time, her skill and in her responsiveness to questions with rapid answers. She sifted, corrected and honed my story to make it worthy of publishing. I feel honored she chose to edit my manuscript and write the foreword to this book. Thanks also to Philip Studdard of Flip Design Studio, who designed the cover and Nola Li Barr who formatted the final manuscript. Kudos to my Beta readers and launch team. I'm grateful for my daughter Jessica who encouraged me to include her battle with Post-partum Depression and laughed out loud at my telling of her escapades.

My final acknowledgment is to Self-Publishing School and CEO Chandler Bolt for intensive courses of study in writing, publishing, marketing and anything to do with self-publishing. RE Vance, my talented SPS coach, helped focus my lens on requirements needed to tell a good story, and the path to publish and market the book successfully. Mastermind Community, the Self-Publishing School online voice of students, authors and writers, provided help choosing the book's title, cover and answers to my questions from writing to creating a web site. The encouragement and support are unparalleled in SPS. I experienced a quantum leap in writing ability. These courses and the school's all-encompassing design made Signs, Whispers, and Miracles come to life. SPS introduced me to people around the world that became writing and author friends.

In the winter of my life, there is such joy in the Lord's gift of a new profession as a writer and author. My favorite Psalm bears repeating:

> My cup runs over.
> Surely goodness and mercy shall follow me
> All the days of my life;
> And I will dwell in the house of the Lord
> Forever
> — Psalm 23:6

WRITE A REVIEW

Thank you for reading my book. If these words touched you, please write an honest review on Amazon. If you feel the book is less than a 4 or 5-star rating, please contact me at vbatejan3@gmail.com. I would like to discuss the issue resulting in the low rating and improve future editions of this book. It is my goal to improve my craft as a writer and I cannot do that without feedback from my readers.

Made in United States
Orlando, FL
14 April 2022

16845352R00240